Paperchase

Paperchase

Mozart, Beethoven, Bach . . .
The Search for their lost Music

by

Nigel Lewis

HAMISH HAMILTON LONDON

First published in Great Britain 1981
by Hamish Hamilton Limited
Garden House 57-59 Long Acre London WC2E 9JZ

Copyright © 1981 by Nigel Lewis

British Library Cataloguing in Publication Data
Lewis, Nigel
 Paperchase: Mozart, Beethoven, Bach . . . The Search for their
lost music.
 1. Grüssau (Monastery)
 2. Music – Manuscripts – East Germany
 I. Title
 780.8'2   ML94
 ISBN 0-241-10235-9

Photoset by Rowland Phototypesetting Limited
Bury St Edmunds, Suffolk
and printed in Great Britain by
St Edmundsbury Press, Bury St Edmunds, Suffolk

Contents

To Angela, with love,
this book is dedicated.

Acknowledgements

The writer who strives for factual accuracy must expect to encounter difficulties in his research, but I think I can claim that the research for the present book was exceptionally difficult to do. The problems were implicit in the terrain, and I draw attention to them, not by way of special pleading, but in order to illustrate some features of that terrain, and, by implication, the depth of my gratitude towards those who helped me across it.

It is sometimes said that there is no such thing as 'investigative journalism', but the phrase usefully distinguishes, I think, between the kind of research which is a matter merely of collating what is already known, or picking up the telephone to hear what people are only too eager to tell, and the kind in which facts must be fought for, despite the reluctance of those in possession of them. In the later stages of this book, where the story moves to the present-day, the difficulties were of this order, and were to be expected.

For other difficulties, I was less prepared. Much of the story is set, and much of the research was conducted, in the twilight between history – where events can be considered to be safely part of the past – and journalism – where they still have repercussions in the present. The dividing line between the two is perhaps nowhere thinner, more shifting, or closer to the present than it is in Central Europe, where the heritage of the war lives on with an intensity which it is hard for the outsider to appreciate, and harder still for him to penetrate. Often in my research, thinking myself in 'the past', I would find myself with a jolt suddenly in 'the present'; often, in speaking to the living, a door would open on to the dead.

This is what Carleton Smith was getting at when he suggested to me once that the book 'would be easier to write in fifty years' time'. Later, there was the retired librarian in East Berlin who jovially offered to help me 'when all of this is history', adding with a laugh, 'of course, I will be dead by then, and so, I expect, will you.'

The same resistance characterised the equally surprising 'Trade Secret', which I describe in the main text without reference to my own frequent encounters with it. There was the scholar in East Berlin who thought that the book could not be written, and the scholar in West Berlin who thought that it should not be written. There was the distinguished British scholar who gave the somewhat tortuous explanation: 'I am sorry that I . . . must decline to give my reasons for refusing to help you. To give you the reasons would be to tell you too much.'

Yet the book *was* written, because there were people prepared to help me. Because of the resistance, however, the result is not quite so much an account of 'one of the most extraordinary episodes in cultural history', as another East German described it to me, as a mystery story with historical overtones; and, of course, it was the mystery which drew me in the first place. One day, perhaps, the history will be written, although that is doubtful.

In the meantime, here is the mystery, and logically, I suppose, I ought first to thank those who helped to make it mysterious. But my greater gratitude goes out, not to those despite whom the story was written, but to those without whom it could not have been written. The circumstances of my research, however, mean that I must refrain from naming many of those who helped me the most. It would be ungrateful to express my gratitude to them individually, and they would not thank me for thanking them.

Others can be named. First among them must be Peter Whitehead, of the British Museum (Natural History) in London. It was from him, one day in 1974, that I first heard of the Benedictine monastery of Grüssau, an acquaintance enlarged by many a subsequent rendezvous 'under the beetle' (the big, black, metal beetle that hangs over the entrance to the museum's Insect Section.) Then there is Professor Dieter Henrich, of the Philosophy Department of Heidelberg University, whom I never succeeded in meeting but whose article on the Grüssau problem (in the West German magazine *Neue Rundschau*, 2/1977) I drew from extensively in Chapter 15. Without his article, and the researches of Peter Whitehead, I might never have embarked on my task and it would certainly have been considerably more daunting.

Other scholars to whom I extend special thanks are Dr. Peter Wackernagel, formerly of the Prussian State Library, Berlin, who supplied valuable personal reminiscences of its wartime evacuation; Dr. Klaus Hofmann of the Johann-Sebastian-Bach-Institut, Göttingen, who helped me to puzzle out the Leningrad Cantata; Dr. Wolfgang Rehm, of the Neue Mozart Ausgabe; Dr. Stanley Sadie, who answered numerous musicological enquiries; William Lichtenwanger, formerly of the American Library of Congress; Nigel Moore, who supplied me with military information; Professor Hugh McLean, of the University of Western Ontario; Professor H. C. Robbins Landon; Thor Wood of the New York Public Library; Hans-Hubert Schönzeler; Graf Dr. Johannes von Moy; and Meinhard von Zallinger-Thurn. Eva Ziesche of the *Staatsbibliothek Preussischer Kulturbesitz* and Frau Renate Gollmetz of the *Deutsche Staatsbibliothek* helped me through the complexities of Berlin's post-war cataloguing.

Other librarians to whom I am grateful are Mrs. Nowak, of the Polish Library in London, where the 'unexpected death' was tracked down; Mrs. Wojakowska, of the Sikorski Library, for her patience; the librarians of the B.B.C., for theirs; and Mr. Järvinen, of U.N.E.S.C.O. in Paris, in whose archives I found the proceedings of the Vaucher Commission. Other material came from a wide variety of organizations – including the Copernicus Society of America and the United States National Archives – and individuals, chief among whom I would like to thank Mrs. Martha Dodd Stern, Herr Friedhelm Grundmann, Mr. Michael Maclagan, Mrs. Mary Radamsky, Count Adam Zamoyski, and Ellen Lentz of the *New York Times*.

For additional information I thank the editors of the *Milwaukee Journal*, the *Salzburger Nachrichten*, the *Neue Zürcher Zeitung* (where I found an invaluable article on Schloss Fürstenstein), and the *Book Collector*. Articles and programmes by me about Grüssau appeared from 1975 to 1977 on B.B.C. Radio 3, in the *Sunday Times*, and on the Canadian Broadcasting Corporation, which broadcast a full-length documentary, *The Grüssau Manuscripts*. My thanks to

Mr. Cormac Rigby of the B.B.C., Mr. Ron Hall of the *Sunday Times*, and Mr. Robert Chesterman of the C.B.C.

Thanks also to Helen Burnett, who typed the book, to my agent, Mike Shaw, of Curtis Brown Ltd., and to my editor, Christopher Sinclair-Stevenson. The following friends merit special mention and campaign medals – Raymond Wolff, for his corrections; Chris Jones, Claire Lister, and my father, N. W. Lewis, for their suggestions; and Robert Eagle, Anita Leslau, Erika Scammel, Stefan Zongollowicz, and Voytek, for their translations. Medals for exceptional bravery under fire go to Angela, Pascoe, and Ned.

The final text is my responsibility, as are any errors that it might contain. One aspect of that responsibility perhaps requires explanation. After careful consideration, I decided to keep footnotes to a bare minimum. This is not only because of the many instances where confidentiality forbade a footnote. There was also the author's responsibility towards his readers – which I felt to be of overriding importance – to ensure that they were not lured by the trees into blindness of the wood. In the interests of clarity, I have kept the undergrowth as sparse as possible, and if in doing so I have erred too much in the direction of sparseness I cannot say that I greatly regret the imbalance.

Nigel Lewis
London, 1981

CHAPTER ONE

The Dynasty

The beginnings go back to the first day of the Second World War, the German invasion of Poland on September 1, 1939. Among the side-effects of this momentous event were the interruption of a young man's promising academic career and the violent disturbance of a family continuum that had flowed uninterruptedly for almost two hundred years.

The family was the Estreichers. The name was originally German, and was imported into Poland from Moravia in 1778, when Dominik Estreicher, a reasonably successful minor painter now virtually forgotten, was invited to teach drawing in Kraków, the old royal capital in the south of the country. So began the family's long association with Kraków, and with its ancient Jagiellonian University, founded in 1364 and named after the Polish royal dynasty which founded it.

By 1939, the Estreichers had become an academic dynasty in their own right, unique in Poland, and, in the words of a Polish art historian, 'typifying the Kraków milieu'. Dominik's son, Alojzy, a Professor of Botany at the Jagiellonian, was appointed its Rector in 1831, a considerable achievement for a family after just over half a century in its adoptive country. Karol, the next in the dynastic succession, brought the achievement to fruition. He was a man of many parts – historian of literature and of the theatre, columnist, author, and critic. But his greater achievements were in bibliography, which here has the sense of listing 'the books of a particular author, printer, country; the literature of a subject', as the Oxford Dictionary defines it. Bibliography does not immediately recommend itself as the most exciting of pursuits, but the importance of Karol's work becomes clearer when we consider its heroic scale and see it in context. There was an underlying nationalism to his bibliographic labours, which he started in 1848, the year of national uprisings throughout Europe. At that time, Poland was still

1

partitioned between Austria, Hungary, and Russia, as she would remain for the rest of his life. But his work helped to give Poland a sense of her own distinct identity down the ages, and to focus her national pride. For his aim was nothing less than to make an *omnium gatherum* of all that had been written by Poles or by foreigners about Poland, from the fifteenth century onwards. He persevered in this for sixty years. Volume Twenty-Two of his monumental *Polish Bibliography* (whose title alone suggests a door-stop from Valhalla) was published in the year of his death, 1908, nicely in time for the achievement of Polish independence ten years later.

In addition, however, his tireless studies laid the foundations for the national importance and the greatness of Kraków's Jagiellonian Library. He was its director from 1862 until his retirement in 1905, and a Polish historian comments that 'Thanks to Estreicher, the Jagiellonian Library's most flourishing period was from 1870 to 1914 . . . A librarian with imagination inspired by love for his country built a mediocre collection into a national monument, a "treasure of intellectual wealth" to use Estreicher's own expression'.

With him, the Estreicher dynasty became part of Poland's cultural and intellectual woodwork. This shows in Karol's face, in which one senses, as one does not in Alojzy's, a donnishness that has become inbred. In a painting of him at the first night of a play he seems abstracted, as though his mind were still on his bibliography, and his body were still in his study, bent over a book.

Karol's bibliographic labours were continued by the next Estreicher, Stanisław, a Professor of Law at the Jagiellonian and its Rector. His son was born in 1906 and named Karol after his grandfather. Physically, neither Stanisław nor the young Karol, as he grew up, resembled the conventional idea of a don. In place of the bookish remoteness that one detects in the face of the elder Karol, their faces reveal a peasant canniness and alertness, and in the younger Karol this was even more marked than it was in his father. Dressed in the right clothes, he could have been taken for a horse dealer. There was a distant resemblance to his great-grandfather Alojzy, in the foxy twinkle around his eyes and mouth, but not in his hair, which lay flat, cropped close to the skull, unlike Alojzy's curly shock, and quite unlike the elder Karol's hairstyle, which was *en brosse*, as though he spent the day worriedly running his fingers through it. Also, the younger Karol's eyes could read people as well as print, whereas one feels of his grandfather that he was happiest buried in a book. There was an instinctive shrewdness about him.

All the same, Stanisław was a dyed-in-the-wool don, and his son set fair to become one. By the end of his childhood, Karol was steeped in his family's past, and in that of Kraków, with which his family was so indissolubly bound. Going on to university – the Jagiellonian, of course – he was regarded as a brilliant student, if somewhat eccentric. But eccentricity was par for the course, conventional donnishness. And as, at the age of twenty-five, he took up an assistant lectureship at the Jagiellonian, a conventional don is perhaps what he would have become; but then, eight years later, came the German invasion, stopping the flow and toppling the Estreicher dynasty.

*

By September 1, the art treasures of Paris had been evacuated and stored away in the Loire valley and the Lot. The Spanish Civil War had set the precedent: for the first time in history, there was the threat of wholesale and random destruction from the air. And the man who had carried out the art evacuation of Madrid, Jacques Jaujard, was also in overall charge of the Paris evacuation. He did his job quickly and thoroughly. Across the English Channel, the treasures of London were also given sanctuary during the war, mostly in the coal mines of Wales.

The British, and especially the French, had a master-plan. Not so the Poles. 'At the outbreak of war,' one Polish account puts it, 'the measures which could be adopted for safeguarding Polish works of art and objects of historic value against the risk of destruction during hostilities were inadequate and limited and covered only a fraction of the appropriate items.' The maces of the Jagiellonian University provide an example of the rough-and-ready nature of the provisions Poland made for the safety of her national soul made material. Only on the first day of the war were they taken from the Rector's office and bricked up in an underground hiding place, where they remained for the duration.

The Polish will to organise was perhaps paralysed by a sense

3

of Poland's extreme vulnerability. Not only did her own terrain, a huge parade ground exposed to the sky, seem unsuitable for hiding things away: there was also a sense of powerlessness and futility in the lowering presence, to east and west, of Poland's traditional enemies. There was a feeling of no escape. The sense of insecurity was made complete in August 1939, when the two Foreign Ministers, Ribbentrop and Molotov, signed the Nazi-Soviet pact. And perhaps Poland knew, in her heart of hearts, that the traditional methods of safekeeping, evacuation to quiet country castles away from the bombing of the cities, were inappropriate for the ruthlessness of the war that was to be waged against her. The danger began with bombs, but far from ended there.

Whatever the underlying reasons, the fact is that most collections stayed where they were, whether packed into crates and stored in cellars, or still accessible on shelves or in showcases. Such things as were evacuated into the country were the few prize pieces: in music, the Warsaw National Library's Krasinski Manuscript 52, the most important source of Polish polyphony of the fifteenth century, or its collection of Chopin's Preludes in the original manuscript. These, extraordinarily, survived the war while remaining within Poland.

The inadequacy of the precautions meant that some collections fell victim to conventional warfare. Destruction by 'conventional' means, however, was to be a tiny proportion of the total losses caused by the German determination to eliminate the very *memory* that there had ever been a proud and independent people called the Poles, the very idea that there had once been a Polish nation.

Poland could scarcely have foreseen the savagery and thoroughness with which this determination was to be put into effect, though Hitler himself had made it clear enough. The reality would defy belief. But that there were dangers it was plain for all to see, and, given Poland's special circumstances, 'it was obvious', as they saw, 'that the ideal method of protection against the ravages of war and pillage was to evacuate the works of art and historic relics to countries far removed from the theatre of war.'

One suitable country was France, with which Poland had long-established émigré connections. Before the German invasion, the National Library evacuated some of Poland's greatest treasures there: the twelfth-century *The Annals of the Holy Cross*; the thirteenth century *Holy Cross Sermons*; the fourteenth-century *Florian Psalter*; medieval illuminated manuscripts; a collection of Chopin manuscripts, fair copies, and other Chopiniana; and one printed work, the only Gutenberg Bible in Polish hands. It requires only a simple effort of imagination to see the significance of this list as a Pole would see it.

Another country that provided a way out was neutral Rumania to the south, and with Rumania, before the war, Poland had signed an agreement providing for assistance if she were occupied. After the Polish lines broke on September 6, the government and the Polish gold reserves moved eastwards, as all able-bodied men were required to do. When the Soviet army invaded from the east on September 17, into Rumania the government and the gold reserves moved.

Rumania was also the destination of objects from the Polish Royal Treasury, most of which was on show in the former royal castle on Wawel Hill in Kraków. Most of the treasury had been plundered by the Prussians during the Third Partition of Poland in 1795, and, consequently, what remained was all the more precious: the Coronation Sword of the Polish kings, dating from the end of the twelfth century; the sword and scabbard, and the hat embroidered with an allegory of the Holy Ghost in pearls, which Pope Innocent XI had given to King Jan Sobieski III after his victory over the Turks in 1683; the gold chain of King Sigismund III; and other things, including the sceptre, sword, and chain of the last Polish king, Stanisław Augustus (1764-1795), which were stored at the Royal Castle in Warsaw.

The Poles have always had a taste for tapestries, and fifteenth century arrases from the Wawel Castle were the most precious of the national heirlooms taken to Rumania. Numerous paintings, gold mugs and cups, clocks, suits of armour, and other items made up the tally.

All travelled to Rumania in a convoy, and Karol Estreicher, drafted into the Polish army specially for the purpose, was one of those seconded to look after them en route. So, at the age of thirty-three, he made his and his family's first decisive break from Kraków.

It was an epic journey. For the first one hundred and twenty miles the objects were carrried by barge. Then they were transferred to waggons hastily assembled. The peasants, like the watermen, worked without pay. At every stage of the journey the roads were bombed. Soldiers travelling with Estreicher were killed when aircraft tried to bomb the lorries carrying the collection the final miles, but none of the actual objects were damaged; at last, its keepers 'half dead with fatigue', the convoy reached the Rumanian frontier, its precious cargo intact.

From Rumania, the collection travelled on by a roundabout route to France, where it joined those things from the National Library in Warsaw mentioned earlier. When the war reached France, and was about to overwhelm her, everything was loaded on to a Polish liner bound for Canada. Arriving in July 1940, they remained there through the war, safe in the keeping of Polish curators.

Karol Estreicher was not among them, however. His destination was London. By November 1939, he was on the staff there of General Sikorski, Poland's Premier-in-exile and Commander-in-Chief of her Home Army. (He was close to Sikorski, and wrote the official pamphlet after the latter's death in 1943, in an aeroplane accident.)

Through the intelligence networks of the Polish underground commanded by Sikorski he kept closely in touch with events in Poland. That November, he heard of the arrest of his father and 183 other professors of the Jagiellonian University. The entire teaching staff of the university had been required to attend a lecture by the Kraków Gestapo chief on 'The Attitude of National Socialism Towards Science'. As the professors sat through the insulting harangue, the Gestapo surrounded the Lecture Hall and heavy lorries drew up outside the main entrance. As the 'lecture' ended, the professors were arrested, lined up in threes, and forced into the lorries. Five of them, including the aged former President of the Polish Academy of Sciences, were treated with special brutality.

After short spells in military detention and in Breslau prison, the professors were taken to Sachsenhausen concentration camp in Berlin. Waiting under the arc lamps in the icy November rain, they were mocked and beaten. Then they were checked into the camp, ordered to undress, and their heads and beards were shaved.

The prison day began at 5.30 a.m. with a cold shower. Daily, there were three roll-calls; daily, all were beaten. On January 16, in a heavy frost, the professors were made to parade for two hours; some froze to death. By the end of January, seventeen were dead, including Karol Estreicher's father. The London *Times* reported: 'Professor Stanisław Estreicher, a leading authority on English and French law, had been approached by the Nazi Government to become President of a Polish 'Protectorate'. Professor Estreicher flatly declined, although aware that prison threatened him if he refused . . . The Germans did not consider either the scientific merits of the famous professor, or his age of seventy-one. The Gestapo simply tortured him to death.'

The mass arrest of the professors marked the opening of a second offensive against Poland, aimed this time not at her sovereignty as a state, but at the very bases of her existence, her traditions, culture, and identity. Intellectuals stood in the front line of the new offensive. On the same day as the arrest – November 6, 1939 – the Jagiellonian Library was closed down. Nine days later a decree was passed 'Concerning the Sequestration of the Property of the Former Polish State within the Government General'. This was the area between the western states of Poland incorporated into the German Reich, and the eastern contested areas occupied by the Soviet Union. Its governor was Hans Frank, the so-called 'Butcher of Poland', who made his residence in the Royal Castle in Kraków. It was Frank who signed this and a series of decrees which, by September 1940, had provided a shabby legal cloak for the suppression of all Polish cultural activity and the looting or destruction of cultural property owned by the state, the church, or privately. Frank himself, at his villa in Bavaria, had Polish-owned art works such as Leonardo's 'Lady with an Ermine' and Raphael's 'Portrait of a Young Man' (which is still missing today), both looted from the private Czartoryski Collection in Kraków.

'We do not intend,' said Frank, 'to continue in any way the work of the Polish librarians.' The first step was to cream off things from the collections and take them back to Germany. A Nazi catalogue published in 1944, 'Safeguarded Works of Art', its cover stamped with the eagle and the swastika, shows that twenty-four different items were officially looted in this

7

way from the Jagiellonian. Most were copper engravings of the fifteenth century, and one from the thirteenth century, the medieval legal work the *Codex Justinian*. This is still missing today, as are most of the other items.[1]

In his London exile, Karol Estreicher noted with the greatest concern the unfolding of German policy in Poland. There must have been a strong personal element to his concern. In less than a year, the Germans had driven him from his country, murdered his father, and begun to undo the life work of his grandfather. The corrosion extended back into the past, as well as poisoning the present: while Poland was occupied, the achievements of the dead would be no safer from harm than the lives of the living. But, to his credit, he used his personal involvement as a means of grasping the problem as a whole. What had happened to his family mirrored what was happening all over the country.

Four generations of Estreichers had contributed to the cultural greatness of Poland. He had grown up, as though it were his birthright, with the expectation that he too would spend his life in Kraków, peacefully adding his contribution. But the war had changed all that. It was not a matter of building, now, but of saving what had been built.

[1]One, the Codex Picturatus, by Balthazar Behem, an illustrated account of Kraków life in the fifteenth and sixteenth centuries, was recovered from Germany soon after the war.

CHAPTER TWO

The Quiet Guests

The range of the German repression in Poland embraced the entire cultural heritage. It was here, as the collective memory of his nation, that Karol Estreicher made his unique contribution.

Firstly, he defined the problem which Poland faced. Looting of art objects is characteristic of all wars but, as Estreicher realised, there was a special fury and at the same time a special detachment and thoroughness to the looting of Poland. Never before had looting been carried out so 'scientifically':

> . . . it must be pointed out that the behaviour of the Germans in Eastern Europe during the present war was very different from their behaviour in the West. East Central European countries were considered by the leaders of the Third Reich and the creators of the 'New Order' as a field for Teutonic colonisation, ground where any act of violence, any plunder, was justified . . . The Germans were sure of impunity . . . with utter ruthlessness, therefore, they proceeded to carry out their long prepared plans.

From the earliest days of Nazi power, plans were coldly laid for the repression, selective destruction, and eventual dismemberment of Poland's cultural life and heritage:

> About 1933, in various German institutions . . . there was a growing and rapidly developing interest in Poland, in her culture, and in Polish scientific institutions and art collections . . . German scholars began to come to Poland, where in the guise of friendly fellow-workers, they gathered information, and accustomed themselves to the tasks which Nazism was putting before them. We remember the visits of those scholars very well . . . the pillage in Poland was methodically planned by the German scholars, who knew Poland.
> The plans were laid before the war . . . All sorts of people took part in their execution . . . but by far the most guilty of

9

all were the German professors . . . Like carrion they settled upon Poland in their party uniforms, and with their academic titles. They pretended to reorganise the Polish academic institutions, but in reality they were systematically destroying them. These German 'Verwaltungs' for libraries, archives, and museums, these 'amts' for education and propaganda, were, if the truth be told, nests of academic gangsters, such as the world has never known before.

Add to this that 'the most valuable objects were usually stolen from libraries and museums during the night, while catalogues and inventories were simultaneously destroyed so that all traces of the looted objects should be eradicated', and we can see that this uniquely scientific looting required a uniquely scientific response. Estreicher provided it. His flat in wartime London soon became the hub of an intelligence operation the like of which had not previously been seen. At the same time, representatives of other occupied countries were setting up their equivalents, but none had the scope of Estreicher's: nowhere in Europe, not even Czechoslovakia, was the threat more immediate or more far-reaching than in Poland. What is more, as one Polish source has it, 'Estreicher was regarded by the Allies as the foremost expert, and material collected by him concerned not only Poland but other occupied countries as well'.

Estreicher's operation can be compared to that mounted after the war by the Israeli hunter of war ciminals, Simon Wiesenthal. Like him, Estreicher was waging a one-man war with index cards and the weapons of research. Like Wiesenthal, his aim was to put right a great wrong, and, like him, he was not really alone but had a whole people behind him.

The bulk of his information was gathered from close perusal of printed German sources, occupation newspapers, catalogues, lists of dealers, and the like. But much else came from the underground, by short-wave radio from Poland, by courier, or by post through Sweden or Rumania. One has an impression of Poland as a nation of art spies, so astonishing is the quality of the intelligence that filtered through to him in London. In some cases, he must have depended on observations made by different people in different parts of the country, in reconstructing the travels of a looted object. Everything was noted down, every little detail, every available German publication gone through with a fine-tooth comb, with the aim of tracing the object's whereabouts after the war was over, and bringing it home.

There is an important difference between the two operations. The murderers pursued by Wiesenthal will die off. So will the looters and assorted 'academic gangsters' whose names and activities Estreicher also carefully noted down (by the war's end, he had listed six hundred). But, so long as the precious objects they stole remain unaccounted for outside Poland, as many still do, Estreicher's operation will retain its relevance.

Nothing, apparently, escaped him in his exile. Often he had to be an obituarist, as was the case with synagogues, Jewish cemeteries, or art objects having a specifically Jewish or Polish resonance. The Monument to the Battle of Grunwald, in Mateki Square, Kraków serves as one example among hundreds:

> Executed by the sculptor, Wiwulski, at the expense of I. Paderewski, in 1910, on the 500th anniversary of the Polish victory over the Knights of the Teutonic Order.
> PRESENT FACTS: Destroyed by the Germans in 1939. The broken fragments lay for a long time in the yard of the Mining Academy in Kraków.[1]

Some of the card entries still bristle with horror, made the more horrific by their brevity. Here is Estreicher's entry on the cathedral at Pelplin, in the western parts of Poland incorporated into the German Reich:

> PRESENT FACTS: Completely looted by Germans. movable objects, i.e. liturgical vessels, works of art, etc., taken to nearby sugar factory and burnt in factory furnaces by order of the Gestapo commandant, Richter. He also ordered the mass murder of all priests belonging to Pelplin Chapter. They were slaughtered in woods near Starogard; cathedral was turned into garage by Germans.

Often, however, the card entries recorded, not the end of a precious object, or of a collection, but a violent new develop-

[1] The Mining Academy itself 'suffered heavily from the German occupation', damage meticulously detailed by Estreicher.

ment in its history – with implications for the future. This was so in the case of the Museum of the Czartoryski Princes, at Goluchow, near Poznań:

> All 'Polonica' remaining in the Museum were destroyed on the spot. The Germans also confiscated and removed from the Museum to Poznań the collection of Greek vases, antique and Renaissance terracottas . . .

At Poznań, however, the trail went cold. The collection of vases and terracottas, well known to scholars throughout the world, remains missing to this day.

Estreicher kept pace with every step of the German *danse macabre* in Poland. In July 1940, a special department of the Government General was set up to deal with libraries. Dr. Gustav Abb, head of the Berlin University Library, was put in charge of it, with the task of Germanising the Polish system. 'He aims at creating,' wrote Mrs. Maria Danilewicz of the Polish National Library,

> in towns which until 1939 were Polish university centres, a complete network of German 'Staatsbibliotheken' which will contribute towards the fulfilment of the 'Great Eastern Mission of German Scholarship' . . . The Nazi authorities are trying to delete and destroy the scholarly achievements of the Polish librarians . . . [They] wish to introduce, instead of living collections, mechanically compiled masses of books. They plan to rearrange many objects, and thus prevent their use by anyone – at least until new catalogues are compiled.

The greatest of those Polish librarians, of course, was the first Karol Estreicher. It takes time to build, but destruction is the work of an instant. The elder Karol had spent nearly forty years building, ordering, and cataloguing the collections of the Jagiellonian Library. It took the Nazis a fraction of that time to disorder and so destroy the living body that he had created.

The process was already well under way by the spring of 1941, when there occurred one of the most subtly humiliating outrages of the entire anti-cultural policy pursued by the Germans in wartime Poland. On April 4 that year, a group of German scholars and officials gathered in the new building of the Jagiellonian Library, paid for by the Polish State and opened just before the war.

12

As an institution, the library had been founded with the university in 1364 and was one of the oldest in the world. Now it was about to be opened as a 'Staatsbibliothek', as though its history had only just begun. The ceremony was organized by Dr. Abb, and presided over by Hans Frank. In London, Estreicher noted the details on his index cards for future reference. Among the dignitaries who attended was Hugo Andres Krüss, director of the Prussian State Library, which shared the same block on the Unter den Linden in Berlin as Dr. Abb's University Library.

Krüss was a mild-mannered, pipe-smoking man, opposed to the Nazis – he was not a party member – but evidently not averse to staying on as a functionary under their rule, and mixing with them in that capacity. In the late 1970s, one of his former employees described him to me as 'a somewhat remote personality, not easily moved, but we all had a great veneration for him. He protected us, and I will remain grateful to the end of my days for that protection.'[1] The veneration was not universally felt, however. According to an American report of 1946,[2] 'Opinions concerning the man's character and abilities vary considerably.' Well they might, given his attendance at the Kraków 'Staatsbibliothek' ceremony.

At the moment of the Jagiellonian Library's lowest fortunes, therefore, the presence of Krüss gives cause to question the moral standing of one of Germany's greatest institutions and one of the pillars of her national and cultural life: the Prussian State Library. Ironically, less than a week after the Kraków ceremony, events in Berlin would force Krüss into a course of action whereby he would have to preside over the dismemberment of his own library – just as Abb was presiding over the dismemberment of Poland's. To understand the scale of the decision and the task that faced Krüss, let us look at the responsibility which he had inherited.

*

In 1661 the Great Elector of Brandenburg, Frederick William, issued a decree ordering the foundation of a library. It was to be built on the River Spree in Berlin, capital of the Mark of Brandenburg, with monies gathered under the compulsory

[1]Dr. Peter Wackernagel.
[2]*The Prussian State Library*, by Richard S. Hill, in *Notes*, The Journal of the American Music Library Association, 3(4) 1946.

13

taxation system he had set up: the nucleus of its collections was to be his own, which must have been small enough, as a letter of 1687 states that Frederick William had inherited so few books that they could hardly be reckoned sufficient for a private gentleman's library.

But the Electoral library prospered with the state of Prussia, and its stocks grew. When Frederick III became King Frederick the First in 1701 its name was changed to the Royal Library of Berlin, and it was under this name that it amassed its priceless collections of music manuscripts. These were built around a collection particularly rich in Bach, belonging to an enterprising scholar called Georg Pölchau, who in 1823 offered them for sale to the library. He proposed that the library start an 'Archive of Musical Art'. 'Apart from the growing financial value of great masterpieces,' he wrote, 'such as those of Sebastian Bach, it is the sacred duty of all culture, art, and institutions of learning to collect and to guard them for future generations.' Pölchau's suggestion was taken up, and for the next eighty-four years the library reaped the rewards of what could be called the Golden Age of music manuscript collection. By the effective end of this Golden Age – Ernst von Mendelssohn's donation of 1908 – the Royal Library possessed the world's finest collection of music in manuscript, by Bach, Mozart, Beethoven, and virtually all the great composers.

The library as a whole continued to grow, against the background of the Prussian emphasis on education, the foundation of a Berlin university in 1810, and the rise of Prussia throughout the nineteenth century. In 1914 it moved into a big new, neo-classical building on the Avenue Unter den Linden, Berlin. Its opening was Berlin's last great royal ceremony before the First World War, and the end of the war saw also the end of royal rule in Prussia. In 1919, the building was renamed the Prussian State Library.

The new change of name brought no deeper changes until 1933. The arrival in power of the Nazis saw the beginning of active state interference in the affairs of the library (since the early 19th century the authorities had exercised only a general supervision over it). They cut its grant, and applied their racial and ideological doctrines. The number of users fell – in the music department, by half in six years. Also in the music department, a large 'R' – for 'Reserved' – was penned in red in the catalogue before every title written by a Jew, and the Mendelssohn Room was dismantled.

To the dangers of interference the war added those of outright destruction. This was driven home after the occupation of Paris in June 1940, when German librarians were able to see for themselves the care the French had taken to evacuate their collections.

Berlin had held on to its collections as long as it had because of an over-confident belief in a speedy end to the war, the defeatist implications of a mass evacuation, and, in the case of the Prussian State Library, because it was the hub of a national network. With its huge stocks, and the pan-German role that it played, it was in effect the country's national library. But these considerations were external to the one which the French had placed first: the physical safety of the unique treasures in their care. The German scholars were impressed, and none more so that Georg Schünemann, head of the Prussian State Library's Music Department. He urged a similar policy upon Krüss and, later in 1940, as a result of his concern, a large number of original music scores were moved to the cellars of the Ministry of Defence in Berlin.

But much more was needed, and the catalyst that set the wholesale evacuation in motion was a direct hit on the library in a surprise British air raid of April 9, 1941. The library was lucky to escape substantial damage; in the same raid the opera house across the Unter den Linden was almost completely destroyed. Still, the point had been made: the library was vulnerable, and would have to be emptied.

The man whom Krüss entrusted with the task was Dr. Wilhelm Poewe, fifty-six years of age and a member of the Nazi Party since the very first day of 1940. Poewe seems to have been a man as colourless as the name of his department – Utilities – would suggest: the complete Prussian functionary. Utilities was the red tape centre of the library, responsible for the upkeep of its collections, the maintenance of its building, and for liason with users and with other German libraries. From his 'roomy but sunless office', Dr. Poewe kept the administrative wheels of Germany's largest Staatsbibliothek turning.

The war, and then the evacuation, transformed this perhaps rather dull, if worthy, job into one that was positively exciting. It meant in effect Poewe's promotion. His responsibility for the

15

evacuation was total. As Krüss wrote in a report to the Ministry: 'When this work is finished ... it will be Dr. Poewe whom we shall have to thank.' 'Never before', comments another who knew Poewe, 'had one man been asked to evacuate a library of millions.' If the evacuation was a military campaign of a kind, then Poewe was the general who fought it. He had served a few months in World War One, 'as a simple soldier'. His war injuries had left him a semi-invalid; his face was scarred, and he had been badly wounded in the chest and lungs. With World War Two he was not a combatant but a strategist. He had worked in the Map Department: now, spreading the maps of Germany in his sunless office, it was with more than a librarians detached interest that he studied them.

The strategy of the evacuation seems to have been fairly straightforward. It falls naturally into two phases, first a comparatively leisurely period up to the autumn of 1943, then — following the stepping-up of the Allied air raids on Berlin — a much more hurried period ending just before the end of the war. In general it is safe to say that fewer, but more valuable, artefacts left Berlin during the first phase, and, because her military success at this time made Germany more confident of her boundaries, that the early sites were the more widely dispersed. Two of the first three, for example, were to remain at the extreme south-western and eastern corners of the entire evacuation map throughout the war. After the Normandy Landings in June 1944, there was an eastward shift to the evacuation, but this was not as marked as the later tendency for sites to contract inwards upon Berlin. Throughout, the bias in favour of southern sites well out of bombing range was more marked than any east-west axis. It was the bombs that were forcing the artefacts out of Berlin: Poewe's priority was to put them in places where they would not be bombed.

The number and geographical range of the sites suggest that Poewe was *intentionally* fragmenting the collections so lovingly, and over so long a time, gathered together in Prussia. To collect is not merely to hoard, but to make whole, and Poewe was sacrificing this organic 'wholeness' in the interests of the physical survival of the parts. Forty-one separate consignments went to twenty-nine sites: in the first four months of the 'leisurely' evacuation up to December 1942, eight consignments went to seven sites throughout the width of southern Germany. This hardly shows a desire to keep the collections together. The French Bibliothèque Nationale, by contrast, had only two main refuges outside Paris.

In the Music Department the fragmentation extended further, to the splitting up where possible of individual works. Peter Wackernagel, then an underling in the Music Department, told me that, 'If a work existed in more than one binding we sent the parts to different places, so that if one went missing from one hiding place the other would perhaps be saved'. This was the case with Mozart's *Marriage of Figaro*, for example, or Beethoven's Ninth Symphony: Beethoven had needed larger manuscript paper for the choral finale (to fit the voice parts), and it was separately bound. The fragmentation did not extend, though, to the mixing of documents from different departments: each did its own packing.

Poewe had also to choose the *Flüchtungsorten*, or refugee places, as Krüss rather quaintly called the evacuation sites, and here, like the French, his preference was for castles. They made up thirteen of the sites. As Dr. Wackernagel put it: 'Books are quiet guests, and the gentlemen of the castles preferred them to the S.S.' Wackernagel himself would spend time in one of the castles.

So it needed a map to show the new horizons which the war opened up for Dr. Wilhelm Poewe; more than that, though, the evacuation took him out of his office and out of the paper world of the librarian, to *places* on the map. 'He has checked the places in question as to their fitness for this purpose.' Krüss reported, 'and has led the transports at great difficulty to himself'.

Of the twenty-nine evacuation sites, six turned out after the war to be in the zones occupied by the Americans and the French, and twenty-three in the East. Gradually, their contents filtered back to Berlin, where they formed the nuclei of two new libraries, one in the eastern part of the city, and one in the western.

The East Berlin Library made its home in the old 1914 building on the Unter den Linden. It was named the Public Scholarly Library at first, and then, from 1954, the Deutsche Staatsbibliothek – the German State Library. The contents of the six western sites were for a long time homeless. For a while

17

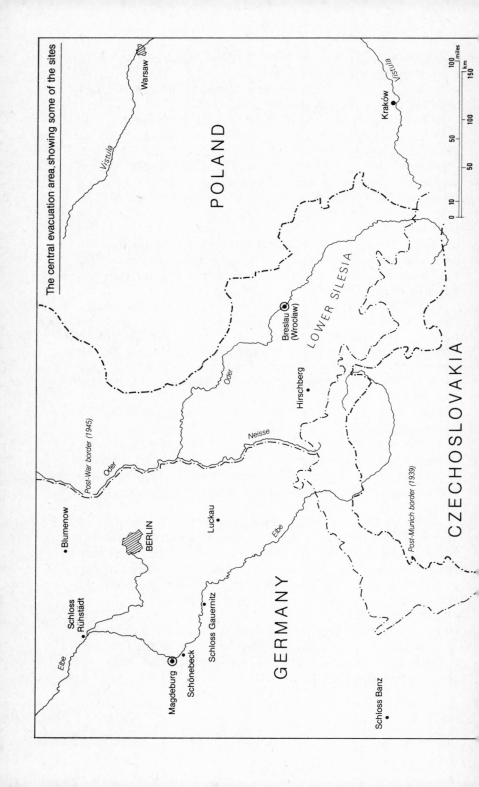

The central evacuation area, showing some of the sites

many were stored in a tent in West Berlin. But in 1978 they were moved into a brand-new building designed by Hans Scharoun and nicknamed by Berliners the '*Bücherdampfer*' — the book-steamship — a reference to the sail-like dormers on its roof and also perhaps to the impression that it had sailed out of nowhere and docked overnight into the present. Its official title is the State Library of the Prussian Cultural Foundation.

So the single library founded in 1661 is now two, a detail in the division of Berlin and of all Germany. If that were the whole story there would be no more to tell; but it is not . . .

CHAPTER THREE

Piquitinga

It was a most obscure problem that led Peter Whitehead to one
of the most powerful mysteries to result from the Second
World War, and eventually to one of the biggest and most
unusual troves of treasure missing in modern times.

But then, the area in which he was expert was an obscure
one too: the family which zoologists know as the clupeoid
fishes and which laymen know simply as the herrings and
anchovies, one of the world's main food supplies. It is an area
that abounds in problems, and that was one reason why
Whitehead had been drawn to it. 'I never got further than the
clupeoid fishes,' he would say, 'since they posed so many
problems. My real intellectual interest lies in solving puzzles. I
got into studying fishes, and fishes provided me with problems
to solve.'

It was such a problem – a fairly minor one, but none the less
tricky for that – that confronted him one morning in the late
summer of 1971. On his desk at the British Museum of Natural
History in London – under the piles of books and papers, and
his own detailed drawings of fish – there was a map of the
world beneath glass. At a glance, he could pick out Brazil and
Berlin, both of them places relevant to his problem: but he was
not yet to know that the most relevant place of all would prove
to be one that was far too tiny and whose name is missing from
modern maps. Nor could he guess at the much greater puzzles
behind the intellectual one that was troubling him that morning.

It had to do with the identity of a fish. Absurd as the layman
may find the idea of a piscine identity problem, to the zoologist
it is of the first importance to be quite certain what species he is
dealing with, and this is not always the straightforward matter
the layman might imagine it to be. Not only are there many
thousands of species, carrying a host of different vernacular

names the world over, but this bewildering variety is echoed within the supposedly cool and clear world of science. There too it is sometimes difficult to be sure which fish is which: one may be lost within another's scientific name: another may have two or more scientific aliases.

So to the zoologist strict rules of scientific naming are vitally important. Natural history uses names to distinguish between different groups of the same, from the Mammals and Reptiles down to the smallest sub-species; and, though nature takes no stock of family trees, the study of nature does. In natural history, the family trees which make up the scientifically known natural kingdom are formed of the researches carried out by zoologists and botanists throughout history, at different stages of knowledge and of scientific development. The study of these family trees is known as taxonomy, from the Greek for a group, *taxon*, and the natural scientist regards taxonomy as another tool of his trade, along with his dissecting instruments and his microscope.

Everything in nature has two Latin names, which act as a retrieval system enabling the natural scientist to work back through published references – or 'the literature' – on the species in question, right back to its discovery by science. On this taxonomic journey, he may discover confusions, duplications, or downright mistakes based on incompetence or on insufficient scientific knowledge.

The complex rules governing scientific names are framed by two international commissions, for animals and plants respectively. They are strict and, within the closed worlds over which they rule, all-powerful: the natural-historical equivalent of the International Court at the Hague. Chief among the rules is the so-called Law of Priority, the cornerstone of the Zoological and Botanical Codes.

The purpose of this strictness is, in Whitehead's words, 'to bring our names into the one-to-one relationship with taxa that we know to be possible.'[1] Because taxonomy is involved with history (as 'the Law of Priority' implies) it is subject, not only to uncertainties all its own, but to the same uncertainties as other branches of historical research. The Law of Priority is administered with a rod of iron with the aim of eliminating these uncertainties as far as possible.

[1]Env Biol Fish. Vol 3, No 22, pp. 153-161, 1978 (Canada)

21

It requires a zoologist or botanist engaged on taxonomic research to go back through 'the literature' and to unearth all references relevant to the taxon and all illustrations or drawings of it: the earliest valid name he finds takes precedence over all later ones. The Law also requires him to take into account any original specimens used in the first description of that species by science. These specimens – known as the types – are the final authority for the identity of a given species, rather like the standard foot or yard. Where the type specimen has deteriorated or has not survived, the Law allows the taxonomist to use an illustration or drawing of the type instead.

One final point fills in the background to Peter Whitehead's peculiar problem that summer morning. The Law of Priority does not go back forever in time, but has a baseline, which for zoology is 1758, the year the Swedish naturalist Carl Linnaeus published the 10th edition of his *Systema Naturae*. This is because of Linnaeus' stature as the first consistently to classify nature into strict groups and the first to employ the two-word Latin system of naming.

The two names of the fish that was puzzling Whitehead, in the course of a long survey he was doing of the taxonomy of the herrings and anchovies, were *Lile* and *piquitinga*. On his desk was a jar containing two specimens of the fish, preserved in spirits of alcohol. To the layman, there was nothing much of interest about them at all: nothing suggests deadness quite as a dead fish does. He might have remarked on the glassy eyes staring sightlessly through the thick glass of the jar, or on the way in which death had dulled the natural silver and given it a greenish tinge: the stripe of deeper greeny-silver down the flanks of the fish might have caught his interest. But Whitehead noticed also the somewhat blunt snout, and the prickly scutes, or large scales, along its belly: sure signs that it was a herring. That was not the problem, and indeed the generic name – *Lile* – indicated as much. No, the problem was one of taxonomy, and it needed special knowledge to know that the name *Lile piquitinga* represented a judgement that was open to question, a forced rather than a natural solution to the problem which the fish presented.

It had been named in 1903 by two Brazilian naturalists, Schreiner and Ribiero, after – as the Law of Priority required – they had gone back through 'the literature'. In Linnaeus, they

22

had come across a fish called *Esox hepsetus*, which he classified as an anchovy. Linnaeus, with the godlike assurance of those who are first in their field, had subsumed three fish with three different names into his *hepsetus*, after deciding that they were in fact all one: a fish that the naturalist Patrick Browne had studied in Jamaica and named *Menidia*, another that he had himself studied in specimen form and called *Atherina menidia*, and *Piquitinga*, a native Brazilian Indian fish name to whose first description by science we shall come. Schreiner and Ribiero decided that Linnaeus had been wrong to lump *Piquitinga* in with the others: after consulting the first description they considered it to be another fish altogether, not an anchovy, but a herring and, what's more, the particular herring that they claimed it to be.

Other naturalists after Linnaeus and before the two Brazilians had been about equally divided, as Whitehead was able to gather from the books on his desk that day. In the early nineteenth century, the French zoologist Georges Cuvier had decided that *Piquitinga* was not the anchovy of Linnaeus, but a herring. Cuvier's collaborator, Achille Valenciennes, at first believed it to be a herring too, but later decided that Linnaeus had been right after all. A Swiss, Louis Agassiz, had also believed it to be an anchovy.

The source of all this uncertainty and disagreement over *Piquitinga* was the ambiguity of Linnaeus' own source material for the fish. This was not an actual specimen, but an illustration, and the same illustration was studied also by those naturalists with opinions on *Piquitinga* who followed Linnaeus. It was, in a sense, the type. But the trouble was that the illustration was too crude for it to be beyond doubt what exactly was illustrated: thus the wide disparity between the judgement of Linnaeus and that of the two Brazilians, two centuries later.

A copy of that original illustration used by Linnaeus also lay on Whitehead's desk. It was from a book called *A Natural History of Brazil*, published in 1648, or more than a century before the Linnaean baseline of the Law of Priority. But, because the confusion in this case stemmed from a possible wrong judgement by the great Linnaeus himself, Whitehead was justified in going back to the 'indication' that Linnaeus had used: to the first scientific mention of *Piquitinga*. In *Piquit-*

inga's case, the Law of Priority ended there, at that seventeenth-century illustration.

It was a woodcut, and crude indeed. Looking at it, Whitehead could well understand the conflicting judgements of the naturalists who had preceded him in the problem. In the seas off north-eastern Brazil where Schreiner and Ribiero had collected their specimens, there were forty or more herring- or anchovy-like fishes, and two – one a herring, the other an anchovy – with that same silver stripe down the flank. The fish in the woodcut could have been either of those, or of the forty; it could even have been another fish altogether.

But Whitehead saw a possible solution to the long-standing *Piquitinga* problem. It had all arisen because of the crudity, and therefore the ambiguity, of the woodcut: *but what about the drawing which had been the model for the woodcut*? That surely would be detailed and defined in comparison: it might even be in colour.

There was, in this case, one last step back in the Law of Priority: back through the production process of *A Natural History of Brazil* to the original drawing. That alone could finally settle the question of whether the right fish had been given the right name. It was at the history of that book – *A Natural History of Brazil* – that Whitehead had been looking that morning.

*

Its authors, Georg Marcgrave and Willem Pies, had been among the entourage of forty-six scientists, scholars and artists that Count Johann Moritz von Nassau-Siegen (Maurice of Nassau) had taken with him during his eight years as the first and last Governor of the short-lived imperial adventure of Dutch Brazil. Later, Whitehead would call this obscure but colourful backwater of history, from 1637 to 1644, 'the first well planned and executed scientific expedition in the New World. In the quality of the observations made, the breadth of the material collected, and the manner in which the results were published, there is no parallel until the Pacific voyages of Captain Cook, over a century later'.[1]

[1]The Clupeoid Fishes of the Guianas, p.191, P. J. P. Whitehead, Bulletin of the British Museum (Natural History), Zoology Supplement 5, London, 1973.

Count Maurice was evidently a man of restless curiosity and many-sided interests. In the intervals between administering the territory under his command, and the military campaigns aimed at subduing hostile Portuguese, he set about creating a little Europe in the country that he loved and later talked about so much that he was nicknamed 'the Brazilian'. First he founded his capital – Mauritsstad, on the island of Antonia Vaz, now the heart of modern Recife: that was his centre. There he built two palaces, an aviary, a zoo, and botanical gardens. He planted a garden in which there were all the fruit trees of Brazil, and collected every kind of animal he could find. Regular wind and rainfall records were kept, and in one of the palaces he installed an observatory, the first in either the New World or the southern hemisphere. Georg Marcgrave was the astronomer.

Today, it is as if those eight years had been nothing but an extended masque, and the period we know as Dutch Brazil nothing but an eccentric dream. What does remain is the scientific and cultural heritage of those years, which first made itself felt after the count's return to Europe in 1644.

Back in the Netherlands, he filled his palace in the Hague with Braziliana. He panelled its walls with Brazilian woods, and hung from them the Brazilian paintings of two of the artists who had travelled with him, Albert Eckhout and Frans Post. Gifts of their paintings, and of cartoons from which tapestries could be woven, helped to familiarise the courts of Europe with the exotic Brazilian landscape, its people, plants, and animals. One of those gifts was made in 1652, to Frederick William, the Great Elector of Brandenburg. Together with other Braziliana, Maurice presented him with two bound volumes of watercolours and an unbound volume of oils, all of Brazilian subjects. Among them were the originals for the woodcuts that had appeared in *A Natural History of Brazil*, published four years before.

Some of the watercolours may have been by Georg Marcgrave who, in addition to his duties as astronomer, had been required to make specimen-hunting trips into the interior and along the Brazilian coast. In the dedication to his part of *A Natural History of Brazil*, Marcgrave declares that he had himself made from life the drawings for the woodcuts with which it was illustrated. *Quorum icones ad vivum ipse fecit*:

Marcgrave's Latin stared up from Whitehead's desk, a challenge. Among those 'drawings from life', surely, was one of *Piquitinga*.

From the Great Elector's private library, Maurice's gift went, in 1661, to the Electoral Library in Berlin. The Brazilian oil paintings were bound into four volumes, making, with the watercolours, six altogether: the first record of them is in the catalogue of the librarian, Johannes Rawe, in 1668, as *Libri Picturati*, A32 to 37.

It was a century before they were first studied in the latter part of the eighteenth century (after Linnaeus): half a century later, they were looked at again. Then there was a long period of neglect until 1938, when they suddenly became the object of intense study by a number of scholars. One reason for the sudden interest was the importance attached to the books by one of the Prussian State Library's staff, Dr. Hans Wegener, who gathered together many drawings that had been misplaced and so helped to draw attention to them.

Wegener's enthusiasm for the Brazilian pictures helps to explain why naturalists who interested themselves in the *Piquitinga* problem failed to study them: quite simply, the existence of the pictures was unknown to them, from Linnaeus onwards. Others studied other pictures, but no one thought to seek out the picture of *Piquitinga*.

The one exception was Achille Valenciennes, but as we have already seen he was in two minds about the problem, and other evidence suggests that he was ill-equipped to solve it anyway. As for Schreiner and Ribiero, either they did not know of the pictures' existence, thought it unnecessary to consult them, or, three thousand miles away in Brazil, were unable to consult them: what is certain is that they did not see the original *Piquitinga* picture.

For the first time, in Whitehead, there was someone who was aware of the problem, equipped to solve it, and able to see a way in which it might be solved. But he had no way yet of knowing that there were obstacles in store beside which the original *Piquitinga* problem would almost pale into insignificance. It would not be long before he found out.

It was easy to discover that with the end of the war the Prussian State Library had been dissolved and replaced by two new Berlin libraries, one for the west and one for the east. In one or other of them the Brazilian books – and *Piquitinga* – would surely be found. He wrote to both libraries.

East Berlin replied first – a reply that utterly dashed hopes of a solution to the problem. The head of the Manuscript Department there, Hans-Erich Teitge, regretted that the books were not to be found in his library, and decisively ruled out hopes that they might be anywhere else. He referred Whitehead to an East German publication of ten years before, in which it was suggested that many of the Libri Picturati – including those that interested Whitehead – had been lost in a fire at the place to which they had been evacuated for their safety during the war.

He had been wondering why the pre-war flurry of interest in the Brazilian pictures had borne no later fruits in natural history. Now he knew why. And it was not just *Piquitinga* that had perished in the fire, but so many of the marvellous works of art which the Dutch had produced from their few years in Brazil. And what else? he wondered.

There was one last, outside possibility: that the *Piquitinga* picture had been reproduced at some time over the last three hundred years or more. A good copy would solve the problem as well as the original, and on the chance of finding one he now began to pin his hopes.

But then came the reply from West Berlin. The library there, too, had no trace in its catalogues of the Brazilian pictures: but this letter, unlike the one from East Berlin, gave grounds for hope, even if the hope was a remote one. According to Hermann Knaus, Keeper of Manuscripts in West Berlin, the *Libri Picturati* and other things in the same evacuation site had survived the war and its aftermath. Of that much he seemed confident, but as to where the pictures were, or how they could be reached, there Knaus regretted that he could be of no help at all: 'We have no news, and they will not return, neither to East nor to West Berlin.'

That was all. The Brazilian pictures seemed to have vanished without trace from the face of the earth. Already Whitehead had been able to see and to appreciate the clean, continuous curve of time that led from the jungles of seventeenth-century Brazil to the Prussian State Library in pre-war Berlin. But he had assumed that the curve would extend unbroken to 1971, to the office in London where he was working on his problem.

It did not. Somewhere, somehow, the continuity had been broken. Now he wanted to know why.

With a growing sense of puzzlement, he enquired again. What about the fire? Knaus replied that there had been no fire. The *Libri Picturati* had been stored first of all in a castle in Silesia, Schloss Fürstenstein, and later in the war at a monastery. They had survived intact. Soon after the war, some of the monks had told him, a convoy had come to the monastery and taken all the things away.

Now Whitehead's puzzlement was complete. He felt himself to be standing at the mouth of a tunnel of indeterminate length. Down that tunnel of time, all those years before, a convoy had gone, loaded with its unusual treasure – not gold, nor precious stones, but priceless pieces of paper, the *Libri Picturati*. Where had it been heading, and would he be able to follow it?

East Berlin proposed a clean and final conclusion to the long history of the Brazilian pictures: a fire. No mystery there. But West Berlin proposed a convoy, and that was much murkier, and not a conclusion at all, but another development. Which was the real explanation? Whitehead's instinct told him that the pictures had survived, but forces he could not grasp as yet had broken the continuity of their history. But, if there had been a convoy, why did the East Germans make no mention of it? Did they not know, or was there another reason?

Meanwhile, his researches had established that there existed no reproduction or photograph of the *Piquitinga* picture, which ruled out the possibility of a short-cut solution to the problem. Only one hope remained – the remote one held out by the West Berlin letter: to find the pictures.

Clearing his desk, Whitehead looked at the map of the world beneath glass. With one finger he traced a line from Brazil to the Netherlands, then from the Netherlands to Berlin. From there he traced eastwards, to the area of Silesia, where the pictures were evacuated during the war. He stopped, and taking a felt-tip pen, wrote a large question mark. Somewhere in that region was the monastery where the continuity had broken and the mystery had begun: the evacuation site. Its name, said the letter from West Berlin, was Grüssau.

CHAPTER FOUR

505 Crates

Before the war, Dr. Krüss of the Prussian State Library had been one of the most ardent admirers of the new building of the Jagiellonian Library; after seeing it again at the Staatsbibliothek ceremony in 1941 his admiration had grown. After the first bomb fell on his own establishment only five days after the ceremony, and the decision was taken to evacuate, he despatched Dr. Wilhelm Poewe to Kraków, to pick up architectural tips that might be incorporated in the structure of the Berlin Library. On his way back to Berlin, Poewe passed through Lower Silesia, in the south-east of the then German Reich, and stopped there in search of evacuation sites.

He found six that were suitable. The easternmost was Schloss Fürstenstein, ancestral home of the Princes of Pless. It dated from the thirteenth century, and rose above the surrounding Waldenburger Highlands 'as if on wings, weightless despite its size', as one pre-war visitor described it.

The castle was built so high up that the River Oder and the city of Breslau, thirty miles north-east, were visible through the haze. It was huge – with five hundred rooms at least. But, for all its massiveness and mountainous position, it was not forbidding. The Hapsburg Empire had softened the hard edges of the medieval fortress and made it a place of pleasure. Terraces surrounded it: one was planted with chestnut trees; on another a stream ran between beds of roses; on a third there were twenty-seven fountains. And, inside the castle, tapestries and portraits made splashes of colour on the grey stone walls.

Industrial, as well as inherited, wealth had helped to pay for all this. Silesia was rich in coal – from its annexation in 1740 it became an industrial powerhouse of Prussia – and the Pless family had extensive mining interests. But in the thirties these began to do badly, and with the worsening of the political

29

climate – the Plesses were opposed to Hitler from the beginning – the family decided to pull out of Prussia. Gradually, they sold off their mines, art treasures, and lands, until, by 1939, the castle was their one remaining possession in the region. Just before the outbreak of war they left for England.

As a result, Schloss Fürstenstein fell vacant. Some of the five hundred rooms were put at the disposal of the Prussian State Library, and over a period of ten days in the autumn of 1941 lorries loaded with its treasures climbed the mountainside to the castle.

*

The material was stored in crates specially ordered by the library, and of a standard size, about 2 x 2 x 2½ feet. They were made of a hard wood, and the lids were nailed down. Inside them were smaller boxes containing individual manuscripts, and in the Music Department, at least, these had been wrapped in padding then sewn into canvas, to keep them waterproof.

How many crates went to Schloss Fürstenstein, and, more importantly, what did they contain? Even at the time, it required specialized knowledge in order to answer this question. The crates did not advertise their contents. On the outside, each was stamped with a hot iron – with the letters P.S.B. for Preussische Staatsbibliothek, and with a number. This number matched that of the evacuation slip which was issued for each crate. The top copy of the slip remained behind with the library administration while the carbon copy accompanied its crate to the evacuation site, listing, as in a game of Chinese boxes, the catalogue-numbers of the objects with which it was packed. Without unpacking the crates, their contents could be determined only by reference to the master copy of the slip and then by reference to the catalogues.

In May 1942, while he was on holiday, Dr. Poewe visited Schloss Fürstenstein, taking with him a list of the numbered evacuation slips. His purpose was to check that the crates and their contents were safe. He would have counted the crates, checking each against its number, then probably have opened some to make sure that their contents were undisturbed. He found nothing to trouble him, neither on this nor on a later check which he made in March and April 1943. The manuscripts were as firmly in place as the castle on its mountain or

30

the black swastika on its red ground, fluttering in the breeze behind the stables.

The quiet guests would not enjoy the hospitality of Schloss Fürstenstein for much longer, but before following them to Grüssau it is necessary to examine more closely the significance of the evacuation slips turned out by Poewe's efficient bureaucratic machine. Had the crates returned safely to Berlin, their wartime documentation and details of the precautions taken to protect them would have no more than curiosity value. When they did not return, the evacuation slips took on an importance greatly transcending their original limited purpose.

They provided the sole record of what had spent the war where, and, by a quirk of the war, all the top copies of them, together with the catalogues to which they referred, ended up in East, not West, Berlin. During the war, the top copies were stored at first in the Unter den Linden building, and later in Luckau, sixty miles south of Berlin. Luckau became the wartime administrative base of the library after the deadline for its complete evacuation in March 1944, and, because it was in an area later occupied by the Russians, it was to East Berlin that all the administrative papers – including the evacuation slips – were returned when the war was over.

The catalogues, too, ended up in East Berlin. Numbering nearly two thousand volumes, they had been evacuated to the archives of Hirschberg, one of the Lower Silesian sites. In January 1945, orders were given for their return to central Germany. The work was hurried, and volumes were lost in transit; a doctor, in a town miles from the route, found children playing in the street with some of them. Most, however, returned safely.

After the war, the library in East Berlin updated the catalogues to indicate, item by item, what had become of the wartime holdings, all of which it regarded, and continues to regard, as its own. The catalogue entries referring to those that had returned to the Unter den Linden were marked in red ink. Those evacuated to the six western sites and today retained by the West – illegally, in East Berlin's view – were circled in pencil, awaiting the red-letter day of their return; only then will the pencilled circles be erased.

Nowhere in the general catalogues was there any indication of the fate of holdings that were not known to be either in East or West Germany. Only in the subject catalogues belonging to individual departments was this marked, in the case of those holdings evacuated to Schloss Fürstenstein, and later lost from Grüssau, by the letters 'Fü'. These were officially regarded as lost, but the revised subject catalogues did not elaborate on the probable nature of the loss.

For the West, it was a major problem to establish what had fallen into *its* hands, let alone to build up an overall picture of the evacuation. It had only the carbon copies of the evacuation slips belonging to the material in its possession, but lacked the general and subject catalogues which were the key to them. The first priority was to make new and separate catalogues covering its own material – a lengthy process. Only when this documentation was complete did it become practicable for the West to ascertain what was neither in its possession nor in the possession of East Berlin. Gradually, over years, a kaleidoscopic picture began to emerge of war losses in particular fields, but – and this is vital – although the documentation of the evacuation was used in drawing up the lists of missing material *no indication was given of the evacuation sites from which particular items had been lost.*

In 1964, for example, the West German specialist magazine *Die Musikforschung* published a list of one hundred and twenty-nine missing Mozart manuscripts formerly in the Prussian State Library and lost as a result of the Second World War. All were lumped together as 'lost', but there are a number of ways in which something can be lost, and as to whether this or that original manuscript was believed destroyed, mislaid, or stolen, the list did not say. Nor did it indicate that a great many of the works had been 'lost' from the same place at the same time. A final point is that, although musicologists have been described as studying *Die Musikforschung* 'as assiduously as fundamentalist ministers study the Bible', no one else reads it. So the problem of Grüssau, the very notion that there was a problem connected with a place of that name, was effectively sealed off and hidden from view.

There was only one institution which, through its possession of the master copies of the evacuation slips, possessed the power to air the problem in full: the Deutsche Staatsbibliothek in East Berlin. It exercised this power by not exercising it, so ensuring that the problem remained hidden. Consistently and firmly, it refused outsiders access to the evacuation slips which were, in effect, its title deeds to the wartime holdings. The Grüssau mystery begins with an apparent absurdity: the victim of a robbery omitting to cry, 'Thief!'.

It was sixteen years after the war before the East Berlin Library first chose to publish information, drawn from the evacuation slips, indicating what had been lost from Grüssau; this publication still gives the most comprehensive picture available of the extent of the loss. The way in which the information was published, however, was hardly calculated to inspire scholars to search for the missing material. Firstly, the outline was so sketchy as to be misleading; secondly, there was the accompanying suggestion that all the material had been destroyed; and, thirdly, it was published in a context in which the spotlight – where war losses was concerned – was very firmly trained on the material retained by the West.

In 1961, an international gathering in East Berlin celebrated the three hundredth anniversary of the Deutsche Staatsbibliothek's foundation as the Electoral Library. The conference air, just two months after the Berlin Wall went up, was thick with denunciations of West Germany's 'barbarism' and its 'illegal' retention of the wartime holdings evacuated westward. Earlier that year, East Berlin had advertised – successfully – for the return from West Germany of some music manuscripts stolen by a dishonest librarian. Why did it not advertise Grüssau in the same way? The holdings retained by West Germany were in place, after all, even if it was the wrong place where East Berlin was concerned. Those of Grüssau, by contrast, had vanished, and their whereabouts were unknown.

Grüssau did crop up in 1961, but the mention of it was extremely discreet. It came in a commemorative volume – or *Festschrift* – handsomely produced and published by the library. It was to this volume that East Berlin referred Peter Whitehead when, ten years later, he came across the *Piquitinga* problem. The first step in his search was to obtain a copy and to look up 'Grüssau' in the index. On page 82 he found a skeleton list of the holdings lost from the monastery. It required some deciphering, even for a trained scholar like Whitehead, but one thing the list did make abundantly clear was that the Brazilian books in which he was interested had had plenty of company in their wartime exile from Berlin:

33

201 crates . . . consisting of 9 crates of *Rara* (mainly from Group Y), 2 crates of art prints, 108 crates of rare prints and manuscripts from the Oriental and East Asia Department, also about 70 Arabic, Persian, and Turkic, as well as 14 Chinese manuscripts. The remaining crates contained genealogical collections, bequests (Hoffmann von Fallersleben, Alexander von Humboldt, Schweinfurth), *Autographa*, the Varnhagen Collection, Lenziana, manuscript collections from various languages, Libri Picturati, Libri c. not. mss., autograph manuscripts by Mozart, Beethoven, Mendelssohn, and Schumann . . . A further 304 crates . . . contained the categories War 1870/'71, Eu-Ez, Zr-Zz, as well as a selection of various special categories (Ac-Ad, R and U).

A grand total of 505 crates! If just one of them had contained the six Brazilian *Libri Picturati*, and just one of those books had contained the picture of *Piquitinga*, how many secrets of research and scholarship had 505 crates contained? Among the Grüssau Manuscripts – as Whitehead at once dubbed them – there must have been the missing pieces of countless jigsaw puzzles. It was simple enough for Whitehead to generalize outwards from his own particular case, and to imagine what an enormous loss this must have been. Why had he never heard of it before? Why was knowledge of this disaster not commonplace among scholars?

He looked again at the list, and recognized the name of Alexander von Humboldt, the eighteenth-century explorer of South America – of the Galapagos Islands in particular – whose work is well-known to natural historians. Surely the papers in his bequest could not be without interest and importance? Elementary research introduced him to other parts of the list: Hoffmann von Fallersleben, the lyricist of the German national anthem 'Deutschland Über Alles', Georg Schweinfurth, the African explorer, Jakob Lenz, the Romantic poet and playwright to whom he supposed the Lenziana referred, and Karl Varnhagen von Ense (1785-1858).

Of all the material lost from Grüssau it was easiest to grasp the Varnhagen Collection. It was known as such well before the war, there were separately published catalogues of it, and it was evacuated to Grüssau in its entirety. In determining what had been lost with the loss of the collection, therefore, there was no need to have recourse to the inaccessible evacuation slips, as there was with the other material. Even when lost, it retained its identity.

The former diplomat, Varnhagen, and his Jewish wife, Rahel, stood firmly at the centre of the intellectual and cultural lives of their day. In the early years of the last century, crucial years in the development of Prussia and the growth of German culture, their home was the main salon in Berlin, and for all those who visited there – the philosopher Hegel and the poet Heine among them – they were in touch with many others, including Goethe and Karl Marx.

After their deaths, their papers went to form the nucleus of a separately administered manuscript collection which by 1911 held the letters and other writings of more than 9,000 important Germans. They included Wilhelm von Humboldt (Alexander's brother, and the founder of a university in Berlin), the brothers Friedrich and A. W. Schlegel (theorists of the German Romantic Movement), Fichte (the exponent of Prussia's primacy over the rest of Germany), Hegel, and Heine – who once wrote that he would be happy to be a dog wearing a collar-tag which read 'I belong to Rahel Varnhagen'.

In that same year, 1911, a catalogue of the collection was published. Listing, not individual items, but groups of them, it ran to just under one thousand pages. But the Varnhagen Collection is not just extremely large. It is invaluable to the study of that period marked by the emergence of the German romantics and of the Idealist philosophy, and the rise of Prussia as a great European power. No wonder that the political philosopher Hannah Arendt, in 1957, opened one of her books with sentences mourning its disappearance.

Most striking of the names in the *Festschrift*'s list, however, were those of the composers, and in particular those of Mozart and Beethoven. They shone from the dry itemization with the brilliance of diamonds in grit. Everyone knew who *they* were; the very mention of them was a loophole for excitement. But scholars learn to resist excitement, and Whitehead saw that the brilliance of the names was no guarantee that any special importance was to be attached to these manuscripts by them. If anything, the value-judgments elsewhere (rare, special, etc.) suggested the contrary. The list did not even give the number of crates that the music had filled. Perhaps there had not been enough manuscripts to fill so much as one out of the 505. They might have been only a few fragments, listed by rote along with everything else.

The names were tantalizing, but no more than that. What Whitehead was not to know was that the *Festschrift*'s tight little list was itself a sort of nailed-down crate, in which the meaning of the music lay locked away. Only special knowledge could prise it open. That could come only from the evacuation slips in East Berlin, and – although Whitehead could not realize this at the time – East Berlin was not talking. There was another maze to be gone through before the lost music of Grüssau could be revealed in all its glory.

Fragmented knowledge of the missing Grüssau music reached the West after the war through several channels. One was the monks; another was Dr. Peter Wackernagel. Their importance in the story will become apparent. Also, knowledge of isolated missing originals was gleaned by western scholars working in East Berlin. These fragments contributed towards, but could not complete, the full picture, which required a wholesale leakage of specialized information from the East Berlin Library. It occurred between 1950 and 1956. Probably during the early part of that period, an American by the name of Carleton Smith – one of the key figures in the Grüssau mystery – obtained from East Berlin a complete list of the missing music. In 1956, Smith leaked it in his turn: some details were published in the Austrian press. But it was a further twelve years before – in 1968 – Smith leaked the complete list. It was published in the London-based antiquarian magazine the *Book Collector*.

By early 1976, Peter Whitehead had been searching for five years, and his was still a search for *Piquitinga*. Inevitably, though, given the variety of the Grüssau Manuscripts, it had broadened. Cross-disciplinary contacts had been made, and through them he came to hear of the *Book Collector*'s list.

On many occasions I have been able to watch the reactions of people seeing it for the first time. Often they have been music lovers, or musicians, but invariably their astonishment falls into the pattern of Whitehead's. Firstly, they find it difficult to believe the sheer quantity and quality of the lost music; then follows a second wave of astonishment, as they wonder why they have never heard of Grüssau before.

CHAPTER FIVE

The Trade Secret

The music evacuated to Schloss Fürstenstein and then to Grüssau was contained in some fifty crates, about equally divided between rare early printed editions and original manuscripts. The latter numbered, at a conservative estimate, one hundred and ninety-six, and were by a total of twenty-two or more composers.

Apart from the four composers given in the East German *Festschrift* there were Johann Sebastian Bach (12 items), Brahms (3), Cherubini (8), Joseph Haydn (13), Meyerbeer (4), and Schubert (the E-flat major symphony). Among the twelve remaining more minor composers in the *Book Collector* list were C. P. E. Bach (6), Telemann (4), E. T. A. Hoffman, Paganini, and Hugo Wolf (one each).

Even with those composers that it *did* mention, the *Festschrift* gave no idea of the size of the loss: Beethoven (17 items), Mendelssohn (11), Schumann (twenty-three songs, twenty-seven letters and two other items) and, most spectacular of all, Mozart (98 different items, or approximately a quarter of all his music known to survive in manuscript).

Nor did it indicate that many of the crown jewels of music had been sent to Grüssau. Chief among them was the entire *Magic Flute*, but the Mozart tally also included Acts 3 and 4 of *Figaro*; Act 1 of *Cosi Fan Tutte*; two acts each of *Idomeneo* and *Die Entführung*; the Jupiter and Prague Symphonies along with nine others; nine piano concertos including some of his greatest; four of the five violin concertos; the G-minor String Quintet; the Mass in C-minor, 'the Great'.

Other crates contained the seventeen Beethoven items, including sketchbooks, notebooks, and letters, as well as musical scores; all of the Ninth Symphony bar the choral finale; all of the Seventh and much of the Eighth; the Piano Concerto No 3;

and the Grosse Fuge, plus four of the other sublime late string quartets.

Almost as an afterthought, one culls from the list famous works like the Mendelssohn Violin Concerto; his oratorio *Elijah* and the *Midsummer Night's Dream* incidental music; the Bach double-Violin Concerto and a clutch of Bach cantatas; four Meyerbeer operas including *Les Huguenots*; and Schumann's Cello Concerto.

*

The whereabouts of the manuscripts were a secret as soon as they left Berlin. In 1942, the Kapellmeister of the Bavarian Opera in Munich wrote to the Berlin Library asking to see *The Magic Flute*. George Schünemann, director of the Music Department, would tell him only that the original was spending the war 'in a little South German corner', adding that it 'cannot be consulted until after the war is over.'

Schünemann's caginess is understandable, given the context of the war. What is more difficult to understand, until one goes into it further, is why his post-war successors should have been just as cagey, if not more so; and only when that is grasped can one approach the trickier question – why did music scholars who came to learn about the Grüssau loss remain largely silent about it?

It was not that they did not discuss Grüssau. They did, but when the subject cropped up it was *sub rosa*, 'between ourselves', scraps of information exchanged in an effort to shed light on the mystery of the music's disappearance. Libraries and monasteries were in the story – the hushed tones of the scholars emphasized the studious, cloistered silence by which it was surrounded.

In the early post-war years, of course, the scholars were as ignorant as everyone else of the exact configuration of the war losses of the former Prussian State Library. We have already touched on the main difficulty – the East Berlin Library's sole possession of the evacuation slips. But, when a true picture of the Grüssau loss began to form, the scholars were the first outside the East Berlin Library to gain a notion of it, and long after the picture had formed they kept that notion to themselves. At no stage did they band together to express their concern over the disappearance, to demand an explanation for or enquiry into it, or to lodge a protest, and such publicity about Grüssau as there was did not have their backing or blessing.

I do not mean that scholars actively conspired to cover up the disappearance of the manuscripts, but that they passively and timidly refused, or were reluctant, to make a public issue out of the Grüssau mystery. The motives for their silence, as we shall see, changed and developed just as the mystery did – the trade secrecy was not static, nor was it completely watertight. But at this point I am concerned only to demonstrate that there was a trade secret, and to isolate one of the abiding motives for it.

Two examples from western books on music show the trade secret in operation. Both date from the early 1970s, by which time – after the *Book Collector* list of 1968 – scholars knew the extent of the music loss. But neither mentions Grüssau, nor the convoy; that information is suppressed. Both qualify the one little word, which in various permutations echoes through the trade secret, 'lost'; but someone who was not already in on the secret would not have been able to guess that there was one. In both cases, the author is really addressing those who *know*, without tipping off those who do not. The first example is from a British book on Mozart[1]:

> Comparative study of sources (the autograph, early MS copies, first and early editions) is now recognised as fundamental, and is specially important for Mozart where the autograph is not extant or was lost in the 1939-45 war.

The reference is brief, as one would expect in a book intended for the general reader, and one must not read too much into it, but, even so, it begs some questions. The inference is clear: although the picture is one of bombed buildings and burning masterpieces, the reader is not to assume that manuscripts 'lost in the 1939-'45 war' are 'not extant'. They have survived, therefore. What the author does not say is why he assumes them to have survived.

The second example is from a more specialist American publication[2], on the collection of Beethoven manuscripts built

[1]*Mozart*, by Alec Hyatt King, Clive Bingley, London, 1970, p.73.
[2]*The Artaria Collection of Beethoven Manuscripts: A New Source*, by Douglas Johnson. In *Beethoven Studies*, edited by Alan Tyson, W. W. Norton & Co. Inc., New York, 1973, p.177.

up by the Viennese music publisher Domenico Artaria. Inherited by his grandsons in 1893, and sold by them in 1897 to the Bonn collector Erich Prieger, from Preiger they went in 1901 to the Berlin library, and from there were evacuated during the war. The author fills in this background, up to the division of the Prussian State Library inheritance, including this collection, between East and West Berlin after the war, but suddenly becomes reticent on the subject of the lost manuscripts. The trade secrecy is turned as tight as it will go:

> What August's sons and Prieger had sought to avoid, a division of the Artaria Collection, was thus accomplished by the war. And regrettably, a considerable number of manuscripts, including some of the most valuable, have disappeared and must for the moment be considered lost.

To grasp what is being said here, one needs to know the trade secret. It makes no real sense otherwise. Only a fool would fail to consider manuscripts which had disappeared as having been lost; but when the author says 'lost' he means something else too. He is defining the correct attitude to be taken 'for the moment' towards that 'disappearance'. Looked at like this, the phrase 'must . . . be considered' takes on an imperative sense: the author is advising, or instructing, his specialist reader to live a little longer with his frustration, and to continue to take at face value the hoary old agreed formula, 'lost'. Specialists are being reminded, in fact, that the trade secrecy is still in force, as late as 1973, although that 'for the moment' holds out the hope that the deadlock may soon be broken.

Given the extreme reticence of those whose work brought them into contact with music manuscripts, it is easy to understand why most musicians and the wider music-loving public remained ignorant about Grüssau. For ten years the world wondered aloud what had become of the paintings of the Dresden Museum (taken in 1945 by the advancing Soviet army of Marshal Koniev, and mostly returned in 1955); it still sometimes speculates on the fate of the Amber Room of Leningrad (looted by the Nazis in 1942, and still unaccounted for). By comparison with these celebrated war losses, the coverage of Grüssau was intermittent, incomplete, and low-key.

Yet the lost music manuscripts were as valuable, both as saleable artefacts and as state property of symbolic significance, as the Dresden paintings and the Amber Room. The first point – their financial value – needs little elaboration. The manuscripts were worth a fortune, and if this was true of them at the time they left Berlin it was a truth reaffirmed with every passing year of their disappearance. The post-war years saw a boom in the original music market centred upon Marburg in West Germany, London, and New York, with the occasional auction in Switzerland. The boom reached a peak in July, 1979, when the manuscript of Mozart's Haffner Symphony (No. 35 in D major, K. 385) was sold for an undisclosed sum believed to be around £400,000[1]. A projection from this of the market value of the Grüssau music is so large as to make little sense. What would nearly a hundred Mozart originals fetch at auction? The whole of *The Magic Flute* or two acts of *Figaro*? If a single heavily-corrected page of music by Beethoven – a sketch for part of the slow movement of the String Quartet Op.59 (described by one newspaper as 'a scribble') – could fetch almost five thousand pounds in 1977, what would the Ninth Symphony go for, or the whole of the String Quartet Op. 131?

The Prussian State paid good money to collect the music manuscripts, and as such they were a national investment. A certain pseudo-mystical materialism and nationalism played their part in the Royal Library's decision – three years before Beethoven's death, when some of the finest music ever composed was coming from Germany – to start the collection. But so had an instinct for shrewd investment. We may recall Georg

[1]Manuscripts of great music rarely appear on the open market, and when they do are usually acquired by institutions committed to collecting rather than to selling. Mozart is the composer whose name figures most often in sales reports, not only because he was very prolific but because of what the East German music librarian Karl-Heinz Köhler calls 'the tragic fate' of the manuscripts which, on his death in 1791, he willed to his widow Constanze. She sold them all to a councillor of Offenbach-am-Main, who wanted to sell them as one collection. He offered them repeatedly to a number of libraries – including Berlin's Royal Library – but was turned down. So he willed them to his five sons, three of whom broke up and sold off their shares of the bequest. In this way many of the manuscripts fell into private hands and were dispersed all over the world.

41

Pölchau's letter suggesting the collection: 'Apart from the growing financial value of great masterpieces . . . it is the sacred duty of all culture, art, and institutions of learning to collect and to guard them for future generations.'

But *whose* culture, institutions, and future generations? The war, the dissolution of the Prussian State by international legal decree in 1947, the consequent statelessness of former Prussian cultural property, and the division of Germany into two republics, brought the question into sharp focus. The war had reminded Germans of what was worst in themselves; their cultural history and heritage reminded them of the best. The post-war political divide turned this into a cultural war resembling the trade wars that other countries wage. From the beginning there was intense competition, with each Germany asserting that it was the legitimate heir to the real, the good, and the right Germany of Beethoven and Goethe. And, where inheritance is in dispute, so is ownership.

East Germany laid claim to the entire holdings of the former Prussian State Library, arguing that they had been evacuated from a building on her territory and that the documentation of their provenance and ownership was held by the G.D.R. The evacuation slips gave East Germany the whip hand; West Germany's lack of access to them left her guessing. East Germany had another advantage in the knowledge that if the manuscripts had survived, these were somewhere in 'the East'; if they were to return, it would surely be to East Berlin.

Had East Germany aired the Grüssau problem it might have implied that the solution to it, and ownership of the manuscripts, lay elsewhere. By keeping quiet, she kept the initiative, and at the same time played down the potentially embarrassing 'eastern' disappearance.

The secrecy, silence, and monopoly of crucial information were willed upon the Deutsche Staatsbibliothek by the East German government – whence, for example, the withholding of the evacuation slips. If the government could have had its way it would doubtless have kept hidden the fact that there was anything missing that could not be accounted for by reference to the 'barbarians' of Bonn. This, however, was beyond its power. The Grüssau Manuscripts should have been in East Berlin – but were not – for the purpose of study. The library of the East German State was open to scholars and legitimate users from all over the world, a part of the international learned community. The seekers after knowledge could not be turned away; but they could be stopped from asking inconvenient questions.

Against this background, the East Berlin librarians had the task of turning the Grüssau mystery into an international trade secret. This put them in an almost impossible position. Each library-user had specific manuscripts that he wanted to study, and the catalogues were open to him. In the catalogue of the Music Department he might notice the letters 'Fü' penned in ink. Asking to study the manuscript, he would learn that it was 'lost'. After the inevitable expression of regret, there would be the equally inevitable question: how was it lost? What was the librarian to say? The catch-all formula of 'lost' was not specific enough, and the little that was known – that the manuscripts had disappeared into eastern Europe, in a convoy, and may have been destroyed, or may not – was not to be told.

Here we have the explanation for the 'fire', of which Peter Whitehead was told by East Berlin. On page 84 of the *Festschrift* he found the reference to it, which suggested that the Grüssau treasure 'probably went up in flames during the fighting'.

There *had* been a fire at Grüssau monastery, not during or just after the Second World War, however, but in 1913, just before the First. The monks called it simply the *Turmbrand* – the tower fire – because it broke out in one of the towers of the monastery church. But only in the wandering imagination of a very old monk could the *Turmbrand* have been confused with a fire over thirty years later.

The second fire never occurred. By 1950 at the latest the East Berlin Library knew that there had been no fighting in the Grüssau region and that the monastery had survived the war intact. By 1954, it also knew that the manuscripts stored there may have survived. It knew about the convoy. But seven years later, in the *Festschrift* of 1961, the fire made its appearance.

That it was a ruse can be seen from another reference to Grüssau, on page 268 of the same *Festschrift* but missing from the index. Significantly, it comes in an article on the music collection by the then music librarian of the Deutsche Staatsbibliothek, Karl-Heinz Köhler. After listing music holdings destroyed at various evacuation sites during the war, Köhler

43

adds that 'the items at Grüssau (priceless autograph manuscripts and early printed material) remain lost right up to now'
(*bislang*). That *bislang*, qualifying the 'lost', shows that Köhler
knew, or at least felt sure that the manuscripts had survived,
just as his 'priceless' shows him to have known how important
they were.

There was no fire, but the library found a fire convenient.
After 1961, it was able to supply inquisitive users who knew no
better with that thitherto absent specific explanation. Nor was
the message lost on those who did know better. Roughly, it
was as follows: 'If you want to be welcome here, keep what
you know to yourselves. Grüssau is *our* property; don't tres-
pass on it.'

The message was effective. The East German authorities
were unable to prevent foreign scholars from knowing about
the loss of the manuscripts, but *were* able to apply pressure to
prevent them from making a public issue of their disappearance. This gave them far more 'crowd-control' than they had
had over the disappearance of the Dresden paintings, which
was plain to the public from the beginning. The paintings, like
the Amber Room, were made to be *seen*, and so it was only too
evident when they were no longer in place. Unlike them, music
manuscripts are not created objects so much as intimate
records of creation. They have their own kind of beauty, and
are sometimes exhibited, but for the most part their beauty is
appreciated only as a by-product of private, specialised study.
The gap in the scheme of things left by the loss of the Grüssau
music was correspondingly easier to paper over and keep
secret. Here we have the clue to the trade secrecy.

The East German authorities saw the loss of the manuscripts
as a domestic political problem, while the scholars saw it
simply as a tragic loss to international scholarship. The trade
secret represented a working compromise between the two
points of view. In keeping it, the scholars were driven not by
self-interest so much as by their imperative need as scholars.

Original scores in the composer's own hand are of immense
importance in the study of music, for much the same reasons as
the scene of a crime is important to the detective trying to solve
it. When external evidence is lacking, there are questions –
such as the date when a work was composed, or the order of
composition of its parts – that can be settled only after detailed

study of the inks, papers, calligraphy, binding, and water-marks of the original. In Mozart's or Beethoven's day, paper was not the mass-produced commodity it is now. It was hand-made, and each piece bore the watermark – as individual as a fingerprint – of the mill which made it. An original score might contain leaves made by mills many miles apart, from different batches of paper bought by the composer at different times. Properly analysed, evidence of this sort can shed important new light on a composer[1]. The post-war years have seen the development of sophisticated new detection techniques: the sub-science of rastrology, or the study of stave-lines – from the Latin '*rastrum*', for rake, meaning the five-nibbed pen used for drawing the lines – which yields valuable evidence on dating; or the bombardment of paper with beta-particles to study watermarks. Using these techniques, scholars are able to gain privileged glimpses into the workshop of genius, and to gather clues as real to them as the strawberry-juice stains on the score of *Don Giovanni* (Mozart wrote much of it sitting in a summer-house).

Strange though it may seem, given the length of time that the works of Mozart and Beethoven have been in the repertoire, their originals are still vital as the one indisputable assurance that the right notes are being played. Mistakes may have crept into the first manuscript copy, to be repeated in the first and subsequent editions. Checking against the original is particu-larly important with Beethoven, whose handwriting was often so impetuous and messy as to be virtually indecipherable, and whose copyists were sometimes less than the best: he was always railing against them. Engrained errors can last a long time: in 1977, Peters Verlag of Leipzig published a revised edition of the Fifth Symphony in which it claimed to have corrected 'numerous mistakes' in earlier printings.

Detective work of this kind requires the clues that can only be gleaned from the originals. It follows that access to them, and therefore to the libraries where they are kept, is of the first

[1]For example, Alan Tyson has shown, by study of the original manuscripts of Mozart's mature string quartets, that Mozart was not being fanciful when, dedicating some of them to Haydn, he called their composition '*una longa e laboriosa fatica*.' It was indeed a long and difficult business, suggesting a Mozart quite different from the divinely inspired recording angel whose fluency never deserted him.

priority. Here we come to the heart of the question: for many of those vital music originals are stored in the East Berlin Library, or other libraries in East Germany and throughout the eastern bloc. To preserve access to them, it was essential for scholars to retain their goodwill, and therefore to bow to their will in certain important matters, such as Grüssau.

An episode in the career of the Haydn scholar Professor H. C. Robbins Landon shows what can happen when a scholar speaks out of turn. In 1959, he wrote an article in *The Times* criticising the conditions in which some original music was being kept in Prague. In this he was doing his duty as a scholar, but that is not how the Czech authorities saw it. To them, in behaving normally Landon was not 'behaving': he was dabbling in politics and propaganda. He was blacklisted and to this day cannot pursue his researches in Czechoslovakia.

It was partly from fear of a similar disaster befalling themselves that scholars remained silent about Grüssau. There was a calculation behind their silence. Many though the lost manuscripts were, and indispensable to the study of this or that piece of music or period in a composer's life, there were many more, equally indispensable, that were not lost; and if active efforts to secure access to manuscripts that were missing meant risking the accessibility of manuscripts that were in place, that was an unacceptable risk. The sacrifice was too great.

This is not to suggest, however, that they decided to forget about the lost music. It was far too important to be forgotten, not only a kind of gold in itself, but a goldmine too, of research secrets great and small. What a German scholar has said of all the Grüssau Manuscripts was, perhaps, especially true of the music: 'With treasures like these, it is the duty of scholars to search for treasure.'[1] Why did Mozart fail to finish the Mass in C minor (K. 427)? When did Beethoven compose his Piano Concerto No.3? What were the different layers of composition in the last two acts of *Figaro*, and what was the correct running order of Act III? Also, there had been shifts in the emphases of research over the period the manuscripts had been missing. The notebooks and sketchbooks of Beethoven, for example, in which familiar themes can be traced back to the germ of an idea, had become a growth area of music research. Beethoven

[1]Professor Dieter Henrich, of Heidelberg University, in 1977.

himself had valued them more than his completed manuscript scores, and five of them had been at Grüssau.

The lost manuscripts were unique, and could not be written off like a bad debt, or a grief that could in time be lived with. Scholars would have found their disappearance easier to bear if there had been photographic facsimiles of them all. For some research purposes, facsimiles are adequate – for example, to gain a heightened sense of the dynamics of a piece of music, a subtler perception of its 'feel'. The original score is a record not only of the final work, but of the process of its composition. The printed score will indicate only the tempi on which the composer finally settled, while the original or a facsimile will show all the crossings-out as well, the hesitations and changes of mind that resulted in the final decision.

But here again there was disappointment. The Grüssau music had been missing a long while. Some of it had been photographed before the war – *The Magic Flute*, for example. But the pre-war photographs were of poor quality, while of the great majority of the missing originals there were no photographs at all.

The absence of facsimiles can be traced to Hitler's seizure of power in 1933. Until 1929, the Prussian State Library had no arrangement for duplication of its music collection; if a scholar wanted to clear up a point in an original owned by Berlin he had to travel to Berlin in order to do so. In that year, an agreement on the exchange of facsimiles was reached with the libraries of London, Paris and Vienna. But in 1933 the agreement was cancelled. The few facsimiles dated from those four years.

So the music scholars, Peter Whitehead, and anyone with an interest in something lost at Grüssau – 'hundreds' of scholars, according to one estimate, in West Germany alone – all had to nurse the same remote hope: *to find the Grüssau manuscripts*!

CHAPTER SIX

Grüssau

It was not only manuscripts that were evacuated to Lower Silesia, but bombed-out businesses, government offices, and people – half a million of them by the spring of 1944. From the west, the nightly air raids built up the pressure – starting in 1943 with the evacuation of women and children from bombardment. From the east, the pressure took the form of prisoners-of-war and captured Jews from Poland and the Soviet Union. Silesia was the place where these two tides converged in a huge cross-current of humanity. The area became in effect a gigantic transit camp: there were camps for forced labour, concentration camps, camps full of P.O.W.'s and others full of displaced persons, and the homeless.

Schloss Fürstenstein too came under pressure, not from people in really desperate straits, but from the president of the railway, who needed a country retreat from Breslau. He took over the castle at the end of 1943, and set about transforming it into the rural headquarters of the railway. A flood of builders arrived to install comfortable new offices: 'You cannot imagine the things that were stolen,' the castle steward recalled.

But others, too, had their eyes on the castle, and in the spring of 1944 it was commandeered by the German Foreign Office for one thousand men of the Death's Head Commando. Now the reconstruction work began in earnest. The castle became a playground for architects, more than thirty of them. At their bidding, the Hapsburg Empire was forcibly replaced by the Nazi. The splendid fountains and terraces were torn up, a lift-shaft was hewn into the rock, granite was broken to make way for marble, while existing marble was painted over red. The Tapestry and Italian Rooms were converted into a special suite in case the Führer should want to pay a visit; in the grounds, huts and barbed-wire fences were built as a transit camp for Jews bound for the concentration camps.

Finally, the whole place was renamed 'The Forest Glade Guest House'.

All these new guests forced out the older ones. The building work was just getting under way when the President-General of Breslau ordered that the 505 crates of manuscripts should be moved, some fifteen miles west, to the Benedictine Abbey of Grüssau.

*

Grüssau was a tiny village whose inhabitants can only just have outnumbered the monks – about fifty-four at the start of the war. There had been a monastery on the site since the mid-thirteenth century, Cistercian at first, and then Benedictine from 1919, when it became a refuge for monks of the Emaus Convent in Prague, expelled by the new Czech government. Twenty years later, many of the monks could remember that biblical expulsion.

But in Grüssau they found a promised land. The surroundings were superb, fine buildings on spacious lawns fading gently into the meadows of the monastery farm. Beyond the meadows were the pine woods, climbing the foothills; beyond those were the heights of the Riesengebirge and out of sight behind them, twenty miles to the south, the Sudetenland. At the centre of everything were the two churches – St. Joseph's, for the parish, and St. Mary's, the monastery church – at right angles to each other in the same square. For miles around, there were only the mountain peaks to challenge in grandeur the two towers of St. Mary's, whose church bells rang out across the shallow valley.

St. Joseph's dated from the late seventeenth century, while St. Mary's was the work of Bohemian craftsmen between 1728 and 1735, and one of the finest Baroque buildings in all Germany. It was very grand indeed, with its Bohemian domes, its 'strong, flowing facade', and its towers 'reaching up like flames'. In the late eighteenth century it had been the setting for performances of Haydn's Masses and *The Creation*.

It was a place that testified to heaven, for which the Nazis had found their own hellish uses. Grüssau was one of the six special camps in the area (another was in the nearby village of Bethlehem), under the command of an S.S. Obersturmführer named Ringmann. In August 1940, the monks were moved out to make way for East European Germans who were being resettled; the 'brutal' and 'feared' Ringmann made the monastery his headquarters. Thereafter, four successive waves of people on the move were camped at Grüssau, including Silesian Jews in transit for Theresienstadt concentration camp.

The manuscripts arrived while the third wave of dispossessed people was in residence. Small though Grüssau was, it had its own railway station, and it was perhaps by rail that the crates arrived, to be taken the short distance to the monastery by lorries. Parking in the central square, the drivers saw the grand facade of St. Mary's festooned in scaffolding. Restoration work had been under way since 1938. Inside St. Joseph's church, the master restorer Johann Drobeck, from Breslau, was working on the cleaning and restoration of some fifty frescoes.

The crates were unloaded, and carried up into the choir lofts of both churches, St. Joseph's first, and then, after they were full, St. Mary's. There they joined approximately the same number of crates – 500 – of objects from Breslau's University Library and possibly its City Library as well. The total of a thousand crates was not, however, noticeable from the nave of either church. In St. Joseph's, they were so piled as to be hidden behind the pillars and the wrought-iron balustrades, while in St. Mary's only the right-hand loft was used.

The bulk of the crates went to St. Joseph's probably because they were considered to be safer there. According to one of the monks, it offered 'a very high security factor'. Church services continued as normal without anyone being aware that they were there, and intruders were kept out simply by locking the doors to the lofts. Even if someone did manage to see the crates – as the monks themselves sometimes did – there was nothing to indicate that they contained anything of special value: their numbers gave nothing away.

Yet there is no doubt that the monks were aware from the beginning of the very great value of the treasures denoted by the numbers. The monastery had been entrusted with a complete and detailed list of the crates' contents. From the Abbot, Albert Schmitt, and from the archivist, Father Nikolaus von Lutterotti, the other monks were able to gain a sense of the treasure too.

In 1954, Father Nikolaus left Grüssau to spend the last year of his life in West Germany, but by then the list had been lost, so he was unable to take with him any more than a memory of it. It is tantalising to speculate on how much more quickly a full western grasp of the Grüssau problem could have been achieved, if that list had made the journey west with Father Nikolaus.

But in the second half of 1944, the monks had other things on their minds. To the west, the Americans and British were moving through France towards the Rhine; much closer, in the east, the Russians were advancing through Poland, reaching the Vistula by the end of July. Germany, like an old painting, was about to be cut from its frame and rolled up. But while they could not but be aware of the canvas as a whole, it was their own little place in it that concerned the monks most.

To them, the war meant the deaths in action of their brothers who had been called up – ten dead by 1944, as well as two fathers, that summer, serving as padres in Rumania and Russia; it meant the still-swelling torrent of refugees, most by then from the east; Ringmann's continuing occupation of their monastery, and their own continuing exile from it; it meant the pall of smoke over Breslau, after the first Russian air raid on October 7.

But the war also meant the end at last of the long restoration work on the two churches. Halfway through October, 'the gigantic scaffolding' on St. Mary's facade was dismantled, to reveal once more the gilding and soft grey, clean white stone; soon afterwards Johann Drobeck finished his restoration of the frescoes.

The monks saw the completion as something of a miracle amid all the gathering destruction and gloom. 'In a time when ancient holy places were reduced to rubble,' said Father Nikolaus in his 1945 New Year's sermon, 'ours survived. More than that, in a time of general destruction, we restored. How it was done will be a mystery to posterity . . .'

On the Feast of Christ the King, the last Sunday in October, the monks sang the Te Deum at a thanksgiving service for St. Mary's restoration. Early in November, Drobeck, Father Nikolaus, and the Keeper of Monuments for the area, Günther Grundmann, met in St. Joseph's to survey the restored frescoes. It was then, 'to my great surprise', that Grundmann saw the depot of crates of the Prussian State Library: the last recorded sighting of them before their disappearance.

On November 12 there was a second thanksgiving in St. Joseph's. The voices of monks and villagers were raised in song; high above the congregation, still safe in their choir lofts, the crates of manuscripts slept on in their silence.

*

From St. Martin's Day (November 11) to St. Joseph's Day (March 19) the Poles say you can be sure there will be snow on the ground. The winter of 1944-45 was no exception. On January 12, the Soviet army, which had been held back to the Vistula since July, crossed the river and began the march westward across the snowbound plains to the Oder. Breslau – one of the towns on the eastern approaches to Berlin proclaimed as fortresses by Hitler – was encircled, and began its long resistance. By the 19th, the Russians were in Lower Silesia, whose population now joined the columns of refugees from further east, moving westward to Saxony, the poorer people in carts or on foot, the women wheeling prams through the snow.

By mid-April the Russians were at the Oder, and by the 24th had encircled Berlin. Since the general administration's move to Luckau in March 1944, Wilhelm Poewe had been in charge of the Unter den Linden building, but in mid-April, Krüss returned to Berlin. There was nothing for him to do there, but then, at the age of sixty-six, he had come to the conclusion that there was nothing more for him to do anywhere. 'For him personally,' one associate put it, 'existence had lost all its meaning.' In 1941, his American wife, Anna, had died. In 1944, his house in Berlin had been bombed. Now he was about to lose 'his' library.

'What will become of me,' he had been given to wondering since Anna's death, 'when I am no longer in charge of the library? I have never been a bookworm, and I never shall be one.' Now there was very little left for him to be in charge of: the library was a virtual hulk, forty per cent destroyed after five direct hits by heavy explosive bombs and innumerable hits by incendiaries, and it was empty, its contents dispersed all over Germany. Outside, the sounds of battle raged as the Russians approached the Unter den Linden. On April 27, Krüss handed over his keys and his papers to Poewe, then went to his office and took poison – a *verismo* death in soft contrast to the

52

Wagnerian struggle only hours away from engulfing the library.

*

An indication of the very great value attached to the original music manuscripts is that they had been one of the library's very first collections to be evacuated in its entirety. There had been music originals in the very first consignment, to Banz Castle in Thuringia in September 1941; by December 1942, most of them were in place in six sites outside Berlin, four in the west and Fürstenstein/Grüssau and Altmarrin castle in the east. The remainder had been in the cellars of the Ministry of Defence in Berlin since 1940; when the Ministry was destroyed in a raid of February 1945, those crates were moved by barge down the River Havel and then down the Elbe to a mine at Schönebeck near Magdeburg, making a total of seven sites for the music manuscripts outside Berlin.

The next priority, the printed music, was divided between these and five other sites. Finally, there was the ordinary music literature, which stayed in Berlin as long as it did only at the insistence of the University Library, which had no music library of its own. But following a huge explosion at the library in February 1944 – when the biggest bomb of all fell through the glass dome over the main reading room – the Music Department decided to go ahead despite opposition. The librarian, Peter Wackernagel, was despatched on a tour of castles in the Mark of Brandenburg, to find a suitable site. All were 'too small, or wrong for another reason', until he came to Rühstädt on the eastern bank of the Elbe, and met its aristocratic owner, Hans-Georg von Jagow, 'a real nobleman in the best Prussian style'. The matter was settled. Wackernagel would live in the castle, whose first floor would be occupied by the quiet guests. They arrived at the castle in mid-July 1944.

The following month they were joined by a very distinguished guest indeed – the original manuscript by Bach of the six Brandenburg Concertos, of which Wackernagel was making a facsimile edition. Late in August, he went to Berlin to collect them. On the way back, the train was dive-bombed. He hid the Brandenburg Concertos under his coat and ran for the cover of the forest, diving to the ground as the 'planes returned to the attack with machine-gun fire.

Even more nerveracking was the arrival of the Russians at

Rühstädt. At first it looked like a disaster. Finding the books on the first floor, they began throwing them down one by one. 'These are all Hitler's,' one of them shouted. 'These books no longer belong to you. They shall all be burnt.'

Wackernagel knelt down and began to pick up the books. He showed them one. 'That,' he said quietly, 'has nothing to do with Hitler. *Das ist Musik*!' Then he found a history, written in Russian, of the Moscow Opera. 'Has Hitler allowed this?' they asked him.

So the gentle librarian charmed the soldiers, first with words, then with music – playing Bach fugues on the village church organ, as a Russian soldier worked the bellows. They nicknamed him 'Piotr Pavlovitch', and came to regard him as a harmless *Musikant*.

Other evacuation sites were less lucky. Sixty miles east, at Blumenow manor north of Berlin, nearly two hundred crates were destroyed in the fighting. Eighty miles south, at the castle of Gauernitz in Saxony, Russian troops removed crates containing 'occidental manuscripts, older printed music, rarities, atlases . . . and a selection of German, English, and Nordic literature'. In Lower Silesia, some three hundred thousand books (including many catalogued under 'War') were destroyed in fighting at the village of Giessmansdorf; twenty miles north, at the estate of Gröditzburg, Prussian State Library holdings 'second in value only to those of Grüssau' were deliberately set on fire by retreating German troops wanting to obliterate records of the eastern forced labour organisation, which were stored in the same place.

On May 7, the last occupants of 'Camp Grüssau' crossed the mountains to the Sudetenland, the escape route to Saxony having by this time been closed by Soviet troops. On the same day, Breslau fell, Ringmann and the other S.S. abandoned their uniforms and escaped, and the occupation of the monastery was lifted. 'Its interior – once so beautiful – looked appalling,' wrote one of the monks. They and the villagers at once started to tidy the dirt and damage left by the S.S.

This work was in progress when the Russians arrived. Not a shot was fired. As in the psalm, Grüssau's help was in the hills – which set a natural limit on military operations – and in its isolation. Irrelevant to military strategy, the monastery proved itself well suited to the strategy of Poewe's evacuation.

The closest the main current of hostilities came to it was in the last week of the war, when the Russians crossed into Czechoslovakia through the mountain passes of the Reisengebirge.

At midnight on May 8, the war in Europe ended. At 5.45 on the afternoon of the 9th, Russian troops occupied Grüssau, 'without a struggle and without damage'.

CHAPTER SEVEN

Introducing Dr. Smith

As Germany was occupied, so the Allied Forces began to discover the wartime hiding places of German gold, currency reserves, paintings and other cultural collections – including those of the Prussian State Library. In mid-April 1945, the American Third Army came across one of the biggest evacuation sites, the Ronsbach potash mine in central Germany:

> The workings are somewhat over 800 metres below ground level and consist of large open chambers with connecting passageways. The bulk of the holdings placed there consist of books from the Berlin library, total number estimated at 1½ to 2 million volumes . . . . a Fräulein Naumann, an assistant from the Berlin Library is living there as a refugee.

In the same way the library's other evacuation sites, both east and west of the agreed demarcation line between the western Allies and the Soviet Union, were discovered and placed under the control of the American Army's Monuments, Fine Arts, and Archives Division, and of the Red Army's Trophies Brigade. It was this brigade that dealt, early in May, with the paintings of the Dresden Museum and their transport into the Soviet Union.

Also in May, the Bavarian town of Bayreuth, the site of Richard Wagner's home, the Villa Wahnfried, and of the annual festival devoted to Wagner's music, was occupied by the Americans. An American Counter Intelligence officer, John Lichtblau, was approached by Winifred Wagner, the composer's daughter-in-law, and presented by her with a list of original scores by Wagner that had gone missing during the war.

On May 10, American intelligence officers broke into a salt-mine near Hallein in Austria, where treasures of the Mozart Foundation in nearby Salzburg had been stored. The treasures – including two gifts to Mozart from the Empress Maria Theresa, a diamond-and agate-studded ring, and a diamond-encrusted gold watch bearing the Empress's portrait – had vanished from the safe where they had been kept. A manuscript minuet, found in a heap of Nazi pamphlets, was all that remained of a small group of original Mozart scores that had been stored in the same place.

All over Germany, similar storage places were being uncovered, containing both German treasures that had been evacuated and foreign treasures that had been looted. As those of the Prussian State Library were found – in the Soviet, American, and French zones of occupation (there were none in the British) – archival and library experts began to sort through the manuscripts and books. As they were checked, they were 'put under the Allies' protection for security purposes'. By the decision of the information control division of the Allied Office of Military Government, no news of the sites and their contents was released.

*

But a music-mad American called Dr. Carleton Smith was able to penetrate the black-out and learn, in advance of the rest of the world, what the war had done to the priceless music collections of the Berlin library – and to other German music. Carleton Smith's experience of Germany went back a good way, to his days as a music critic and broadcaster in pre-war Berlin, Bayreuth, and other centres of musical life. His first German visit had been in 1930, to Berlin to see Richard Strauss and Strauss's publisher, Adolph Fürstner. The same summer he paid his first visit to Bayreuth, for the festival. There he picked up again with Wagner's son, Siegfried, whom he had interviewed for the radio in Chicago, and with Siegfried's wife, Winifred, whom he had met in New York. In Berlin and Bayreuth, on this and later pre-war visits, he cemented his acquaintance with the conductor Wilhelm Furtwängler – who knew Smith from a winter season he had done in Washington in the late twenties. On occasions he stayed with Furtwängler at his villa in Potsdam, near Berlin; on his last visit before the war – in 1938 – he stayed in Berlin with Heinz Tietjen, co-intendant with Winifred, after Siegfried's death in 1930, of the Bayreuth festival.

These and other friendships with Germans who had remained in Germany had been discontinued since the outbreak of war. In the summer of 1945, as soon as he could after the war was over, Smith took up these friendships once more. Through them he learned for the first time of the wartime dispersal of German music.

Winifred told him that the missing Wagner scores had been given as fiftieth birthday presents to Hitler in April 1939. Among them were the original scores in Wagner's own hand of *Die Feen*, *Das Liebesverbot*, and *Rienzi*, fair copies by Wagner of the first two operas of the Ring Cycle, *Das Rheingold* and *Die Walküre*, and orchestral sketches for parts of the final two – *Siegfried* and *Götterdämmerung*.

In the 1860s Wagner had given these originals, drafts, and fair copies as Christmas and birthday presents to his patron, King Ludwig II of Bavaria. On Ludwig's death they went to his heirs, the Wittelsbacher Ausgleichsfond, in Munich. In the late 1930s they were bought by the German State Chamber of Commerce and presented to Hitler.

Hitler, a lover of Wagner's music and an habitué of the Bayreuth Festival, was delighted with the gift, but apparently had no idea that the scores were the originals themselves until Winifred told him at the 1939 festival the following July. He was, Winifred told Carleton Smith, 'flabbergasted, speechless, beside himself with joy' at the news.

After that, it seems to have been difficult to part Hitler from the scores. In the early years of the war, Winifred suggested to him that they might be safer kept in Bayreuth, in the Villa Wahnfried: he replied that they would be safer with him. In the early spring of 1945, Winifred's son Wieland tried to contact Hitler personally, to plead with him that the manuscripts be moved to Bayreuth: that attempt failed too.

Had the Wagner manuscripts perished in the Berlin bunker together with their owner, in the *Götterdämmerung* of Hitler's and the war's last hours? Or had they survived? This was the question which Winifred – the guardian of the Wagner family tradition – wanted answered, and which she was powerless to pursue. As a friend of Hitler (who remained unrepentant in her admiration of him until her death early in 1980) she was in disgrace and undergoing de-nazification. Smith, by contrast, was the well-connected – the very well-connected – citizen of an occupying power, and was known to her. He could serve as a bridge.

The same question mark hung over the past and future of Wilhelm Furtwängler, who had continued his conducting career in Bayreuth and elsewhere in Germany under the Nazis. From him, in the summer of 1945, Smith heard the same refrain of priceless music manuscripts displaced and perhaps destroyed as a result of the war. The music, this time, was that of the Prussian State Library. Furtwängler knew of the music collection's evacuation and dispersal throughout 'Greater Germany' from his old friend Dr. Peter Wackernagel (who was at this time still at the Rühstädt site) and doubtless also from the former chief music librarian, Dr. Georg Schünemann (who had died in December 1944).

Carleton Smith had also known Schünemann, and could claim, as he could not with the Wagner manuscripts, a special relationship with the original music collections of the Berlin library. He had seen and studied them on his pre-war German visits; during his visit of 1938, he spent a whole week on the Unter den Linden, studying the scores.

One wonders how Schünemann regarded Smith. Probably as something of a dilettante nuisance. 'Schünemann would bring me the scores,' Smith says. 'He was aggressive and domineering, and I didn't much like him. He knew so much, though. Sometimes I couldn't read Beethoven's handwriting, and had to ask him: he would always explain what was written.'

It is hard to picture Smith, as a young man, working his way methodically through the scores. One sees him, rather, sitting in the music reading-room surrounded by a heap of them, leafing through this one or that as the whim took him. 'I regarded libraries,' he says, 'as treasure-houses.'

Now, from Furtwängler, he learned how the contents of the biggest treasure-house of them all had been scattered to the four winds.

At this early stage, Furtwängler would not have singled out the Grüssau site for special mention – if indeed he knew of it. It was simply one of a number of places from which *all* the treasures had yet to return. The safety of the music collection as a whole was in question, and the obvious dangers that existed were aggravated by the difficulty in obtaining information. Grüssau had yet to attain its special status.

But we can guess that Furtwängler would have singled out

some of the library's thousands of original scores – the symphonies of Beethoven, for example, with which his own name as a conductor was so closely associated, and in particular the Ninth, which Beethoven's factotum Anton Schindler had sold to the library in the early 1840s. Perhaps Furtwängler mentioned too *The Magic Flute*, and perhaps he knew the story of how Franz Espagne, the music librarian in the 1860s, had had to battle with the Prussian Government to buy it for the Royal Library. Was a Russian soldier, even then, using the Queen of the Night's aria to light a fire? Was a G.I. from South Dakota applying the Ode to Joy to the tip of his cigarette?

The missing original scores of Wagner and the displaced music of the Berlin library powerfully complemented one another. A dramatic image began to form in Smith's mind, of the creativity represented both by the music originals, and by the care taken in their collection, torn apart by war; pages of great music caught up in the whirlwind of exploding bombs . . .

Later evidence would augment the image. In Finland, Sibelius would tell of some of *his* original scores that had been with the music publishing firm Breitkopf and Hartel, in Leipzig. The firm had been bombed: had the originals survived? In Austria, he would learn of the disappearance of the Mozart treasures from their salt-mine storage place near Hallein . . .

But the missing Wagner scores, the music of the Prussian State Library, and, later, the music of Grüssau, would remain the core of the image. And, as this image evolved, so an idea began to emerge, a plan suitable for the times. Someone had to be responsible for finding the missing music, for piecing the shattered collections together again . . . Who better suited than he?

And Carleton Smith knew just the person to approach with his plan – the music-loving 'country boy from Missouri' who was the mightiest of all his connections: Harry S. Truman, President of the United States.

CHAPTER EIGHT

Waltz in A

If Smith had had to conceive of a President expressly for the purpose, he could not have imagined one to whom his plan was more likely to appeal.

Throughout his time in power, and afterwards, Harry Truman was fond of saying that if he had made the grade as a pianist he would never have gone into politics. Sessions at the piano – playing Chopin for a bored but polite Winston Churchill, Paderewski's Minuet in G for Stalin (incorporating the 'turn' that Paderewski himself had taught him), or the Missouri Waltz for some voters – punctuated his political career.

As a boy, Truman was known as the one piano pupil in his home town of Independence, Missouri, who never dodged his lessons. His teacher wanted him to pursue a musical career, but when he was seventeen Truman decided he was not good enough and abandoned his piano studies. Not the piano, however: 'He plays it for relaxation whenever any big international or domestic problem arises,' a newspaper reported in 1945.

The public was then just getting to know the new American President, who had taken over after Roosevelt's death in April. In July, Truman set out for Germany, to attend the Potsdam conference, the last of the 'Big Three' meetings. For a fortnight, together with Stalin, Churchill, and later, Clement Attlee, Truman presided over the future of post-war Germany, reparations (or war damages, including the fate of the German fleet), and the division of Europe and the world into 'spheres of influence'. Even today, one is staggered by the immensity of the issues on the conference agenda.

Only one of them need detain us here: the question of Poland's western boundaries. The problem went back to the first month of the war – the time of the Nazi-Soviet pact – and the invasion of eastern Poland by the Soviet Union. Polish territory beyond the River Bug was incorporated into Byelo-russia and the Ukraine. At the Yalta conference it had been agreed in principle, pending a final peace conference, that Poland should be compensated in the west for this land lost in the east. The country was to be shunted westward – how far was never agreed. There was talk at Yalta of the Oder and Neisse rivers as the new boundary, but just how vague this was can be judged from the confusion at Potsdam over whether the western or the eastern tributary of the Neisse had been meant. A further complication was the Yalta decision that German territory was to be occupied only by the four powers – the Soviet Union, the United States, Britain, and France – each with its own zone of occupation. Poland was not listed among the occupying nations.

But, by Potsdam, that is what she had effectively become. Polish soldiers and a skeleton Polish administration had followed the Red Army into Silesia and Pomerania up to the Oder and the western Neisse: the so-called Oder-Neisse Line. As well as suiting the Poles' desire to gain more land, it suited Stalin to push the area of Soviet control as far west as possible and to have a large portion of eastern Germany under the thumb of what was about to become a client state. At Potsdam, he pressed for official recognition of this *fait accompli*, as Truman described it, while disclaiming responsibility for Poland's occupation, in defiance of Yalta, of part of Germany. He did say, however, that the Polish back-up had helped the Red Army by providing a secure rear for the advance on Berlin.

No clear conclusion or agreement was reached on the matter. The Polish boundary question was left to become another bone of contention in the cold war. Potsdam, and the war, would end without the expected peace treaty, with Poland in *de facto* possession of territory its rights to which would thereafter remain open to question.

*

The boundary question became part of the Potsdam discussion on reparations, and was shelved amidst talk of tons of coal, millions of people who would have to be moved, fed, and housed, and tens of thousands of square kilometres.

Grüssau – a speck on the map between the western and eastern branches of the Neisse – appeared nowhere on the agenda of Potsdam. Nor did the manuscripts stored there. But even if they had they would doubtless have been overlooked in all the global horse-trading that was going on. It is interesting to note, though, that music did play a distinct if minor role in the conference.

A sort of musical war was waged between the Big Three, started by Truman (with a pianist and a violinist), escalated by Stalin (two pianists and two violinists), and finally oom-pahed to kingdom come by Churchill (the whole of the Royal Air Force band).

Truman opened the hostilities with a dinner party for Stalin and Churchill at which his favourite pieces were played. Among them was Chopin's Waltz in A-flat Major, Op. 42, which Truman had first heard as a boy played by Paderewski himself at a concert in Kansas City (it was after that concert that Paderewski taught him the 'turn'). It had been, ever since, the composition to which he most consistently returned. Truman had requested it, but the pianist did not have the score, so one was found in Paris and flown to Potsdam for the occasion.

So the cold war got under way to the sound of music. The most powerful men in the world, at the whim of one of them, sat through the waltz he had heard as a child.

*

During the fortnight of the Potsdam conference, the Polish army was completing the last stages of an operation to clear the new border area of Germans. They were deported west, and in their place Polish military posts were set up in the border villages. The monks were just a few of some seven and a half million Germans contained within this ring of foreign military power. Soldiers were everywhere: the First and Fourth Ukrainian Fronts of the Red Army were based at Liegnitz, less than fifty miles north. In their region, bordering Czechoslovakia, the Polish army was represented by the First Armoured Division, and then, from the first week in July, by the First Army, numbering perhaps 70,000 men. In the late summer, Polish soldiers began to harvest the crops that German peasants had planted.

The military presence was backed up by an administration. As early as April 2, the Polish plenipotentiary for Lower Silesia issued his first order. On May 20, a Polish civil administration was set up in Landeshut, to whose area Grüssau belonged.

Clearly the Poles were settling in, and for the monks another exile – like that from Czechoslovakia in 1919 – was in the offing.

*

In Berlin, just as the Potsdam conference was ending, the Russian authorities asked Wilhelm Poewe, the architect of the evacuation, to write an account of his life and career. In effect the former Nazi was being asked to draw up a defence brief for himself. Poewe was in no doubt over which aspect of his life to stress:

> I was in charge of the organisation and management of the evacuation of the three million volumes of the Prussian State Library, a duty that is unique in the history of librarianship. It was to save German cultural knowledge from destruction.

Perhaps the Russians were impressed by this, but unfavourably so, because on August 28 they arrested him. Poewe was taken to Sachsenhausen, the concentration camp in north Berlin which the Russians turned into a camp for ex-Nazis. There, under the arc-lamps known as 'the sun of Sachsenhausen', the saviour of German cultural knowledge ended his days 'in deepest darkness'. Nothing more was ever heard of him.

*

'Mr. Truman was more interested in the manuscripts than anyone ever knew,' says Carleton Smith. '"Everyone's worried about the missing paintings," he said once, "but no one seems to know about the music".' Smith adds that he started his search 'by order of Truman', and that each time he saw Truman until his death in 1972 he always asked after its progress.

Smith first broached the subject of Germany's music manuscripts in a meeting at the White House soon after the President's return from Potsdam. The two men had met only once before, when Truman was Vice-President, but one imagines that they hit it off well together. They had a lot in common.

Smith, like Truman, was a mid-western country boy, born in 1908 in Bement, Illinois, a small town which had started as little more than a railway stop in the cornfields of the American 'bread basket'. And, as with Truman, music had played an

64

important part in his life since early childhood. He began by learning from his mother, a devout Catholic who was organist of St. Michael's Roman Catholic Church in Bement, and from the priest, Father Selva, who taught him to read music. But for the most part he was self-taught.

Smith's father, a grocer, could not afford the machinery of the technological revolution of the early years of the century. But there were people down the road in Bement who could, and they gladly turned their drawing-room over to the musically-minded youngster. There, at his request, the black servant wound the Edisonograph and the horn gramophone and changed the discs and cylinders – Chaliapin on the Russian Red Label, Columbia's Grand Opera and Victor's Red Seal series, Mary Garden with Debussy at the piano, and, of course, Caruso. By the time he was twelve, Smith claims to 'have heard and to know all the recordings issued in the United States'.

From 1920, the first radio broadcasts from Pittsburgh helped to bring more music into the Illinois cornfields. But this was not enough for Smith. He actively sought a greater intimacy with the music which was his godhead and the performers who were its high priests. At the age of four we find him backstage at the Chicago Opera, sitting on Mary Garden's lap; later, like Truman again, and at much the same age, he met Paderewski. Then Furtwängler, Siegfried Wagner, Richard Strauss, Sibelius . . .

Concern for the displaced music manuscripts gave Smith and the President of the United States something else in common. Truman was quick to respond. One of his first acts was to authorise the flamboyant Dr. Smith to visit Hermann Goering in his cell at Nuremberg, so that Smith – who knew Goering from Bayreuth – could ask him about the Wagner manuscripts. The initiative came to nothing. As for the Berlin music Smith was able to draw on his own experience to involve President Truman in a sense of the dangers facing it. 'When I told the President that I had had these manuscripts in my hands . . .' The sentence tails off, as Smith's sentences, and often Smith himself, tend to do. But the meaning is clear enough: the former music critic was presenting himself to Truman as a living link with the originals.

Smith has given as one of the abiding motives for his long search for the missing music 'the sentimental desire' simply to see the manuscripts again. 'The musical manuscripts meant a lot to me,' he said. In them he detected 'signs of fresh creation'. Beethoven's, in particular, were 'so living'. 'For me,' he has written:[1]

> there is something mystical and thrilling about a piece of paper that has received directly from the pen of a genius the fresh statement of his creative vision. Here we can study the origin of a dream, the changes, the crossings out, the after thoughts, all of which contribute to the growth of a master-piece. The original is often an immensely personal and graphic embodiment of a composer's musical imagination . . . One doesn't have to go far into the dense jungle of Beethoven's manuscripts to know that this impetuous, im-pulsive hand – now and then stabbing the pen right through the paper – is far different from the clear sure flow of Mozart or the orderly, even inspirations of Schubert.

This emotion in the presence of great music as its composer actually wrote it down is real and quite valid. Smith himself tells how, in 1950, he went to see George Bernard Shaw when he was dying, taking with him a manuscript page containing a piece of melody by Mozart. 'It is like looking into sunlight,' said Shaw. Or as Tchaikovsky emotionally remarked, after studying the original score of *Don Giovanni* in Paris: 'I felt as though I had pressed Mozart's hand.'

The scores represented in a sense the consummation of the drive to get on closer terms with music that had impelled Carleton Smith ever since his childhood in the Illinois corn-fields. First the music, made accessible on disc or on crystal set; then meetings with the musicians, in the flesh; finally the virgin, disembodied *sources* of the music, the original scores, 'mystical and thrilling'. Smith wallowed in the Prussian State Library's treasure-trove of original scores just as he had wallowed in the recordings when a child in Bement. In Berlin, he consolidated the musical self-education that a Berliner – Emil Berliner, inventor of the gramophone – had enabled him to pursue in the cornfields.

No other explanation seems adequately to fit a disturbing implausibility that we here encounter in Smith's story. Tchai-

---

[1]The *Smithsonian Magazine*, Dec. 1975, p.88.

kovsky could claim only to have held hands with Mozart. Smith claims to have gone to bed with Bach.

He says that on his pre-war visits to Berlin he was able to borrow original scores from the library and take them overnight to the American Embassy, where he was staying. He enjoyed this privilege through his friendship with William E. Dodd, Roosevelt's ambassador in Germany from 1933. Smith had first met Dodd as a child, after a debate in the Bryant House in Bement, where Abraham Lincoln had also debated. He met him again when he was a student at the University of Chicago, where Dodd, before becoming an ambassador to Germany, was a history professor. 'I decided,' he says, 'that Mr. Dodd was not only a brilliant historian, but one of the nicest men I had met. I idolized him.'

He met his 'idol' again in Berlin, after 1933, to discover that Dodd was 'great friends' with the director of the Prussian State Library, Hugo Andres Krüss, and with Krüss's American wife, Anna (who was also from Illinois). Ambassador Dodd was able to ask Krüss to let the originals out of the library for the study of the visiting young American who was so mad about music. One which spent the night in Smith's room was the original of Bach's St. Matthew Passion, whose performance under Mendelssohn in 1829 had started the modern Bach revival. Smith remembers staying awake all night worrying that the embassy might burn down and the precious Passion be burnt with it.

Anyone familiar with the way in which a great library is run will at once be struck by the unlikelihood of Smith's story. Peter Wackernagel, who worked in the Music Department at this time, says that while minor manuscripts were sometimes allowed out of the library it would have been 'absolutely impossible' for Smith or any other individual to take out music manuscripts of the first quality, such as the St. Matthew Passion.

Wackernagel can recall only two occasions on which top-flight manuscripts were lent out. One of them was the Passion, lent to London in 1935 when Hitler was making friendly overtures to Britain; the other was *The Marriage of Figaro*, lent to Vienna in 1941.

It would have been most unprofessional of Krüss to have 'ordered' the overnight loans, as Smith says he did, and of the then music librarian Schünemann to have allowed them. Friendship with the American Ambassador seems insufficient excuse for such irregular behaviour, especially when the favour was not directly for the ambassador himself. And would Dodd really have made so special a request of the head of the Prussian State Library? Was he so anxious to impress his young compatriot? Or is the anxiety to impress rather to be laid at Smith's door?

'A fantastic figure', one of Smith's oldest acquaintances remembers him, 'connected in my memory mainly with music and mystery as to what he was up to . . .' But here we have evidence that some at least of Smith's fantasy may be of his own making. Smith's story of the overnight loans can only have been true if he was staying at the American Embassy, as he says he was. But Dodd's daughter, Martha Dodd Stern, asserts that although she remembers Smith in Berlin he 'did not stay with us at our home'. So the notion of a tripartite understanding between Smith, Dodd, and Krüss regarding the originals simply breaks down.

Similar evidence of a white lie emerges from Smith's story that he was present when Dodd presented his credentials to Hindenburg, in August 1933. Setting it against Dodd's own diary record[1], we find that, to have overheard what he says he overheard, Smith would have had to be seated on 'the preferred sofa' which we know only Dodd and Hindenburg to have occupied. Martha Dodd Stern recalls that 'these occasions were much too formal' even for her or her mother's presence, and has no memory of having been there on that important day; Smith remembers both women as having been present.

Smith was simultaneously suggesting to Truman a greater intimacy both with the music of Berlin and with the former American ambassador to Germany than he had in fact enjoyed. The story of bedtime with Bach was a sales point which served to dramatise both the 'mystical thrill' of the original scores and Smith's relationship with them. Presented like this, the leaves of music became, as it were, communion wafers made holy by the touch of Bach's, Mozart's, and Beethoven's hands; concern for them, and the search for those that were

[1] *Ambassador Dodd's Diary, 1933-1938*, edited by William E. Dodd, Jr. and Martha Dodd, London, Victor Gollancz, 1941, pp.43-44.

missing, became a sacred quest. The Passion had survived the night in Smith's bedroom, but had it survived the war?

Smith was not just an experienced music critic, but a qualified accountant, with a degree from the University of Illinois behind him, business studies at other universities, and wartime experience as an adviser and 'image builder' for big American corporations. He had tried his hand at selling jeeps to the Soviet Union (a pair of jeep-embossed gold cuff-links was sent to Stalin), working in South America for the Rubber Development Corporation, and joining in the 'drive for better homes' for Celotex.

The Passion story has the same gimmicky ring as that of the jeep-motif cuff-links. Smith was doing some image building, seeking to impress Truman – the successful politician but failed pianist – and 'sell' him the plan he had in mind: the safeguarding of Germany's music.

That plan fitted perfectly into the prevailing American outlook just after the Second World War. The United States was determined not to retreat into isolationism as she had done after the First, but on the contrary to involve herself closely in European reconstruction and world affairs. The Soviet threat helped to inspire and give added edge to this determination. The jockeying for power and spheres of influence that had marked Potsdam was to be prolonged into the Cold War.

The key year in this was 1947, when the President outlined to Congress his 'Truman doctrine', advocating a turning away from isolationism and the Monroe Doctrine, whereby the United States had largely confined her international interests to the American continent. In 1947 the Marshall Plan for European recovery was launched: the United States was to supply raw materials, goods, and capital subsidies and credits to the tune of 14 billion dollars by 1953. And in 1947 the National Arts Foundation of New York – director, Carleton Smith – came into being.

A side-effect of the outgoing, buoyant mood just after the war ('dollar imperialism', the Soviet Union called it) was that it created an unusually favourable climate for American philanthropy. The philanthropic ideal, nourished by special provisos in the American tax laws, was seen as an assertion of free enterprise and a bulwark against Communism. In 1946, in a speech launching a charity drive for Jewish victims of Nazism,

Smith's old boss at the Rubber Development Corporation, Bernard Baruch, said that 'if we want to retain the system of personal initiative, we must support private charity; the two go hand in hand. Abolish private charity and the state takes over, in a grim, organised, statistical way . . .' In 1947, President Truman endorsed the American system of philanthropy: 'We cannot hope to be worthy of the continued blessing of Providence if our prosperity is used selfishly for our own personal gratification.'

Against this background of altered American foreign policy and government encouragement of philanthropy, late in 1947, the National Arts Foundation started operating in New York. The city is the capital of American philanthropy: a report of 1970 stated that nearly a quarter of all American foundations were based in New York State. (By then, however, the National Arts Foundation had moved to Liechtenstein.)

In 1973 the Director of Arts of the Rockefeller Foundation, Howard Klein, reported that 'there are some 22,000 foundations now engaged in making presents of money'. Foundations in America, he said, 'are the passers-on of money from a central source to people and organisations which spend the money'. But there is more to a foundation than a mere clearing-house. Foundation executives ('for the most part, vicarious millionaires,' says Klein, 'many with little or no private fortune . . . well educated, intellectual, and some are self-made action types') are also expected to show vision. 'The foundation,' wrote Douglas Dillon in a report to the Tax Institute in Washington in 1971, 'is the only element in private philanthropy that can continually explore new and high ground.'

Carleton Smith certainly fits the stereotype of the foundation executive as 'vicarious millionaire': he has described his profession as 'spending other people's money'. And the National Arts Foundation fits the idea of the foundation as a philanthropic 'passer-on' dedicated to the exploration of 'new and high ground'. A *New York Times* report of December 1948 described it as 'a non-profit group to stimulate public interest and participation' in the arts, and as 'endowed by private funds, the donors to which prefer at present to remain anonymous'.

But in other ways the foundation strikes one as anything but typical. To begin with there is the ambiguity in its name, which

70

was, says Smith, suggested to him by President Roosevelt (who, Smith adds, did much of the initial work in getting the foundation started). Despite the name, it is a private not a public body, but there are times in its short history when, for a private body, it seems to be working uncommonly in tandem with American Government agencies. One newspaper report of 1949 even adds the prefix 'American' to its name. This harmony with government is most in evidence when one considers the foundation's 'foreign end'.

Less than three years after the foundation was set up the *New York Times*'s designation of it had altered to 'a philanthropic organisation concerned with the interchange of art and artists among countries'. By then, the foundation had set up its 'newly begun foreign activities committee' and the trustees had voted Carleton Smith as its 'co-ordinator'. To these 'foreign activities', of course, belonged the search for the Grüssau Manuscripts.

Here we come to the heart of the matter, for Carleton Smith quite clearly conceived the National Arts Foundation which he directed as bringing a cultural dimension to the Marshall Plan. In October 1948, on his return from a 'three-month trip to every country in Europe, including Russia', Smith said that the Marshall Plan was succeeding, but that while the United States was filling the stomachs of Europe the Soviet Union was poisoning European minds.

On November 4, the night of President Truman's re-election, Smith went to see him at the Mühlbach Hotel in Kansas City, Missouri, and reported on his trip. 'As part of the Marshall Plan,' he urged Truman, 'foreign countries should be encouraged to portray themselves to America, and America should teach a greater understanding of her purposes. We're winning the economic and military conflict, but losing the war of ideas.'

Here we find the first evidence of uncanny coincidence between Smith's 'private' views and official policy. For, just over a month after the Mühlbach Hotel meeting with Truman, Smith gave a press conference at which he unfolded 'plans for a quasi-governmental organisation that would interpret American thought and culture to the world and stimulate public interest in the United States':

71

. . . Secretary of Defense James Forrestal has requested such a plan, Mr. Smith said, for presentation to the Hoover Commission for Government reorganization, of which the Secretary is a member, and through it to the Congress. The projected cultural body, he added, would tap our best artistic resources and channel them through the State Department for the benefit of the foreign peoples. . . . The plan might be a forerunner, Mr. Smith related, towards establishment of a quasi-governmental department of arts, on a level comparable to the National Science Foundation.[1]

Quite clearly, the National Arts Foundation had its part to play in this 'quasi-governmental' organisation, which as clearly derived from Smith's criticisms of the Marshall Plan and President Truman's acceptance of their validity.

Smith would later date his roving portfolio to find displaced music manuscripts to the early part of 1948, but it was almost exactly a year later, after this press conference and after the start of the National Arts Foundation's foreign activities committee in the spring of 1949, that the search really got going in earnest. As an important but unusual contribution to the post-war cultural reconstruction of Germany it fulfilled the philanthropic goal of worthwhile exploration of new and high ground, while providing some cultural under-pinning to Marshall aid. Nearly four years after his post-Potsdam conversation with Truman in the White House, Carleton Smith was about to realise his plan.

[1] *New York Times*, Dec. 9, 1948.

CHAPTER NINE

A Thousand Leads

It is important to remember that Carleton Smith started out with the aim of overseeing the return to the proper places of *all* music manuscripts displaced by the war, not just those of Grüssau. Only gradually would the tiny Silesian village come to assume a commanding position in the picture with which he began – of the whole of Europe littered with lost and displaced music. The quixotic image emerges of Smith hunting for needles in a huge overturned haystack. 'Mr. Truman made it possible for me to go to every country from Finland to Portugal,' he says. Elsewhere he writes, 'We were told of secret caves in East Prussian castles, of an estate near Marienbad, of a monastery a few miles up the river from Kraków.' According to *The Times* in October 1953, 'Mr. Carleton Smith has just concluded a tour of Soviet-occupied Austria in search of missing manuscripts.'

Smith's chosen parish was indeed a wide one, but he was not alone in it. Firstly, there was until 1953 the powerful figure of President Truman in the background. The President 'said he would see to it that scholars were instructed to search them [the manuscripts] out in the American Zone, which he did. He was also helpful in opening doors for me in the other occupied zones . . .' Then there was Smith's mysterious army of ancillary workers, none of whom he will name: 'The foundation employed musicologists, searchers, spies and informants in a dozen countries from Finland to Spain. My task was to supervise and co-ordinate their work. In all, hundreds of people – official and non-official – joined the search, working together or alone.' Speaking specifically of the Grüssau search, Smith adds, 'We hired a large number of people in the Catholic church' (presumably because of the Benedictine background).

Nor did Smith go about his searching in silence. He was,

73

from the beginning, the one obvious exception to the trade secrecy – in the first place, of course, because he was not himself in the 'trade' of music scholarship. Evidently he judged publicity to be both in his own best interests, as an advertisement for the constructive work he was doing, and in the interests of the search itself, to let as many people as possible know that the scripts were missing. 'I made a lot of noise,' he says. 'I used every opportunity afforded me by press, radio, and television to create hell about the manuscripts.'

Smith was at his noisiest in the late 1940s and throughout the 1950s, then (except for one brief blast of noise in 1965) virtually silent in the 1960s, the period when the Grüssau mystery went deepest underground. He woke up again in the 1970s, only to fall finally silent in 1974, when he stopped searching, and secrecy claimed him too. There has not – as far as Grüssau is concerned – been anything new from him since.

Making a noise had come naturally to Carleton Smith ever since he took his first train-ride to Chicago to see the opera. Across the road from Smith's grocery lived a former railroad worker, George Tracy; through him the boy got free rides in the train's engine, and as a special treat he was allowed to pull the whistle and hear it shrieking out across the endless cornfields. 'All my life I've been pulling that whistle,' he wearily told me once.

Over Grüssau, Smith 'pulled the whistle'. 'Appeals were broadcast throughout Germany and the countries of eastern Europe, offering rewards to anyone furnishing information that would help lead us to the Grüssau manuscripts ... We circulated enquiries in Armed Services publications and in the press of the United States and other western countries on the odd chance that some manuscripts from Grüssau might have been found by members of the forces occupying western Germany at the time when the material disappeared.'

Smith, the former journalist turned 'image builder' and expert publicist, had an undoubted gift for placing stories in the press: the chorus of whistles which he raised presents one with the problem of separating those that mean something from those that are merely attention-seeking. The problem is compounded by his secretiveness since 1974, and further compounded by an apparently incurable vagueness. 'Carleton was always extremely vague about his activities,' says someone who knew him very well in the 1930s, when he was far too young to plead old age.

So it is as well to tread carefully. What, for example, shall we make of his claim that 'over thirty years, we followed perhaps a thousand different leads'? Does he mean Grüssau, or all his manuscript searches? My impression here is that Smith had in fact comparatively few leads to Grüssau, and that most of the tally is attributable to the Wagner manuscript search, which has yielded nothing to this day.

Albert Bormann, the brother of Hitler's chief lieutenant Martin Bormann, 'came to see me one night, at my hotel in Munich, under another name', and told Smith that at the end of the war the Wagner originals were not with Hitler in the Berlin bunker but had been stored elsewhere by his brother. Where, he did not know. Neither did Albert Speer, nor Hitler's personal servants.

Winifred Wagner reasoned that Hitler would have kept the scores somewhere within easy reach. If they had not been destroyed in the Berlin bunker or removed from there by the Russians, there was always the chance that they were somewhere in the bunkers of Obersalzburg, Hitler's home near Berchtesgaden in Bavaria, in one of the hundreds of rooms and tunnels that the Allies had sealed up. In 1976, a team of German technicians armed with ultrasonic equipment scoured these bunkers, looking for cavities that might contain the manuscripts: but the sound of Wagner's scores eluded their sophisticated machinery. In 1977, the Mayor of Bayreuth received an anonymous telephone call saying the scores were in Vienna; but there the line, and the trail, went dead. Three years later, Winifred, the dynamo of the search, died too.

Other leads were in pursuit of the Mozart treasures lost from the salt-mine near Hallein in Austria. This search was to be more successful, though its success cannot be attributed to Carleton Smith. From Vienna, in July 1949, he launched a 'world-wide appeal' for their return; a year later, he offered a reward for them.

But the first results were produced by another appeal, late in 1954, by the Mozart Foundation in Salzburg, pre-war home of the treasures. Soon after sending a list of them to the U.S. Information Agency, on the chance that they might have crossed the Atlantic, eight Mozart manuscripts from the

Hallein hoard were found in mysterious circumstances in a Salzburg museum. At much the same time an Austrian contacted the Mozart Foundation saying that a Polish soldier had offered to sell him Mozart's watch in 1945. The watch, the ring, and the rest of the Hallein hoard remain missing.

Our sense of the true scale of Carleton Smith's search, and those 'thousand leads' of his, diminishes dramatically if we consider that his reckoning included *all* the Berlin Library's original music, and all the sites to which it was evacuated. If he was counting also the library staff who processed these sites, we will wonder also at the true numbers of his private army of helpers.

On the one hand, in 1949, Smith spoke of his National Arts Foundation as 'seeking to verify the existence of all the autograph manuscripts of the great German composers from Bach to Brahms'. Elsewhere, he speaks of a series of trips to Dresden and Leipzig during the 1950s which resulted in his 'verifying the existence of certain valuable autograph manuscripts'.

But to verify the existence of something is by no means the same as to search for and to trace it, and on the other hand we find in *The Times* of October 1950:

> That National Arts Foundation. . . . has been engaged for two and a half years in the task of tracing lost musical manuscripts. It has already found or located 10,500, which, whenever possible, have been restored to their owners or brought to a safe place.

This became the basis for a passage in the ninth edition of *The Oxford Companion to Music*, stating that 'the Native [*sic*] Arts Foundation of New York generously set itself the task of locating' music autographs displaced by the war. But in the tenth edition this passage was expunged, and if we look at a later newspaper report, in the *Daily Telegraph* of July 1953, we begin to see why. Now the claim has grown, and we are given to understand that the search started in 1948 had all along been a five-year programme:

> Dr. Carleton Smith, director of the National Arts Foundation of New York, yesterday gave to the trustees, who are visiting London, the results of the Foundation's five-year programme to restore original musical manuscripts displaced during the

war. Over 12,000 compositions, among them the only manuscripts of Bach's St. Matthew Passion, Mendelssohn's
Songs Without Words and Schubert's Goethe Lieder, have
been returned to their owners.

This indeed shows the foundation's generosity – to itself.
The three scores mentioned – the Bach (again), part of the
Mendelssohn,[1] and the Schubert – were returned to East Berlin from their evacuation site in 1946, two years before the
earliest starting point of Smith's five-year programme. The
National Arts Foundation of New York may have verified
their existence to itself, but it had nothing whatever to do with
the survival and return of the music.

*

It was February 1946, nine months after the end of hostilities,
before Dr. Peter Wackernagel was allowed to leave Rühstädt
and return to Berlin with the holdings in his keeping. He
brought them back as he had taken them, in a convoy of
lorries: he travelled in front, carrying in his hands the original
of the Brandenburg Concertos.

The library was a ruin. Many of his old associates, like Dr.
Krüss, were dead, others had disappeared, like Dr. Poewe, and
others had fled westward. The remainder, in the absence of
heating, worked in their overcoats and gloves in the huge,
freezing shell of the building. At the entrance there was a sign
in Russian:

> Entrance to this library is absolutely forbidden unless in
> possession of a permit issued by the Kommandantura.
> By order of Marshal Zhukov.

The ordinary music literature from Rühstädt was the first
part of the evacuated library holdings to return to Berlin. The
failure of the Four Powers to agree on their future had resulted
in a deadlock preventing their return. A British librarian serving with Signals in Berlin summed up the situation:

> . . .The Americans will not agree to their return unless the
> Soviets guarantee to carry out similar removals within their
> zone, and so on. Even intersector removals within Berlin

[1]The remainder of Songs Without Words was at Grüssau.

itself are not allowed. Thus, a Four Power agreement will have to be reached in the matter before an answer can be given.

An American music librarian, Richard S. Hill, who was in Berlin over the same period, laid most of the blame on 'the Russian system of strict censorship and their firmly closed borders over which only a rumour can float . . . No Frenchman, Englishman, or American could discover what the Russian policy was to be, and as a result the only thing that they could do was to do nothing.'

In the spring, unilateral action by the American general, Lucius Clay, held out the first hope of an end to the stalemate. The American Third Army, in the last days of the war, had found twenty-eight freight cars in a railway siding in Czechoslovakia. In them were some 350,000 volumes – one of the last shipments of the evacuation – which had failed to reach their evacuation site. The cars were shunted first to Headquarters in Frankfurt, but then, on Clay's orders, were sent to East Berlin, where they arrived late in April. For three days, the Unter den Linden library's staff formed bucket lines to pass the packages of books into the building.

'Now that the jam has been broken,' wrote Hill,

> . . . it turns out that the Russians, like everyone in the U.S. Zone, were intending all along to return the books evacuated to their Zone, and were only waiting for the matter to be settled at the top in the Control Council. 'Rumor' . . . has it that the Russians will bring up the question at a meeting of the Control Council in the near future, and if agreement can be reached, the books may be on their way back from *all* evacuation points sometime in September.

As it happened, Hill's estimate was unduly pessimistic. In the first week of July, the Commander of Soviet Occupation Troops in Germany, Marshal Sokolowski, issued an order that the contents of sites in the Soviet Zone should be returned to Berlin. A few days later, the Allied Office of Military Government lifted its embargo on news of the evacuation sites. For the first time in public, the *New York Times* painted a picture of the wartime dispersal of Germany's music. The article also made the first public identification of Grüssau with music manuscripts. Appropriately, perhaps, given the hide-and-seek that was to come, it was a stunning piece of misinformation: all the music stored in the monastery, the article said, had been 'salvaged'.

The following month, a convoy of lorries pulled up at the Unter den Linden library. In them were the crates of scripts that had been evacuated to Schönebeck, across the Elbe. 'I wanted to see as quickly as possible,' Peter Wackernagel remembers, 'what boxes were there. I remember thinking, "In this box with that number must be the Matthew Passion." I pulled the nails. It was a great day for me – the 28th of August, 1946, Goethe's birthday – when I saw the Passion again.'

The stalemate was broken at last. In the west, it was decided to gather the material together in the principal towns of the provinces to which they happened to have been evacuated: Tübingen in the French Zone, and Marburg in the American. This took place after a law concerning former Prussian cultural property was passed by the Allied Control Council in February 1947.

So, score by original score, catalogue number by number, everything was accounted for . . . all but the scripts in the eleven evacuation sites beyond the Oder-Neisse line. Peter Wackernagel, by then head of the Music Department, had an interest only in those things which had gone to Grüssau (late in the war, the music in Altmarrin Castle had been taken to the Schönebeck mine).

Sokolowski's order had specifically disclaimed any power of commitment regarding the sites beyond the two rivers, in accordance with official Soviet policy towards the area as expressed by Stalin at Potsdam. So Wackernagel was not allowed to ask for the manuscripts back, only whether they existed or not. He wrote, but received no answer. He asked Furtwängler to petition Russian officers for him, without result.

Had the manuscripts at Grüssau – the most spectacular of all the music – been destroyed? It was unthinkable, but it was possible. He remembered the Russian soldier at Rühstädt: 'These are all Hitler's . . . They shall all be burnt.' He had been there to reply, but who had been at Grüssau?

Information was hard to come by. Through a friend in the Roman Catholic Church – Dr. Karl Forster, choir master of St.

Hedwig's cathedral in Berlin – he succeeded in finding out that there had been no fighting in the region. So the manuscripts had cleared the first survival hurdle, at least. Had they survived? But, if so, why was there no answer to his enquiries? As time drew on, so did his sense of *'ein undurchdringliches Geheimnis'* – an 'impenetrable mystery'.

CHAPTER TEN

The Benedictine Rescue

In February 1946, as Peter Wackernagel was settling in again at the Unter den Linden library, the Minister responsible for Poland's new western and Baltic 'Recovered Territories', Władysław Gomułka, made it clear that Germans were to be moved out of these areas and Poles from the east moved into them. 'It is not a question of thousands of people to be transferred,' he said, 'but of millions. This operation will involve literally the whole people.' At the May Plenum of the Polish Communist Party, he underlined the message: 'During the current year the entire German population must be removed from the Recovered Territories. We must settle there three and a half million Poles, of whom two and a half millions must be settled before harvest time, otherwise the crops will spoil.'

In 1946 the monastery was a community of some forty fathers and brothers. In the middle of May, all but three of them were turned out of Grüssau and out of Silesia. Together with many of the villagers, they were taken to the British Zone of occupation.

The three allowed to remain could all lay claim to nationalities and passports other than German: Brothers Florian Windisch and Günther Veith (Czech and Austrian) and the archivist, Father Nikolaus von Lutterotti (Italian). This accident of nationality was to be one of the most significant factors in the slow revelation of the Grüssau mystery. Without it, the chances are high that it would indeed have remained as 'impenetrable' as Peter Wackernagel considered it to be.

Eleven years later, the former Keeper of Monuments in Lower Silesia, Günther Grundmann, praised Lutterotti's decision to remain behind: 'By staying on in Grüssau [he] proved his conviction in the homeland of his church and became the consolation and help of all those who needed him.' But Lutterotti's diaries after the expulsion reveal a rapid erosion both of the region's German identity and of the need for his continued presence:

June 21, 1946: 'I preach twice every Sunday and public holiday and thrice celebrate Mass, but soon the last people of Grüssau will have to leave . . . Then the creative pause I so badly need will arrive for me. I can still manage the "Ora et Labora", and that's all a monk needs.'

September 3, 1946: 'People from Grüssau . . . were expelled from their homeland on the thirtieth of August and . . . found a place near Münster. Now there will be a few changes . . . I can only now give sermons in the morning, but after Vespers and the Holy Blessing (at three o'clock) I have introduced since May a Sunday reading at the sacramental altar . . . I go up [to Schömberg] every Saturday to hear confession . . . I'm now giving religious instruction in Grüssau, but there are only five children . . . Since May I have grown many more grey hairs. If this goes on, I'll soon be white. If only one grew wise at the same time! The harvest was very good . . .'

September 9, 1947: 'It's all grown very quiet here . . . Grüssau is almost empty [of Germans]. But . . . there are still people here who need me . . . I am now covering Friedland, Schömberg, Albendorf, Landeshut, and Liebau. Mostly on foot . . . from time to time I get a horse . . . but during harvest that isn't always possible . . . Apart from that, one can't turn up the purest of the pure with a horse-and-cart: one has to come like the Good Shepherd . . . I still have about thirty believers whom I can tell of God's word in German.'

*

In the first week of September 1949, four months after becoming co-ordinator of the National Arts Foundation's foreign activities committee, Carleton Smith arrived in Frankfurt on the fourth leg of a 'musicology tour' which he was making through Europe. By this time he had visited Vienna, where he launched his appeal for the Mozart treasures of Hallein, Prague, where he looked for displaced music manuscripts, and Bayreuth, where he discussed the revival of the festival with Wieland Wagner.

By this time also he knew, from Wilhelm Furtwängler, about the still-outstanding missing manuscripts of Berlin, and in Frankfurt he first started to make a noise about them. But he was still feeling his way. The original scores, he told reporters, were 'said to have disappeared' and he hoped to be able to travel in the Russian Zone and find out more there: Furtwängler's overtures to the Russians, of course, had by this time failed. The news agency Reuters described Smith as 'head of an American commission searching for missing music manuscripts', but it seems clear that Smith at this time still saw the problem as a relatively simple one of verification rather than prolonged search. 'All we wish to do,' his secretary said, 'is to establish if the missing scores are in existence and are not destroyed and that they are returned to their proper keeping places.' Doubtless Smith was hoping that his 'quasi-governmental' status would give his enquiries added weight.

It is doubtful if Smith yet connected the missing music with the monastery of Grüssau. We find him talking, not of monasteries, but of castles. The Ninth Symphony and *The Magic Flute*, he said in July, 'may have been shipped along with other treasures to seven castles scattered throughout Germany'. By September he was firmer: 'He pointed out that it was known that the original scores . . . had been hidden in castles in eastern Germany.' The number of castles – seven – and their location suggest that he was thinking of other Lower Silesian sites. Possibly Furtwängler had confused things – they are certainly complicated enough.

But, at about this time, the stir created in the press by Smith's visit came to the attention of the expelled monks of Grüssau. Since 1947, they had been based in the town of Bad Wimpfen, on the River Neckar in south-western Germany. In memory of their old home, they called their new one Grüssau also.

By 1948, the monks had heard from the three still in Silesia of the convoy that had come to take the manuscripts away. The abbot – Albert Schmitt – tried to draw the disappearance to the attention of the German authorities. In Lutterotti's absence, he made another monk – Father Andreas Michalski– responsible for archival matters, and authorised Father Michalski to press the question with the Culture Department of the Military Government in Frankfurt. Father Michalski and the abbot then got in touch with Carleton Smith. The manuscripts, they told him, had been 'taken east'.

Wilhelm Furtwängler had written to Dr. Wackernagel telling him that Carleton Smith would be contacting him, and a few days later they met in Berlin at a dinner party given by

Robert Murphy, Political Adviser to the U.S. Military Government, at whose home Smith was staying.

Wackernagel told Smith of his enquiries about the missing manuscripts and also of the Unter den Linden library's gift to Poland, only a few days before, of seven original preludes and études by Chopin. The gift had been ordered for September 1, the tenth anniversary of Germany's invasion of Poland. It had incensed Wackernagel; the scores, he said, were the legitimate property of the German people. This was his first big break with official policy on the Unter den Linden – a break which was to become final the following year.

Carleton Smith's 'musicology tour' of Europe ended with an open letter to Stalin and the Premier of Poland, Józef Cyrankiewicz:

> May I ask your help in our search for some of Europe's most precious cultural treasures? . . . Knowing your personal interest in all cultural expressions, I request travel facilities and the co-operation of your experts in locating these remaining lost treasures of Europe's cultural heritage.

Smith told reporters in Berlin that he had twice interviewed Stalin on cultural questions before the war, and felt sure that he would give all possible help. But Stalin did not reply to the letter, nor did Cyrankiewicz. The solution was not going to be so simple after all.

Certainly, by 1950, Dr. Wackernagel had become convinced that there was to be no solution. He told the scholar Christa Landon, 'We shall never see these manuscripts again. Tell your husband [H. C. Robbins Landon, who was interested in Haydn material at Grüssau] that it is very unlikely.' But it was in 1950 that Carleton Smith's hopes of a solution soared higher than they were to do for a very long time – only to be brutally disappointed,

This was the year when he visited Grüssau – on October 2. For a long while I puzzled over this visit. What was the purpose of it, when Smith already knew, as he clearly did by then, that the scripts had been taken away from the monastery? Was it possible that he was interested not so much in Grüssau as in those 'seven castles' in the same area? He might have believed that the Germans had left some of the things in Schloss Fürstenstein during the war, or that the post-war convoy had made for one of the castles. This fitted with a later reference by Smith: 'We traced diligently all leads that came to us and visited all indicated hiding places including those uninhabited Silesian castles which local authorities would permit us to visit.'

In visiting Silesia, the diligent Dr. Smith was evidently pursuing a lead concerning the castles. But a tantalising passage from a *Times* report datelined Paris, October 9, 1950 (just after the visit) suggested another and stranger strand of reasoning in the background: 'Several weeks ago Dr. Smith was told in Rome that the manuscripts were still at Kloster Grüssau . . .'

The mention of Rome suggested Roman Catholic sources, part of that small army of hired churchmen whom Smith, himself a Roman Catholic, had marshalled for the search. But another and apparently better-placed Roman Catholic source – Abbot Schmitt – had specifically told Smith that the manuscripts were *no longer* at Grüssau but had been 'taken east'. Two sources within the same church, it seemed, were at odds with one another.

Had the 'noisy' Dr. Smith anywhere expanded on that intriguing reference to Rome? Eventually, in the Frankfurt edition of *Die Neue Zeitung* ('The American Newspaper in Germany') for September 29, 1950, I came across the astonishing headline:

MANUSCRIPTS OF BEETHOVEN'S NINTH SYMPHONY AND MOZART'S MAGIC FLUTE FOUND AGAIN

. . . The manuscripts . . . the director of the National Arts Foundation of New York, Carleton Smith, said in Rome on Saturday, have been found again . . .

Smith, who has long been travelling Europe in search of lost music manuscripts, was informed by Benedictine monks in Rome that according to the Benedictines of the Abbey of Grüssau, Lower Silesia, now in Polish occupied territory, both manuscripts have been safeguarded . . .

All earlier searches for these two manuscripts were fruitless. Smith personally wrote to Marshal Stalin . . . without receiving any answer. Also, U.N.E.S.C.O., which was asked to help in the search, had no success.

85

So it was not just a question of churchmen of the same church disagreeing, but of Benedictines disagreeing. In Rome, Smith had stumbled upon an extraordinary twist in the Grüssau mystery: the story of the Benedictine Rescue.

Nearly thirty years later, Father Michalski would comment on reports of 1950 that the manuscripts had been safeguarded. "I certainly couldn't begin to say by whom they are supposed to have been safeguarded,' he would say, 'but at any rate it was not by any German authority whatsoever.' Maybe Father Michalski had not heard of the Benedictine Rescue, or maybe he did not think of the Benedictines as 'a German authority'. The point is that towards and just after the end of the war there was no German authority in a position to try to save the manuscripts: only the monks of Grüssau.

The story goes like this . . .

Amidst their other wartime preoccupations, the monks worried also about what would become of the manuscripts. Over the centuries, the Benedictines had come to see themselves as a civilising force, taming barbarians and draining marshes, building cathedrals and copying manuscripts. Spreading God's Word had meant also spreading literacy and culture. (Incidentally, Ksiaź castle, as the Poles were to rename Schloss Fürstenstein, irresistibly suggests to Polish minds the words both for book – *ksíazka* – and for monk – *ksiadz*.)

But by 1944 the tide was clearly turning. 'The barbarians' were rolling back the carpet of culture that the monks had helped to spread eastward. Consider how the monastery archivist, Father Nikolaus Lutterotti, would have seen the position.

The war had made him the man on the spot directly responsible for treasures infinitely greater than any his own archive could boast, and by the winter of 1944 – at the latest – it would have been clear to him that they were in terrible danger. To the west, he would have seen the culture that had created and that valued the manuscripts, to the east, an uncomprehending 'barbarous' horde, hating the Germans and their works.

Günther Grundmann describes him as having been 'as faithful a scholar of Silesian art history as he was a responsible friend and guardian of Silesian monuments'. But now he had in his keeping treasures of a far wider than Silesian significance, things that were sacred not only to all Germany but to the whole of the civilised world. The responsibility of the crates in the loft of St. Joseph's must have weighed on him.

The progress of the war left him increasingly alone with this responsibility. Did he try to contact the Prussian State Library? But there would have been nothing, anyway, that the library could do. No one site could be considered any safer than another, and anywhere was safer than Berlin. Transport was at a premium, too, and manuscripts were low on the list of priorities.

In February 1945, Günther Grundmann managed to borrow a diesel car from the Wehrmacht, and fled west with treasures belonging to the Prince of Hesse. (The 'silent, sour-faced' Grundmann, as an American officer described him, turned up at Banz castle in Hessen, incidentally another of the evacuation sites.)

It could have been at this time that Father Lutterotti decided to act. His anxiety, his sense of being cut off from Berlin and therefore of being completely responsible for the treasure, would have reached a high point in the mid-winter of 1944–45, after the Russian advance from the Vistula but before the Russian arrival in the region. But it could have been later, after the mass exodus from Lower Silesia but before the Russians and then the Poles consolidated their occupation. It might even have been after the expulsion from the monastery in May 1946, but it would have become more difficult to act the longer he waited.

On the other hand, the activity and concern of the abbot and Father Michalski, and, later, Father Michalski's apparent ignorance of any safeguarding operation, suggest that knowledge of it may have been confined to Father Lutterotti and the two brothers in Silesia, and that it may have taken place after the expulsion but before the arrival of the foreign convoy.

At some point, however, it was decided to hide away as many crates of manuscripts as possible. They had been safe at Grüssau as long as a German victory was the war's anticipated end; now they needed to be physically hidden from view, where the conqueror could not find them, in a place suitable for defeat.

Lutterotti knew such a place, but its size and the transport problem severely limited his ability to act as decisively as the situation seemed to demand. He had to choose very carefully which crates of manuscripts he was going to save. He chose the music. Consulting his list, he picked out some four to six crates, containing perhaps forty catalogue entries. Which, we do not know, but we can venture that the Ninth Symphony and *The Magic Flute* were among them. These, the most valuable and best known of all the manuscripts, also figure by name in the report from Rome of 1950.

The crates were taken down from St. Joseph's choir lofts, and loaded – probably on to that very horse-and-cart, belonging to the monastery farm, which Lutterotti thought it impure to use when visiting his parishioners. They were taken eastwards, in the direction of Waldenburg. At a small parish church a few kilometres from the town the crates were unloaded, then hidden behind the altar.

So, by the time the foreign convoy came to the monastery, important things were already missing from St. Joseph's. The monks had done their bit – as much as they could in the circumstances – to save the culture that was being overrun.

The story of the rescue suggests that the monks were much more deeply involved in the Grüssau mystery, and in the history of at least two of music's greatest masterpieces, than has hitherto been realised. How many monks are supposed to have taken part in the action we do not know, nor which monks they were, nor the name of the church. Nor can we be sure that Father Lutterotti was in charge: but it is likely that he was, and I am assuming so. What we can say is that according to this version of events the monks acted, and in secret, so becoming party to a secrecy all their own.

*

In 1950 Carleton Smith somehow got wind of the story of the Benedictine rescue. It probably reached him in a garbled form, and he may have had only an inkling of it, but one moment with him sticks in my mind. Early in 1979, as I was speaking to him of the help which Dr. Wackernagel had from 'the gentlemen of the Catholic Church', he interrupted me and said that this was 'a crucial phrase'; discretion forbade him from telling me any more.

One's impression is that Smith returned from his 1950 visit

to Silesia and Grüssau – the visit which had promised a quick and sensational end to the mystery, and which he had prefaced with an announcement that the treasures were 'found again' – deeply disappointed. He found the former monastery inhabited by Benedictine nuns of Polish origin; part of it was turned over to a workshop where the nuns made church ornaments. But he found no manuscripts, neither there nor in the nearby castles. Nor did he have any joy in Warsaw, where he enquired next. The Polish government, he told a press conference in Paris a week after visiting Grüssau, 'had refused to give him any information concerning their whereabouts ... the answer in every case was that nothing was known of the manuscripts'.

Smith in his Paris press conference was the first publicly to speak of a convoy and to put an approximate date to it – 1947. But ambiguity surrounded both 'facts' from the very beginning. The expelled monks of the new Grüssau had them at second hand from the three who had stayed behind in Silesia, with whom they were not properly in touch until 1954. And the incorrigibly vague Dr. Smith had them from the expelled monks (if he saw Lutterotti, Windisch, or Veith in Silesia, he has never said so). The press in turn had them from Dr. Smith, so some distortion on the way would not be surprising.

But the confusion was more than a mere matter of words and reporting. In a letter of 1975 Father Michalski first gave the date of the convoy as 1946, but later corrected it to 1947; in 1977 he gave the year as 1946 again. As to the convoy, it was evidently an army one, but whose army? According to the *New York Times* in 1950, Smith had 'learned that [the manuscripts] had been removed by Polish army officers', while according to the London *Times* correspondent at the same press conference the culprit was 'the Red Army'.

The confusion existed in Smith's own mind, and in the minds of the monks who were his informants. Three years later, Smith appealed to Mr. Malenkov in Moscow; six years later to Russia and Poland jointly. In 1977, Father Michalski would specify only that 'an eastern power' was responsible, because 'it cannot precisely be said whether it was Poland or Russia that took the treasure'.

So although Carleton Smith in Paris roundly 'accused the Polish Government of making off with a group of valuable music manuscripts . . . among the most valuable of the musical heritage of western Europe', he had by no means abandoned the Russian option.

CHAPTER ELEVEN

Shadow Play

In 1955, the Swiss auction firm, Haus der Bücher of Basel, put up for sale a group of manuscript letters by well-known composers. A dealer in London spotted in the catalogue three letters by Hugo Wolf. To find out more about them, he telephoned the Wolf scholar Frank Walker, who said, 'There must be something wrong here. I saw these letters in the Prussian State Library in 1938.' Walker got in touch with the Deutsche Staatsbibliothek in East Berlin, which in turn sent a telegram to Haus der Bücher claiming the letters as its property.

The telegram arrived on the eve of the auction. Dealers and auctioneers met to discuss whether the letters should be sold. At last, despite the opposition of a West German dealer who insisted that a sale was perfectly in order, the Wolf letters were withheld and returned to Berlin. Not so the other letters, although the London dealer was 'convinced, as other people were, that lots of them were also from Berlin'. But, whereas the Wolf letters had been documented as Berlin property by Frank Walker, in his book on Wolf, similar documentation was lacking for the other letters, or was impossible to assemble in time, so they were sold and snapped up by the dealers.

Apparently, the old Prussian State Library had been somewhat slack in its cataloguing of manuscript letters. And thousands of letters were known to be among the manuscripts lost beyond the Oder-Neisse line, from Grüssau and other sites. The Basel incident raised the suspicion that whoever had run off with the 'eastern manuscripts' was testing the market by offloading uncatalogued ones. Countries, institutions, and individuals who have lost art treasures make a point of studying auction catalogues to see whether they have resurfaced, but that is difficult to prove when you cannot show that you ever owned the objects. Were the Wolf letters a clue to the resurfacing of the Grüssau manuscripts?

The real explanation is rather different. The letters had been brought to Basel by a big fellow describing himself as a 'grocer from Wiesbaden'. They had been in his family for generations, he said, and he produced an official-looking document proving as much.

Two years earlier, Carleton Smith had reported that a former music librarian, Joachim Krüger, who in 1950 had succeeded Peter Wackernagel as head of the East Berlin Library's Music Department, 'may be living at Wiesbaden'. Krüger is surely the most unusual and colourful music librarian in history: confidence trickster, secret agent, thief, and, evidently, consummate actor. It was through his acting ability that he obtained the music library post in 1950. He acquired for himself a shining reputation as a staunch member of the governing Socialist Unity Party and as the heart-and-soul secretary of the German-Polish Friendship Society, and on the strength of this a government minister recommended his promotion. In fact, by his own later admission, Krüger was a member of the Gehlen Organisation – Hitler's anti-Soviet intelligence network which the Americans took over almost intact in 1945. Equipped with false identity papers provided by the Americans, according to his own account, he was sent to spy in and against East Berlin.

On May 1, 1951, under cover of the May Day celebrations, a lorry pulled up at a side entrance of the library off the Unter den Linden. Quickly, Krüger and the driver loaded three or four crates; minutes later they were across the sector boundary in West Berlin.

The crates were packed with music manuscripts and letters. One of them – containing twenty-seven Beethoven scores, all but two of the 139 existing 'conversation books' through which Beethoven communicated with his friends after his deafness, and other manuscripts – Krüger gave to the Beethoven House in Bonn. The contents of the others served to start him off on a new career as an antiquarian dealer, and as a 'grocer from Wiesbaden'.

Krüger was certainly a resourceful crook. On another occasion, a piece of music printed by Petrucci of Venice – the world's first music publishers – came up for sale. A dealer bought it and placed it on his shelves, only to discover after a few years that the stamp 'The Royal Library, Berlin' had mysteriously appeared on the flyleaf and some of the pages:

Krüger had wiped out the mark with chemicals whose effect had at last worn off.

To complete the Krüger story, he was arrested in West Germany in 1959 after he was caught stealing from other libraries; in 1961 – just before the Berlin Wall went up – the Beethoven House reluctantly returned to East Berlin the treasures Krüger had stolen and given to them.

The Haus der Bücher incident illustrates another difficulty arising from the lack of a central forum for the Grüssau search. The search would anyway have been a shadow play, but the absence of any centre where clues could be pooled and sifted meant that it was a shadow play without unity, acted out on different stages in different theatres by *dramatis personae* who often had no idea who the others were or even that there *were* any others. Only in a narrative account do we have a semblance of unity. There was no concerted search. Carleton Smith and his National Arts Foundation came the closest to providing the forum that was needed; but because we have been following his progress it does not mean that all interested parties were following it or, more importantly, contributing to it, at the time.

If we had to pick a date when the several plots and the sub-plots of the shadow play really began to thicken, it would have to be 1955. Briefly, that year, Basel was a stage where suspicion flickered and the shadow was strongest. But inevitably, at that period, most of the suspicion was steadily aimed eastwards, at the new enemy, the Soviet Union. And the elucidation of the brief shadow at Basel was simple in comparison to the problems searchers faced in the deep shadows that seemed to loom around the state Churchill had dubbed 'a riddle inside a mystery wrapped in an enigma'.

There were strong grounds for connecting the Soviet Union with the Grüssau disappearance. Strongest of all was the knowledge that Lower Silesia had been occupied not just by the Polish army, but by the Red Army too. More than that, the Russians had reached the area first, and the monastery, and had been in overall charge of military movements. The feeling that Poland was an obedient Soviet satellite – incapable of taking such momentous action by itself, at any rate without Moscow's permission – fed the suspicion that the Soviet Union was behind the disappearance.

And were not vanishing tricks involving military convoys something of a Soviet speciality? Was it not in a convoy that the priceless paintings of the Dresden Museum had vanished? The certain knowledge that the Red Army had taken the Rembrandts, Van Dycks, Tintorettos, Poussins, Raphaels, and Vermeers, the stubborn refusal of the Russians even to admit that they had them, the long unexplained absence of the treasure, offered almost exact parallels to Grüssau. The mystery of the manuscripts bore the Soviet stamp. President Truman implicitly drew the parallel when he told Carleton Smith, 'Everyone's worried about the missing paintings, but no one seems to know about the music.'

Speculation went further than the idea of Soviet appropriation of the manuscripts, however, to the belief that the Russians had destroyed them. This had a basis in horror stories involving the Red Army and art treasures, some of them specifically musical. In Soviet-occupied Austria, in 1945, a truck loaded with music manuscripts was stopped at a Soviet roadblock, and the music scattered at the wayside like so much waste paper. Among the manuscripts was the original of a Haydn Mass[1]. In the castle of Liegnitz, in Silesia, Soviet soldiers kept themselves warm in the bitterly cold winter of 1945 by burning music that had been evacuated there. Manuscripts from the Kirchenmusik-Institut in Berlin and the Ritterakademie in Liegnitz went up in smoke.

The city of Liegnitz, just fifty miles north of Grüssau, was the headquarters of the occupying Red Army, as it still is today under its Polish name of Legnica. Had the trucks that arrived at Grüssau come from there, and returned there with the manuscripts? As late as the 1970s, I heard speculation that the Liegnitz castle fire had been the fate of Grüssau paper treasure. How much more plausible such a fate seemed in the 1950s, when there were plenty of horror stories in circulation. Knowledge of the convoy was no insurance against this brand of pessimism: the fact that the manuscripts had been taken away did not necessarily mean that they had survived. The image was still one of the horny hands of soldiers, rather than the soft, white hands of scholars or of monks.

[1] Many of the manuscripts, including this one, were found and saved by a 'music-loving forester'.

The lasting power of this pessimism can be seen from the case of the 'Neue Mozart Ausgabe', or N.M.A., the complete new edition of all Mozart's music which began publication in 1955. The International Mozart Foundation in Salzburg had been considering ways to celebrate the two hundredth anniversary of Mozart's birth in 1956, and eventually settled on the N.M.A. as both the most fitting tribute to Mozart and most appropriate contribution to the 'Mozart Year'.

The old edition had long been out of print, and many copies of it had been destroyed during the war; also, it dated from the late nineteenth century, and the need was felt for a new edition, free from the editorial excesses and excrescences of that period, which let the music speak for itself. As Yehudi Menuhin put it, twenty years after the project got under way:

> Personally, I cannot begin to describe the sense of awe and inspiration which strikes me whenever I open the volumes of the Bach, the Mozart, or any other Ur-text edition. Instead of taking an edited version, too often revealing more the vanity of the editor than the truth of the music, one becomes in fact a worshiper in a great church and is part of a consecreation of time and place. A great human value is restored . . .

Work like this is a labour of love requiring care and time, and a span of fifteen years was envisaged for the N.M.A.; but when Menuhin wrote the above (in 1975) the project was still incomplete, and for that the continued absence of the Grüssau manuscripts was largely to blame.

The founding general editor of the N.M.A., Ernst Fritz Schmid, had been one of the first scholars to learn of the missing Grüssau music, when he was working on Haydn originals in Berlin soon after the war. The problems that faced him then were tiny in comparison to those of the missing Mozart (the autograph originals of about a quarter of all his known music).

Scholars were reasonably fortunate where the lost Haydn originals were concerned. For example, of the four complete Haydn symphonies at Grüssau, three existed in facsimile. The Dutch scholar Anthony van Hoboken had all of No. 50, his Photogramm Archiv had all of Nos. 99 and 101 ('The Clock'). H. C. Robbins Landon also had a score of the fourth missing

Symphony, No. 98, which another scholar had corrected against the original before the war. So Professor Landon had comparatively few problems with existing original sources in writing his massive study *The Symphonies of Joseph Haydn*, which was published in 1955. (In an appendix he gave the missing four symphonies, and the missing part of No. 73, as 'whereabouts unknown', adding in brackets '(Poland?)'. This was hardly shouting it from the rooftops, but it is worth noting as the earliest case I have come across of a scholar drawing attention to the missing music.)

The quantity alone of the lost Mozart manuscripts meant that a far different situation faced Schmid with the N.M.A. Of the great majority of the missing works there existed no facsimiles at all; facsimiles of others were of poor quality and unreliable; and not one of the originals had been examined in the light of the most up-to-date musicological techniques. So the authoritativeness of the planned new definitive edition, if not its completeness, was under threat from the beginning. The uncertainty of Grüssau bedevilled the project, and, as a British music scholar has remarked, 'the consequent effect upon editorial policy may be imagined'.[1]

According to one of the editors, Wolfgang Rehm, who started work on the N.M.A. in 1960, even then 'the general feeling was that the manuscripts no longer existed. One story was that Russian soldiers had taken them away and destroyed them, not even knowing what they were'. The strength of this feeling can be seen from the N.M.A.'s publication, not only of *The Magic Flute*, for which the pre-war facsimile was used, but of Mozart works lost at Grüssau of which there were no facsimiles. Normally, it would have been unthinkable to publish these editions without consultation of the existing originals; but, in the conviction that they no longer existed, or after years of futile hoping against hope for them to turn up, the editors made do as best they could.

The N.M.A. was pessimistic even though the indications are that it actually started life knowing about the convoy. The editors heard the story from the Austrian count, Johannes von Moy, who had worked with the International Mozart Foundation in Salzburg since 1950 and who is today its vice-presi-

[1] Alec Hyatt King, of the Music Department of the British Library.

dent. Count Moy had a step-cousin who lived near Bad Wimpfen, the post-war home of the expelled monks of Grüssau. The step-cousin spoke with the monks, and, as the count remembers it, was told of the convoy by the Prior. Father Nikolaus Lutterotti was not only the Archivist of Grüssau, but its Prior, and if he was indeed the source, we can narrow the date down to 1954, when he came to Bad Wimpfen, or 1955, when he died. It was in 1955 that the first volume of the N.M.A. – *Works for Two Claviers* – was published.

The new edition was not only a two hundredth birthday present to Mozart, but a first birthday present to the new state of Austria. On May 15, the Austrian State Treaty was signed, under which the Soviet occupation of the country was to be ended. Only a few days earlier the International Mozart Foundation had announced the rediscovery after almost a century of the original 'Eine Kleine Nachtmusik'. The find vividly illustrated the claim made by the promoters of the N.M.A. that new editorial matter had become available in the eighty years since the last complete Mozart edition.

But editorial matter available then had in the meantime become unavailable, and despite the good omens the Grüssau gloom prevailed. Only with the first gleams of hope that the manuscripts had survived did the pessimism begin to turn into frustration. The daughter of Friedrich Gehmacher, president of the International Mozart Foundation until his death in 1976, remembers that the missing Mozart originals were a nagging subject of conversation in the family circle, like an itch that would not go away.

*

After the disappointment of his 1950 initiative, Carleton Smith turned away from Grüssau to other projects, large and small. They ranged from helping to revive the Bayreuth festival and launching big money arts prizes, down to overseeing a new tombstone for Bach, arranging an American tour by 'the singing priest of Argyll', and taking Sibelius boxfuls of his favourite Portegas cigars. (Some scholars still remember him as 'Cigars-for-Sibelius-Smith'.)

His involvement with music manuscripts, and those of Grüssau, was comparatively intermittent and low-key in these years. He obtained the list of the Grüssau music from the East Berlin Library, and, in 1951, was the first to report the news of

97

Joachim Krüger's manuscript theft. In that year he also reiterated his appeal to the Soviet Union and Poland. In 1953, he announced the results of his 'five-year programme' of manuscript reclamation, and, following the death of Stalin, addressed an appeal to Malenkov, the new Prime Minister.

But 1955 raised the possibility of developments even more promising than those opened by Stalin's death. First, there was the mood of reconciliation surrounding the Four Power summit meeting in Geneva, at which Eisenhower, Truman's successor as President, conferred with Stalin's replacement as First Secretary of the Soviet Communist Party, Nikita Khrushchev. Then, in the summer, hundreds of paintings from the Dresden Museum at last emerged from hiding. At a ceremony in August, the Deputy Soviet Minister of Culture declared: 'We are glad that the forces of the heroic Soviet army saved these valuable treasures from ruin.' In this unabashed manner, as the result of a secret policy decision, ten years of speculation were ended. Was there just such an arbitrary and enigmatic ending in store for the mystery of Grüssau? By the middle of September Carleton Smith was in Moscow.

Again, from this visit, we have evidence that the activities of Smith's private National Arts Foundation were synchronised with American official policy. On August 1 Harrison Salisbury of the *New York Times*, a specialist in Soviet affairs, had announced that the State Department intended to set up 'a unit on cultural ties with the U.S.S.R.'. The groundwork for this, he said, had been done by President Eisenhower at the Geneva summit, and the President was understood to be personally interested in the programme. Plans were already 'in full swing', and the State Department had been 'deluged with ideas'. 'The task of studying proposals,' Salisbury wrote,

> . . . has fallen to the East European office of the State Department . . . But the burden has become so heavy that . . . the State Department therefore has decided that special facilities and personnel will be necessary to handle the job efficiently. It was expected that a special section in the department will be organised for this purpose.

Four days later, Carleton Smith set off for the Soviet Union. With the approval of the Soviet Embassy in Washington, he

went 'to pave the way for an exchange of painters and enter-
tainers', and had before him a heavy programme of meetings,
not just with the artists, but with the Soviet Minister of Culture, Nikolai Mikhailov, and representatives of V.O.K.S., the
Soviet department dealing with foreign cultural relations.
Towards the end of September, Smith was able to say that 'a
programme of American-Soviet cultural exchange featuring
top musicians, dancers, and singers is rapidly moving towards
completion'. In the first week of October he said that an
agreement in principle had been reached on an exchange of
200 paintings between the United States and the Soviet Union.

Are we to construe this as a purely private visit by the
director of a private American foundation? The delicate balance of Smith's peculiar 'quasi-governmental' status seems
nowhere more weighted on the governmental side than here –
weighted, perhaps, with that burden which the State Department had decided to farm out to 'special personnel'. We even
find Smith making the final arrangements for *Porgy and Bess*
to visit the Soviet Union, a tour which Harrison Salisbury's
earlier report said 'the State Department might finance in part
with foreign cultural funds'.

This is significant because it subtly affects our perception of
the context in which Smith pursued his search for the Grüssau
manuscripts – a search which he did not forget on his visit to
Moscow. He pursued the matter both officially and unofficially. By October 12, he had his official answer from the Minister of Culture: 'We have consulted with Soviet musical experts
and they have no knowledge of the whereabouts of these
manuscripts. We are certain they are not in the U.S.S.R.'

Smith's unofficial contact was made as soon as he arrived in
Moscow. 'I was met at the railroad station by a competent and
highly interested musicologist, who rode with me to my hotel.
He interrogated me at length about our searches and current
knowledge, and then he said that he thought these manuscripts
were in Poland. I should look there. I tried very hard for years
afterwards to get him, but I never could find him again. He was
permanently "absent" and my efforts to reach him by letter
met with silence. He'd disappeared in Russia.'

So, in 1955, the compass needle of Carleton Smith's search
stopped going round in circles and started to point in the
direction of Poland. He pursued the suggestion of the anony-

mous musicologist, and, on his way back through Warsaw, lodged an enquiry with the Polish Minister of Culture. He assured Smith that a thorough search for the manuscripts would be made in Poland.

In the same year, however, another compass needle found its true north, not in Warsaw, but in Moscow. The East German composer, conductor, and head of the composers' union, Leo Spies, was visiting the Soviet Union. Later, he told his former pupil at the Felsenstein Oper, Meinhard von Zallinger-Thurn, of an extraordinary experience that he had had in Moscow. A door was opened, and he saw before him 'a great stack of crates'. They were hard wooden boxes, nailed down and branded with the initials P.S.B., 'obviously containing those manuscripts which were captured in Grüssau'.

CHAPTER TWELVE

The Leningrad Cantata

Leo Spies had fallen into a trap which was almost, if not quite, the subtlest of the Grüssau search. Two years later, with considerably less excuse, Carleton Smith was to fall into it too, in a blunder which leads one to question the quality of the intelligence which reached him from his private army of informants.

By the beginning of 1956, he was doubting whether the promised Polish search would yield anything. In Warsaw, the Minister of Culture had told him that he would question all relevant Polish institutions about the matter, and that he hoped eventually to have 'good news'. But nothing more had been heard since.

The search looked like it was about to peter out again. But Smith was determined to keep it alive. His belief was that the Geneva summit and the return of the Dresden paintings had created a 'political climate . . . changed enough to justify hope of a favourable reply – at least an assurance that the manuscripts are still in existence'. But the thaw was precarious; he had to act quickly before the cold war winter set in again.

The two hundredth anniversary of Mozart's birth – January 27, 1956 – afforded an ideal opportunity. At the very hour of the anniversary, Smith was in Salzburg to play Mozart's clavicord in the house where Mozart was born. (Later in the year, ex-President Truman did the same.) The incident is a further telling example of that spiritual nearness to music that Smith had sought in the 'mystical and thrilling' original scores of Berlin. And, as the sound of his playing filled Mozart's house, the self-made director of the National Arts Foundation must have taken special pleasure in the knowledge that his appeal for those original scores was even then reverberating round the world:

> The ears of the world are filled today with the immortal
> melodies of Mozart; everywhere in the world music lovers

are listening to his music; all eyes are turned towards Salzburg . . . When will it be deemed fitting to let us know that the irreplaceable manuscripts in Mozart's own handwriting have not been destroyed? . . . For seven long years the National Arts Foundation has been trying to find out whether they were abducted or lost . . . It is the foundation's hope that the whereabouts of the missing manuscripts can now be settled. Scholars and performers of music wait in readiness for their discovery. They are versed in the study of original scores. Many of these which have 'gone missing' have never been photocopied . . . Will you please let us know whether the manuscripts of Mozart's *Jupiter* symphony, his *Magic Flute* and *Titus*, the first two acts of *Seraglio*, the last two acts of *Figaro*, and the first act of *Cosi Fan Tutte*, can be found in your lands?

The tie-in with the Mozart celebrations made this Smith's most successful appeal in terms of media noise, but as before, the ears that mattered remained deaf to it. It was aimed, despite the solemn assurances Smith had been given in Moscow, at both the Polish *and* Soviet Ministers of Culture. Either he did not believe the assurances, or he did believe the manuscripts to be in Poland, and was playing at politics – in the hope that the Soviet Union would exert pressure on its satellite – by appealing also further east. If that is what he was doing – and it seems likely – the tactic did not work. The echoes of his appeal died away, and silence fell once more. In 1957, the British librarian F. J. Hill reported, 'Of books and manuscripts evacuated to Pomerania and Silesia, no information has been received.'

In that year, however, Smith's confidence in the changed political climate proved to be justified. In October, on his return to New York after a six-week visit to Europe, he announced:

> that representatives of the foundation in Berlin had told him that the manuscripts of Beethoven's Seventh and Ninth symphonies, Mozart's operas *Titus*, *The Magic Flute*, and two acts of *Figaro*, and many other important musical manuscripts had been returned by the Russian Ministry of Culture to an East German delegation which was visiting Moscow.[1]

[1]Reported in *The Times*, October 7, 1957.

This was the blunder referred to earlier. It shows just how confused and lost Carleton Smith had become. As with the 1956 appeal, we notice how his possession of the list from East Berlin has helped him to get his sense of what had been lost into sharper focus: many of the missing works are now listed individually. But his sense of their whereabouts is vaguer than ever before. Within two years he has gone round in a full circle: first believing the manuscripts to be in the Soviet Union, then in Poland, then appealing to both states, and finally proclaiming that he had been right the first time, and, as in 1950, triumphantly announcing that the manuscripts had been found again.

As in 1950, however, Smith had jumped the gun. The Soviet Union *had* returned to Berlin manuscripts of the former Prussian State Library – on September 30, a week before Smith's announcement. But they were not those for which Smith was looking.

Marshal Sokolowski, in his order of July 1946, had specifically mentioned the castle of Gauernitz, in Saxony, as one of the sites from which library holdings were to be returned to Berlin. This was done, but, as we have already noted[1], not before the Red Army had sorted through the three hundred crates in the castle and returned with a selection of them to the Soviet Union.

These, surely, were the crates which Leo Spies saw in Moscow in 1955, the year when the return of the Dresden paintings signalled a change in Soviet policy towards the G.D.R. (two years earlier, in 1953, the Soviet Union had dropped all claims to war reparations from Germany). Soon after the re-emergence of the Dresden treasures there was 'a decision by the government of the U.S.S.R. to return to the G.D.R. all German cultural holdings which had been taken into custody by the Soviet Union'[2]. One of the first fruits of this decision was the return to Berlin, in 1957, of crates abducted twelve years before from Gauernitz castle – which Carleton Smith confused with Grüssau.

In January 1958, more of the Gauernitz crates were returned, and in that year Smith was personally assured in a

[1] Page 54.
[2] The East Berlin Library's *Festschrift* of 1961.

conversation with Khrushchev 'that if Russian musicologists had any clue of the whereabouts of these lost manuscripts the *world* would know'.

In 1958, however, a clue emerged from Leningrad which suggested that Khrushchev was not speaking the truth. A Hungarian music scholar was studying at the national library in Leningrad. He filled in a form asking for a manuscript and waited for the library attendant to bring it to him. When it came, he opened it to find that a mistake had been made: it was not the manuscript he had asked for, but a Bach cantata, and on it was the mark 'The Royal Library, Berlin'. He had it in his hands for perhaps half a minute, before the attendant realised his mistake and took it back.

In December, H. C. Robbins Landon visited the Hungarian National Library in Budapest. Over lunch, Jenö Véscey of the Music Department, who had heard the story over the grapevine of Hungarian scholars, told him of the Leningrad Cantata. From Landon, the story spread to a wider audience. Bach cantatas were known to have been evacuated to Grüssau. Was that half-minute glimpse in Leningrad a clue to their whereabouts, and to those of all the Grüssau manuscripts? The Berlin library mark was a sign that the cantata could not have reached Leningrad through conventional channels.

Landon brooded on the story until 1962, when he saw a way of pursuing it. The tenor and teacher Professor Sergei Radamsky arrived in Vienna to make arrangements for his first visit to Russia since 1936. The Polish-born Radamsky had taught singing at the Moscow Conservatory between 1927 and 1936, was a fluent Russian speaker, and a friend of Shostakovich. It was this friendship that led to his becoming *persona non grata* in 1936. Shostakovich's opera, *Lady Macbeth of Mtsensk*, had been staged with great success in Leningrad and then disastrously in Moscow, Stalin describing it as 'noise, not music'. This led to a witch-hunt against Shostakovich, but Radamsky stood up for his friend and questioned Stalin's abilities as a music critic. His visa was withdrawn, and he was given two hours to leave the country. Twenty-six years later, the death of Stalin and the denunciation of the Stalin era by Khrushchev had enabled him to renew that visa.

Landon met Radamsky in Vienna and told him about the missing manuscripts and the 'serious concern' over their survival or whereabouts. He told him about the Leningrad Cantata, and asked him to speak to Shostakovich about the affair. Radamsky agreed to do this.

Radamsky's autobiography, *The Persecuted Tenor*[1], records his trip to Russia in April 1962, and his meeting with Shostakovich. But it omits any enquiry about the manuscripts. Shostakovich said he would pursue the matter, and later told Radamsky what he had found out. 'Yes,' he said, 'we have these manuscripts, but we don't want them returned to Berlin. We feel they are safer here.' (This was a time of great international tension in Berlin.)

Dr. Landon relayed this information to the then head of the International Mozart Foundation in Salzburg, Bruno Hantsch, and together they went to see officials of the Austrian government. Soon afterwards, the question was raised with the new Soviet Minister of Culture, Ekaterina Furtseva, when she was passing through Salzburg. Mme. Furtseva's reply was that the manuscripts were not in the Soviet Union. After this, Landon gave up all hope that the manuscripts were going to re-emerge, and, according to him, the N.M.A. followed suit.

The whole episode is very puzzling, but from the perspective of twenty years later it may be possible to explain it. The Leningrad Cantata was, I believe, like the Basel letters and the crates of Gauernitz castle, a red herring, not planted on purpose but built into the Grüssau story.

Let us first consider the possibility that the Hungarian scholar's experience in Leningrad was distorted and exaggerated through hearsay. What if it was not a manuscript of Bach that he saw, for example, but an early printed edition of a Bach cantata? Whatever he saw, he saw it over the period during which the Soviet Union was returning material that had been at Gauernitz, and 'older printed music' is known to have been evacuated to the castle. The cantata could have been a printed score which, emerging from its hiding place in the Leningrad Library in the upheaval of the Gauernitz returns of 1957–8, fell by mistake into the Hungarian's hands.

But if it was a *manuscript* that he saw, the possibilities are fewer. There is only one manuscript of a Bach cantata officially

[1]Sergei Radamsky, *Der Verfolgte Tenor – Mein Sängerleben Zwischen Moskau und Hollywood*, Piper Verlag, Munich, 1972, pp. 262–267.

known to be in Leningrad, and that is No. 188, together with a fragment of No. 80. But neither of them bears the mark of the Royal Library, Berlin, and we can dismiss them from the reckoning. A more intriguing possibility is that he saw another manuscript which has long been in the Leningrad Library, of a work which was once thought to be by Bach but which is now regarded as the work of another composer, possibly Telemann. This is the *Little Magnificat*, which is entered as B.W.V. 21 in the appendix to the complete list of works by and works attributed to Bach. The *Little Magnificat* manuscript, unlike that of Cantata No. 188, provides rich openings for a misunderstanding.

On its flyleaf there is a certificate authenticating it as the work of Bach – a certificate drawn up in 1857 by the then director of the Berlin Royal Library's Music Department, Siegfried Wilhelm Dehn, and signed by him. Beneath his signature, Dehn wrote 'Custos der Königliche Bibliothek in Berlin'. It is quite possible that the Hungarian scholar – in the few seconds he had the manuscript in his hands – mistook the certificate for a mark of ownership, and jumped to the conclusion that it was one of the lost Grüssau Manuscripts.

However, neither of these explanations – that the Bach cantata was a printed edition, or that it was the *Little Magnificat* – squares with the remark which Shostakovich made to Radamsky: 'Yes, we have these manuscripts . . .' Now, the Leningrad Library has long been rumoured to be the storage place of former Prussian State Library holdings lost in the war. Priceless material from the East Asian Collection, in particular, is thought to be there. The rumours were reported by the West German *Frankfurter Allgemeine Zeitung* in 1974[1], and they are backed up by the statement of Shostakovich in 1962. The East German *Festschrift* of 1961 also supports the notion that the Soviet Union, despite its 'decision . . . to return to the G.D.R. all German cultural holdings', held on to some, just as it held on to a number of the Dresden paintings even after 1955. The *Festschrift* makes it clear that there is material from Gauernitz still missing, 'presumably . . . lost during the chaos of the last years of the war'. This is a euphemism for looting.

Is the Leningrad Cantata a clue to the presence of other

[1]March 1, 1974, 'Wem Gehört Die Nofretete?', by Peter Jochen Winters.

looted German music – not from Grüssau – in the Leningrad Library? Is it, in fact, a clue to quite another paperchase? At the cost of some Russian credibility, which there is already cause to question, this, as we shall see, is the one explanation that makes proper sense of the conversation between Shostakovich and Radamsky in 1962.

In 1968, the Johann-Sebastian-Bach-Institut in Göttingen issued a list of missing manuscripts by Bach. One part of it is devoted to material lost as a result of the war, and in it there are eight cantatas. All are given in the *Book Collector* list of the same year as having been evacuated to Grüssau. If the Leningrad Cantata was a clue to another paperchase, therefore, it cannot have been one of these.

It is not out of the question, however, that it may have been another Bach cantata altogether. Bach wrote a great many cantatas – the exact number is disputed – and the Bach Institute does not claim that its list is definitive. 'Strictly speaking,' says Dr. Klaus Hofmann of the Institute, 'it was no more than a by-product of [our] work on sources, [and it] in no way claims to be complete.' There is the possibility, therefore, that another cantata failed to return from the war, and that its loss was not advertised by the East Berlin Library.

But, if that is so, from which evacuation site could the cantata have come? Another, apart from Grüssau, to which we know that Bach cantatas were sent was Schönebeck, on the western bank of the Elbe, in an area occupied first by American and then by Soviet troops. And we know that there was some looting of the Schönebeck mine. In 1965, when ten missing Mozart manuscripts mysteriously turned up in Tübingen, in West Germany, the East Berlin Library claimed ownership of them, saying that they had been looted from Schönebeck by Americans. This makes it clear that music manuscripts were among the objects looted.

We know this also from Dr. Wackernagel. When the Schönebeck crates returned to Berlin in August 1946, he 'found some of the boxes opened and others partly broken. I don't know by whom. Some of the things were missing. Only the binding was there, the manuscripts had gone'. Significant here is that phrase 'I don't know by whom'. The Schönebeck mine could have been looted either by Americans or – as it would have been impolitic for East Berlin to suggest – by Russians.

Viewed against this background, the Leningrad Cantata could be a clue, not to the Grüssau mystery, but to the where-about of the much smaller Schönebeck losses. If Carleton Smith, by then a veteran of the mystery, could confuse Grüssau with Gauernitz, how much easier for two novices to be misled by the much more deeply camouflaged false trail of Schönebeck. The names of the two sites would have meant little or nothing to Radamsky and Shostakovich, and they could quite easily have talked at cross purposes. Radamsky would have enquired after music manuscripts from Berlin, said to be in Leningrad. In his reply, discreetly passed down from official quarters, Shostakovich confirmed that this was so.

But they lacked the all-important precise vocabulary of the evacuation. There probably were, and still are, in Leningrad manuscripts belonging to Berlin, and musical manuscripts among them, but if so — as Mme. Furtseva told the Austrians — they were not the treasures of Grüssau.

*

I have left out the most important premise behind this interpre-tation, for the reason that — as the Leningrad story itself shows — it was not generally shared at the time. But it was at about this period, the early 1960s, that it began to develop, to reach virtual certainty by the middle of the decade.

Dr. Landon was led by the Leningrad Cantata to revise his earlier guess, and to believe that the manuscripts must be in Russia. Through him, others came to share the same belief. It was reinforced by the outcome of a Party-to-Party request to the Poles from the East Germans in the mid-sixties. The reply was that the manuscripts were 'not on Polish soil'. The West Berlin music librarian Dr. Rudolf Elvers was one who took this as a veiled reference to the manuscripts' presence therefore on *Russian* soil, in Leningrad.

But, over the same period, others engaged elsewhere in the search were moving in precisely the opposite direction, and coming to believe that it was time to remove the brackets and the question-mark from Landon's exceedingly tentative '(Poland?)'.

CHAPTER THIRTEEN

The Need For Proof

In August 1960, Professor Schmidt-Görg of the Beethoven House in Bonn broadcast to the eastern bloc countries over Radio Free Europe appealing for information about the Ninth Symphony and other Beethoven manuscripts lost at Grüssau. Reports of the appeal carried the rider: 'Experts believe the missing manuscript [i.e. the Ninth Symphony] is in Poland.' This was the first open suggestion that Poland and no one else had absconded with the treasure.

The rider sounds authoritative, but it was still a stab in the dark. Its air of confidence derived from the elimination of the Russian option over the five years since Landon's guess. The reasoning is simple. If the manuscripts had survived – and that was a faith shared by all the searchers – they were either in Poland or in the Soviet Union. But both had denied having them; therefore one was not telling the truth. Which? The return of the Dresden paintings and the Gauernitz crates helped to win western acceptance that there really had been a change in Russian policy, and that, as Khrushchev told Carleton Smith, if Russia had the manuscripts 'the *world* would know'. This tended to eliminate the prime suspect, the Soviet Union, leaving only Poland.

The proof was still lacking, but with the strengthening of this suspicion the first broad phase of the search effectively ended. Its epitaph might be Carleton Smith's retrospective: 'We thought for many years the manuscripts were in Russia, because the Russians had the great paintings of Dresden.' The Russian option would not be considered seriously again, except as a lever on Poland. This was clearly Carleton Smith's intention when he appealed to Brezhnev and Kosygin in 1965, by which time he firmly felt the manuscripts to be in Poland.

Smith's noisy paperchase had been possible only when its tramping-ground, and the butt of his accusations, was 'the

East'. The singling out of a particular nation state, when it had already denied having the manuscripts, and when there was still no proof that it had them, required a different approach. Especially so when the state was Poland.The nuances of this complication will become apparent, but for the time being it can be summed up simply. The manuscripts of great music by German composers had been lost as the result of a war which had begun, we will hardly need reminding, with Germany's invasion of Poland. It had been the occupied country for which the Nazis reserved their greatest cruelties. They had murdered its people, suppressed its universities, arts, press, and even its language, destroyed its historic buildings and statues, and ripped apart and looted its national and private collections. They had dynamited the Palace of the Kings in Warsaw, and just for good measure dynamited the remaining rubble. Even old trees had not been spared in the effort to flatten Poland and the Polish spirit.

In approaching Poland, it was as well, indeed imperative, to remember her experience of the war, and great tact as well as humility were clearly essential. Carleton Smith had no cause to feel war guilt, but perhaps he too was influenced by these considerations to lump Russia into his appeal of 1965, so as to blunt the accusation. And of course he was not yet sure.

At the same time, however, deference to the recent Polish past was insufficient reason for abandoning the search altogether. The manuscripts collected by Prussia belonged also to the world, and the motives for wanting to know that they were safe and for wanting access to them remained as strong and as real as before. The difference was that the whole imbroglio became enormously more complicated. The elimination of Russia from the reckoning enabled searchers to concentrate their energies in one and the same general direction; but that still left ample territorial space into which 505 crates could vanish, and introduced moreover new political difficulties.

It is no accident, therefore, that over this period we find governments beginning to engage in the search. There were three. All shared the burden of war guilt, but otherwise there were important differences in their positions. The two Germanies were involved in the East-West power struggle, and each could lay claim to ownership of the manuscripts, while the third, Austria, was a neutral state whose interest in the search was a paternal concern for the missing Mozart treasures.

None was able to raise a furore over the disappearance: the much more obvious furore of the recent past coupled with the lack of any solid proof made the situation too delicate for that. But, here, East Germany enjoyed great advantages. Firstly, through her possession of the evacuation lists, she was able to give Poland chapter and verse as to what had been lost, which West Germany was unable to do. Secondly, her alignment was broadly the same as Poland's. And thirdly, as a consequence of this, she had had diplomatic relations with Poland since becoming a republic in 1949.

All this gave East Germany the machinery needed to pursue the search – as it had to be pursued – discreetly, through 'the proper channels'. As a result, her government was certainly the first to engage in the search, with what lack of success may be judged from the evident necessity of the Party-to-Party request of the mid-1960s.

West Germany's position was the weakest of the three. It was 1972 before Bonn and Warsaw exchanged ambassadors, and until then she simply had not the means to pursue such enquiries. Her one strength during the sixties was her trade relationship with eastern bloc countries. In 1963, an agreement was signed with a number of them, including Poland, and Polish trade missions were opened in West German cities.

In the early sixties, the then Federal Minister of the Interior, Hermann Höcherl, made contact with the monks of Bad Wimpfen and learned from them of the missing manuscripts. According to Father Michalski, he took a particular interest in the problem, and tried to carry matters further. West German Foreign Office records show how far he succeeded. The contents of the six western evacuation sites were among the material held in trust by the West German 'Prussian Cultural Heritage Foundation' set up under a law enacted in 1957. When government officials applied to the Foundation, according to a later West German Secretary of State for Foreign Affairs, they found that it 'does not possess any evacuation papers and has only fragments of former catalogues'. The absence of 'any official record regarding the relocated contents of the former Prussian State Library' forced the government to fall back on the fatalistic formula under which the lists of

111

missing things were drawn up: 'Since 1946, the original scores . . . have been considered lost after their evacuation to Silesia.'

The result of this 'continuing confusion', as the Secretary of State put it, was that it made 'any adequate proof impossible.' In 1975, a Minister of State at the Foreign Office summarised the situation: 'Up to now there have been no discussions with the Polish government about this matter, as we have no precise information.' (In fact, there was precise information by then, but it was privileged and could not be used in negotiations.)

Without 'adequate proof' the government could not make representations, and without diplomatic relations it could not make discreet enquiries. The result was paralysis. During West Germany's *Ostpolitik* and after 1972, the monks at Bad Wimpfen were asked to keep quiet about the Grüssau manuscripts, so as not to prejudice the diplomatic overtures that were at last being made. These must have been extremely tentative, however. According to Father Michalski, 'because of political considerations, they were not willing in Bonn to pursue the matter more widely'. Foreign Office papers say that the Warsaw Embassy 'repeatedly sounded out the Polish authorities, however without results', as we may assume the East Germans to have been doing by then for more than twenty years.

Austrian involvement came about in direct response to the needs of the N.M.A. The Austrian government's position was perhaps the purest of the three, a foreign policy extension of the national Mozart-worship. Untainted by questions of ownership, its interest in the missing manuscripts corresponded exactly with the interests of scholars. Having diplomatic relations with Poland, it was able to enquire, and its enquiries were made out of a disinterested desire to know only that the manuscripts were safe and would one day become accessible again. An additional advantage was that it was concerned with only one part of the missing treasure – the Mozart originals – and was able to be highly specific as to what it was.

This was thanks to Carleton Smith, who, twelve years before publishing his list of the missing music, allowed the Austrians to see it. That was in 1956, the year he issued his appeal from Salzburg. From that year, too, we can date the merging of Smith's private search having governmental overtones into the fully-fledged governmental search of the Austrians. In his 1956 appeal there is for the first time a note of identification with the needs of scholars ('Scholars and performers of music wait in readiness . . .'). Smith clearly had the beleaguered N.M.A. in mind. The appeal met with the approval of the then Austrian President, Theodor Körner. He told Smith that it helped to suggest a measure of independence from the Russians, who had only just pulled out. Three or four years later, Smith, the then Austrian Foreign Minister, later Chancellor, Bruno Kreisky, and the instigator of Smith's search, ex-President Truman, met at a lunch in Kansas City, Missouri. Afterwards, Smith spoke at length on his ten years of searching for the manuscripts. Truman played the piano for Kreisky – Chopin's Waltz in A perhaps?

These informal links were strengthened in 1960, when Austria conferred on Smith the Order of Merit. Two years later, he took up a public affairs consultancy to the Austrian Foreign Ministry. This was the period when Mme. Furtseva was asked about the manuscripts; the same questions were put to Khrushchev, when he was visiting Austria.[1] Again he denied that the treasure was in the Soviet Union.

So the Foreign Ministry in Vienna came to open a file on the Grüssau manuscripts. It is reticent as to its contents, and will say only that 'Prominent Austrian personalities repeatedly enquired after the manuscripts in question with the Polish authorities in order to render possible research by Austrian scholars . . .' We know that 'prominent personalities' ranged from the Mayor of Salzburg, who visited Poland in an attempt to find the manuscripts, to the upper echelons of government: successive Austrian Presidents and at least one Foreign Minister took up the matter with their Polish counterparts.

It matters little that we know no more than that. It can confidently be stated that the Austrian government's search, like those conducted by East Germany, and later West Germany, achieved precisely nothing, unless it was to press home the high seriousness with which the disappearance of the manuscripts was regarded.

*

Without proof, there could be no progress in the search. If Poland had the manuscripts, yet had denied having them, it

[1]Khrushchev was questioned by the Austrians on July 4, 1960, when he visited the house in Salzburg where Mozart was born.

followed that their retention was a matter of policy and a state secret. Alteration of this situation required the full authority and diplomatic skills of a government, or governments, able to deal as equals with the government of Poland. But, until there was proof, the most governments could do was to ask disingenuous questions. At the same time, they were powerless to gather proof for themselves. The same set of factors which gave a government the weight and authority to act effectively deprived it of the freedom to act informally. If proof was to be gathered, there was digging to be done, accusations to be levelled, tricky questions to be asked.

This was the province of the individual searchers, and, as though on cue, these years saw a sudden growth in their numbers. There were reasons for this. In 1959 and 1963, the lists were issued of the missing holdings of the old Prussian State Library's Manuscript Department. In 1964, the list of missing Mozart manuscripts appeared. And, as the sense of what had been lost was sharpened by these definitive lists, so the surviving holdings of the old library were assuming two distinct identities in East and West Berlin. In 1964, a first consignment of manuscripts and objects that had been evacuated westward was returned to Berlin, not to the Unter den Linden, but to a special archive in the western part of the city. The process continued throughout the sixties, reaching completion in 1977. By 1978, all were housed in the brand new library building of the Prussian Cultural Heritage Foundation.

At the same time, the Grüssau problem gained definition. A collection can be compared to a chemical suspension that is left standing. The war had shaken this one up, and made it murky. It had been decanted into separate containers, in which it was settling down once more, and clarifying. Library-users applied at the Berlin archive to discover that things they wanted to see had been 'lost'. Some wanted to find out more. In 1964, soon after the final list of lost things from the old Manuscript Department appeared, Dr. Luise Charlotte Pickert enquired at the Bad Wimpfen monastery. She wanted to see if she could trace through her own efforts a group of twenty-eight letters which the painters Franz and Christian Riepenhausen had written to their father. After the extent of the Mozart losses became known, a Mozart-loving nurse called Ruth Hörber also got in touch with Bad Wimpfen. She went further than Dr.

Pickert, pursuing the matter with the Polish trade mission in Cologne and later in Poland itself.

Those were just two of the West German searchers. The most persistent and important of them, however, was a professor of philosophy, Dieter Henrich. He first came across the Grüssau problem in 1960, when he was in Berlin on his first professorship. At the time he was studying Hegel and the First System Programme of German Idealism, and was a regular user of the East Berlin library. There he 'became acquainted with the catalogues and with the problem', and he adds, 'the search became more intensive when I discovered that there were in the Varnhagen Collection unpublished manuscripts of Hölderlin's friend and pupil Isaak von Sinclair'. This gave him the same sort of insight into the problem, and the same sort of motive for solving it, that the missing *Piquitinga* picture would later give Peter Whitehead.

Professor Henrich brought to the search a scientific exactness and a sense of historical perspective that had thitherto been lacking. His search was not as colourful as Carleton Smith's had been, and would be again. Nor did it have the luck that Peter Whitehead's was to have. But he pursued it with a diligence and a concern for detail that enabled him to pin down the problem with clarity. As we have seen, there were no short cuts. Great staying power, as well as a sense of mission, were needed to follow what had become a quest. Professor Henrich had these qualities, too. 'With treasures like these,' as he put it, 'it is the duty of scholars to search for treasure.'

Having come across the problem, he did not relax his grip. His aim was ambitious: to provide documentation so meticulous as to put beyond doubt both what was missing and who had taken it. He eventually succeeded in this, but, ironically, his success came at the precise moment when the vital breakthrough was achieved elsewhere. His painstaking documentation arrived too late to influence events.

The required proof was to come from unexpected quarters, in a series of dramatic developments. Carleton Smith was to play a part in the process, which began in the mid-sixties but took time to reach fruition. In 1965, no more than a hint of it came perhaps to Smith's attention, and perhaps prompted his appeal of that year. It was addressed to the Prime Ministers of the Soviet Union and Poland, and the First Secretaries of their

Communist Parties. In his appeal to the Poles, Smith mentioned that the National Arts Foundation 'had reason to believe' that the manuscripts might be in or near the city of Wrocław, formerly Breslau, in Silesia.

This was the first time a particular Polish location for the manuscripts had been suggested. As such, it represented an advance in confidence on the rider to Professor Schmidt-Görg's appeal of 1960. But Wrocław was yet another false trail. The game of hide-and-seek had shifted from the map of 'the east' to that of Poland, but the blindfolds were still on.

There were two grounds for the Wrocław theory. The first was that holdings from Grüssau had indeed been transferred to Wrocław – not the crates of the Prussian State Library, however, but *the library of the monastery itself*. This numbered more than forty thousand volumes. From the monastery, they were moved first to St. Matthew's School in Wrocław, then to the Ossolineum Library.

The monastery library in itself could have misled Carleton Smith, as it later misled at least one West German scholar and a member of the Bundestag in Bonn. A second reason could have been the Rü-Be-Pol operation, as it was called, which took place in 1965, partly from Wrocław. This is that 'hint' at the truth mentioned above, to which we shall return in due course.[1]

False though it was, at the end of the sixties the Wrocław theory gained currency. In 1967, the standard German reference work *Riemann Musik Lexikon* said in its entry on the Berlin library that 'the parts evacuated to Silesia (including the Meyerbeer Bequest) have since been located in Breslau'. This gave rise to a flood of enquiries addressed to Wrocław.

Again in 1967, Smith repeated the Wroclaw theory, with the proviso that it was 'not capable of verification'. He added: 'We believe [this priceless music] has not been destroyed, and that some evidence of its whereabouts will be forthcoming.' Significantly, Smith chose to publish this, not in a newspaper, but in a small-circulation antiquarian magazine, the *Book Collector*, which is published from London. He had already done all he could to alert the public to the loss of the manuscripts; but

[1] The Breslau University holdings evacuated to Grüssau could also have been behind the misunderstanding.

116

the time for that was over. As the search began to get to grips with the supposed heart of the problem, it was necessary to go deeper.

The article was published in 1968, together with the list of the missing music which had been in Smith's private possession for almost twenty years. Now, the *Book Collector* has a special relationship with the eastern bloc countries and a fairly wide readership within them. Was this why Smith chose it as his outlet? In Poland, for example, according to its editor, Nicholas Barker, 'More copies circulate than are sold there. We've made a special practice of taking articles from the eastern bloc. I don't know who gets copies on the unofficial subscription list. We just bundle them off.'

Since at least 1964, an unofficial subscriber to the *Book Collector* has been Karol Estreicher. After the war, he had returned to Kraków and resumed his interrupted association with the Jagiellonian University; in 1968, when he received the issue containing Carleton Smith's article, he was an Associate Professor in Art History.

Reading the article, did he allow himself a smile? He might well have done so, and not only because he knew a thing or two both about convoys and about what it was like to search for missing art treasure. Dr. Estreicher had a more specialized reason for smiling: he knew about the Grüssau Manuscripts, and had done for more than twenty years.

CHAPTER FOURTEEN

Meeting 19

In 1944, with the war's end in sight, Estreicher's grisly file was published as a handbook, *Cultural Losses of Poland*, almost two hundred and fifty pages of small print listing acts of destruction and looting. Even today, it exudes an overwhelming sense of brutality.

This portable memory of all that Germany had done to Polish culture was Estreicher's work, but his achievement went further than information-gathering. He also drew conclusions from his work, and stated them powerfully. Estreicher was the first and most influential exponent of the idea of cultural revindication, and here we come across his first connection with the story of the Grüssau Manuscripts.

On the face of it, one would not think that the idea of revindication needed any expounding. It is a technical, topical term which means simply the return to its country of origin, or the country legally owning it, of an object looted from it and taken elsewhere.

This is straightforward enough when there are only a limited number of objects at issue, when the legal owner can prove his right to them, and when they can be traced to the places where the looter has hidden them away. It becomes more complicated – much more so – when the looter has helped himself to countless things, has destroyed the catalogues listing them and proving their ownership, then hidden them away in many secret places. To this we may add the problem, where Poland was concerned, of convincing others of the almost incredible extent and ferocity of the German destruction and looting. Estreicher faced precisely this problem with two British experts, the archaeologist Sir Leonard Woolley, and the head of the Victoria and Albert Museum, Sir Eric Maclagan.

Matters become more complicated when we move beyond revindication to reparation, the compensation for something destroyed or lost apparently irretrievably. Reparation is a concept which it is hard to apply in the cultural field, for the reason that woks of art are unique and there can be no accurate comparisons of their relative value. We can express the difficulty as follows. If a tractor is stolen or destroyed, another tractor of the same make, or its money equivalent, will serve as compensation. But if a mother loses her child, she cannot be offered in exchange another child of the same sex and age and similar appearance. Art works are material objects, like tractors; but, unlike tractors, they bear much the same relation to the culture which had produced them, or adopted them, as a child does to its mother. By the same token, a kind of grief is involved in their loss which reparation can go some way towards assuaging, but cannot assuage altogether. In the cultural field, revindication is obviously greatly preferable to reparation.

At the turn of 1942–43, Estreicher visited the United States, and from the report which he presented there[1] we know what his views were on these matters at that time. Here are some extracts from it:

> Simple justice demands that he who plundered, destroyed, and murdered should restore damages.

> I am against the destruction of the cultural resources of defeated Germany – but I declare that the guilty ones must be punished with all the severity of the law and that they must restore and repair the damages done in their nationalistic fury.

> International law, the Hague Convention, and other international agreements distinctly oppose the looting and destruction of art and culture. The Germans introduced a new law, the law of the stronger, permitting the looting and destruction. We must think about new methods of repairing the damages inflicted by plunderers.

In these statements, Estreicher crosses the borderline from revindication into reparation, and no one reading them in the

---

[1] 'The Destruction and Plunder by the Germans of Works of Art and the Necessary Cultural Revindication Resulting from it.'

119

light of his detailed documentation would argue with them or with the strength of his feelings. When it comes to discussing the form that reparation should take, however, he has remarkably little to say, only that 'we must at once declare that . . . the damages must be paid for in kind', and that 'if the Polish libraries have suffered through German lootings, they should be repaid by "Polonica", of which there are plenty in Germany'. Others after him would tackle the question of cultural reparations in more detail.

Obviously, for something destroyed, reparation would be the only recourse. But Estreicher's energies, and hopes, were channelled in a different direction: his emphasis was on total revindication of looted things by squeezing them, as it were, out of their German hiding places. In discussing revindication, he comes up with specific, practical proposals for 'new methods' befitting the 'new laws':

> In the terms of the armistice, clauses should be introduced which would have real value. They should provide first of all for the compulsory management of all German museums and collections until such time when it is proved that they do not contain looted objects . . .

> Immediately after the armistice all sales of works of art . . . should be stopped in Germany.

> Without training . . . of a group of specialists who would be able to become supervisors of museums and collections in the most important German cities, it will be impossible to take from the Germans what they have stolen.

Note especially the last statement: Estreicher, from the wealth of his experience, is saying that total revindication would not be possible unless his stringent proposals are put into effect. But note also that he is making two assumptions: firstly, that the war would end with an armistice, when it would not; and, secondly, that there would still be one Germany, when there would in fact be two. The politics of the Cold War would intervene to prevent the implementation of his proposals (which, again, strike one as eminently reasonable).

There would be no 'squeeze' of the kind he wanted, no clauses with real bite to them, no compulsory management, no lasting embargo of German arts sales, and no thoroughgoing vetting of German collections. And, as he had prophesied, revindication suffered as a result.

Reparation, too, would be unsatisfactory. Immediately after the war, a Polish Bureau of Reparations approached the problem in a series of pamphlets setting out the facts, and the Polish claims deriving from them. They stressed, firstly, that 'We should not feel able to accept an equivalent in money or industrial products':

> Having lost objects expressive of culture, we demand only analogous objects. They may be highly valuable according to current catalogues. But for us, our heritage has been priceless . . . it is beside the point to try to fix up the 'market' value of the reparations due to us . . . We want only objects capable of influencing art and culture development in general.

This elaborates upon Estreicher's 'damages in kind', but leaves open the problem of defining the 'analogous objects' expressive of Polish culture. What could they be? The question was tackled in most detail by the Polish philosopher Tatarkiewicz, in one of the pamphlets. Firstly, he at once rules out 'any objects which are "true German property". Here belong objects that Germans themselves have produced. The Reich is the right place for these'.

Eschewing simple material compensation, the Poles aimed at Estreicher's 'simple justice'. Tatarkiewicz outlined three categories of art objects which it was proper for Poland to expect: '(1) Objects that bear some connection with Poland, e.g. the sculptures of Veit Stoss[1], or those that once formed part of a Polish collection; (2) Objects purchased by Germans with funds derived in part at least from Poland, as had been the case with pictures secured by the two Saxon kings of Poland for the Dresden Gallery; (3) Objects that have been secured for German collections by purchase, but otherwise do not stand in any close relationship with German culture. This is so, for example, of works of Greek or Italian art.'

Reasonable arguments, once again, put forward with admirable restraint. But once again denied. Under the terms of the

[1]Known in Poland as Wit Stwosz, he was born in Nuremberg, in Bavaria, but lived and worked in Kraków between 1477 and 1489.

Potsdam agreement, reparations to Poland were to be made as a percentage of those received by the Soviet Union. All Soviet reparations, moreover, were to be drawn only from the Soviet-occupied zone of Germany. This made Poland in effect dependent upon Soviet charity, at the same time as it prevented her from staking claims in the western-occupied zones. It was difficult to penalise East Germany for a looted art work that might remain missing in the west. It was difficult, in other words, to hold either Germany fully accountable. We may note here that when East Germany gave Poland a group of Chopin manuscripts in 1949 (to mark the tenth anniversary of the outbreak of war) it was *voluntarily*.

If we consider the commonly-held Polish view that the Soviet Union welshed on its reparations commitment *as a whole* regarding Poland, we can easily imagine how great was the short-fall in the specific field of culture. The possibility of rectifying this was lost in 1953, when the Soviet Union, dropping all further reparations claims against East Germany, thereby dropped Poland's as well.

Then, in 1955, it effectively buried the idea of cultural reparations within the Soviet bloc by returning the Dresden paintings. The return could be called an act of symbolic *realpolitik*, designed to stress the importance of post-war solidarity between the Warsaw Pact countries over sources of division and conflict dating from the war. At the same time, it affirmed Soviet regard for East Germany as a separate state. With the Dresden return, the Soviet Union signalled that an era had ended. Setting aside its own heavy war losses in the cultural field, including the Amber Room, it wrote off a still unresolved part of its past.

The world had changed, and it was necessary to change with it. Poland's history since the war is to a large extent the history of this adjustment, in which she has tried to come to terms with one of the most contortionist realities that any country has had to confront: that her bitterest enemies, to west and east, partitioners and oppressors of Poland throughout her history, must also be her staunchest allies; and that the most Roman Catholic country in the world must be nominally Communist. Poland provides an extreme case of conflict between the inner, emotional and religious realities recognised by her people, and the outer, political necessities willed upon her people by her

122

government. She has had to live with this conflict, in one form or another, for much of her history, and as a result a pattern of behaviour has evolved which we may recognise as distinctively Polish and which has enabled Poles to cope with ordinary lives which inevitably have a great deal of play-acting in them. The pattern is difficult to define. As with the Czechs, 'the reed that bends but does not break', as Hitler's gauleiter called them, there is a good deal of pliability in the mix: instinctive secretiveness and cunning, a kind of self-exiled 'inner' dissidence. But where the Poles are markedly different, and why they sometimes tend to despise the Czechs, is in the degree of defiant 'outer' expression they allow themselves and will not allow to be taken away. It is as though they cannot bear to spend all their time lurking opaquely on the stitching side of the tapestry of life, but must sometimes come out from behind it and be seen for what they are. This can be as a violent, hang-the-consequences assertiveness in private home or drinking-house. But, more often, it is peaceful, in the form of religious devotion or cultural pride; for it is largely in their religious and cultural lives that the Poles, throughout their troubled history, have found dignity under domination, continuity in chaos. In church, theatre, cinema, or art gallery, for a time at least, the intolerable conflict between 'inner' and 'outer' is resolved.

The question is too complex to explore here in greater detail, and perhaps sufficiently well-known not to need more than a sketch. Suffice it to say, that latitude of expression of the 'inner' does not extend to the country's political life[1]. There the 'outer' reigns supreme. Those who govern Poland have willed the Polish paradox through to an artificial resolution: the right motions have been gone through, the right noises made, the right agreements and treaties of friendship signed with all the right-thinking People's Republics, including East Germany. Poland has behaved. Old enemies are friends. In her foreign relations, if not in the minds of her people, the war has been forgiven. Poland has seen where her best interests lie, has buried the hatchet, and changed with the times.

In one part of herself, however, Poland did not change, but remained arrested in time, unable to make the transition. Her

[1]Until the emergence of the Solidarity free trade union movement. However, as I write, it is not at all certain that this will be allowed to survive and develop.

culture had been one of the two most cohesive factors in her history and national life, and – unlike Roman Catholicism – one with which Communists and non-Communists alike could identify. The damage and humiliation inflicted upon her culture had been too great, the compensation too small, revindication only partly successful, reparations pitifully inadequate.

Estreicher's 'simple justice' remained as remote as ever, and, unlike the Russians, the Poles did not write off the grudge. Instead, it was officially, but secretly, incorporated into the national policy – secretly, because the authorised version was that accounts had been settled, the war forgotten, and there were no grudges. This one, therefore, did not permit of robust outward expression – as a bone of contention between two Soviet satellites. But in this instance, at least, one river of the national feeling – a river of resentment – ran right to the top of the Polish hierarchy. The cause of the 'inner' reality, one could say, was championed for once by the exponents of the 'outer'. Here, at least, there was Polish unity.

The river runs right up to the present day. For this is not ancient history. The grudge is very much alive, and will remain so until the reason for it is removed. It is as timeless as the vases of Gołuchow, or the portrait by Raphael, stolen and missing these forty years.

As timeless as great music.

*

In the middle of the war, however, there was every reason for Karol Estreicher to feel sure that the best that could be done would be done. In April 1943, at the end of his visit to the United States, the Director of the Metropolitan Museum in New York wrote to the Polish ambassador in Washington:

> Dr. Estreicher has been in constant consultation during the past five months with the leaders of the art world in this country, and has given us much valuable information . . . concerning the restitution and salvage of the artistic heritage of Europe. As a result very largely of his visit, a committee has been formed . . . which is co-operating with various agencies of the United States Government in developing a pattern of how we may be able to act in these matters when called upon . . . Without his visit I am sure that any plans or activities undertaken by the American institutions would have been delayed many months.

The committee was formed in January 1943, and met for the first time in June. Two months later it was merged into the Roberts Commission set up by President Roosevelt and chaired by the Supreme Court Justice, Owen Roberts. Its main purpose was to collect up-to-the-minute information, along the lines pioneered by Estreicher, and to produce detailed maps, culturally orientated, for use in military operations. But the main achievement of the Roberts Commission was the establishment by the Americans of their Monuments, Fine Arts and Archives Division (or MFA & A). This was a group of specially-trained officers who travelled with the troops and alerted them to the whereabouts of museums, collections, and so on, and ensured that they escaped damage. After the battle was over, they supervised the care and vetting of art works, and tried to establish whether they had been looted, and if so, from where.

According to one of the officers, the establishment of the Roberts Commission was 'the first time in history that a country had taken such precautions to safeguard cultural monuments lying in the path of its invading armies'. The next important initiative was the creation, in London, of an inter-Allied commission largely composed of representatives of the occupied countries and chaired by the French professor, Paul Vaucher. It started work in April 1944. Finally, full awareness of the war's cultural dimensions was achieved when Churchill, soon afterwards, started a British counterpart to the Roberts Commission, chaired by Lord Macmillan of the British Museum.

All three commissions worked closely together in gathering information and pooling it, co-ordinating the work of protection in the last victorious months of the war, and the work of revindication when it was over. But we should note that they had limited powers. The Roberts Commission, for instance, being a Presidential body, 'was not attached to any Government Department, but had an independent existence; this also meant that it had little authority'.

Estreicher, by whose initiative this chain reaction of commissions had come about, and whose work provided the model for much of their activity, was a member of the one chaired by Vaucher. From its records he emerges as perhaps its most knowledgeable and active member. At Meeting No. 10, we find him singling out one particular Polish art-work and urging that it be regarded as a special case, part of the cultural heritage, not merely of Poland, 'but of Europe itself'. This was the magnificent altarpiece which the king of Poland commissioned in 1477 from Veit Stoss, for Our Lady's Church in Kraków. It was regarded by the Poles with reverence, not only as a beautiful work of art, but as one of their most sacred objects, and Estreicher called its removal by the Germans in 1939 'the most striking example of plunder' among all the thousands documented by him. He gave its return to Poland top priority, and when, as 'Major Estreicher', he was appointed as Polish representative for revindication in Germany after the war, the altarpiece was the first thing he asked for.

From a German guidebook of 1943, he had found that the German destination of the altarpiece was the birthplace of Veit Stoss, Nuremberg, in Bavaria. But his researches had also shown that Bavaria, together with Austria and Silesia, was the area where the densest concentrations of looted art would be found. And so, as the war ended, it was for the U.S. occupied zone of Bavaria that he made.

He was right to do so. In Munich, MFA & A had set up a collecting point, and all over Bavaria, according to one of its officers, 'repositories are springing up like mushrooms . . . Most of it is loot'. Within a year, some five hundred depots had been uncovered, but, according to another American officer, there were 'very few objects from Eastern Europe'. Estreicher, nevertheless, found rich pickings: Polish ecclesiastical vessels of gold and silver in the Reichsbank in Frankfurt, paintings from the Polish National Museum in the castle of Tambach. Later, he would supervise the return from Bavaria of a huge collection of looted Polish art – but still only a proportion of the total tally – in twenty-six railway carriages.

The richest Bavarian find was the Kraków altarpiece, but it was not discovered by Estreicher. Armed with his handbook, he went first to Höchst, near Frankfurt, to study the files of MFA & A, then on to Munich and Nuremberg. There, he was shown the altarpiece. It had been hoarded, together with other Veit Stoss sculptures, in an underground bunker, and there, opposite the bombed remains of Dürer's house, an American officer had happened upon it. Everything was miraculously there, and intact – the central panel, the painted figures of

126

hollow wood, ten feet high, the predella. In the darkness of the German bunker the gilding burned as, from his earliest childhood, Estreicher could remember it burning in the sacred, perfumed gloom of Our Lady's. It would take ten trucks to carry it all.

The triumphant return came later, at the beginning of 1946. There were problems. Firstly, as one American officer put it, 'progress was naturally slow. Men and materials were lacking; and the question of the Fine Arts was only one of many problems facing the United States Army in Germany'. Secondly, the roads into Poland were badly damaged, and 'internal conditions in Poland were too unsettled'. Thirdly, for the above reasons and perhaps also because of a certain caginess towards Poland since the Potsdam conference, Poland was fairly low down on the list of countries to receive the first 'token restitutions' which were to start the overall process. Western countries were served first: by the autumn of 1945, for instance, Belgium had been returned its 'Mystic Lamb' by Van Eyck, as its token restitution.

Estreicher took advantage of the delay to visit Poland for the first time since his traumatic departure six years before. In the first week of September, he returned to London in time for Meeting 19 of the Vaucher Commission.

The minutes of this penultimate meeting are crucial to our story. From them, it becomes clear that something less than total revindication – or restitution, as the Allies called it from their point of view – was being considered even at this early stage. The inter-Allied politics of the cold war, inaugurated at Potsdam only the month before, had arrived to clog the works with red tape and complicate the execution of 'simple justice'. The problem was delicately summed up by the American representative:

> Originally, the United States authorities had felt, as had this Commission, that the Restitution of Cultural Material should be the province of some body, possibly an international body. Yet difficulties, mainly connected with Reparations, had arisen, and after the Potsdam Conference the American authorities decided to take what action they thought fit, without waiting for an international agreement.

To both Estreicher and the Czech representative (who complained that the Reparations Commission sitting in Paris had given him too short a deadline to supply a list of Czech losses), 'the Chairman pointed out that Reparations were not within the scope of this Commission'.

The Vaucher Commission, in short, was having to come to terms with its limited powers. 'After the Liberation of Europe,' said its British secretary, it had been faced 'not so much with the problem of protection as with the restitution of Cultural Material. The Commission had been anxious to centralise information on looted works of art, send it to the Military Authorities in Germany, and receive their information in return. The unofficial status of the Commission had, however, made this project impossible. It had been considered necessary to regularise our position.' The secretary and others had therefore drafted proposals for 'an official Allied Secretariat' on cultural restitution, but the scheme 'had unfortunately failed to materialise.'

On the same note, the French representative, Major Charles d'Orange, pointed out:

> That it had originally been proposed to establish a Secretariat for the Restitution of Cultural Material under the aegis of the Control Commission at Berlin. Later the material difficulties of such a proposal had been realised: facilities in Berlin were few and far between and communications were difficult. It was therefore agreed that the Commission at Berlin should decide on policy and that the work of compiling inventories of looted objects should be carried on elsewhere.

Most interestingly, Major d'Orange went on, 'It was sometimes argued . . . that as 70 per cent of the works of art looted could be found and identified, there was no need to bother about the remainder. But the remaining 30 per cent were often valuable works of art . . .'

Indeed; and the figures given by d'Orange deviate by only ten per cent from the net result as far as Poland was concerned. Today, nearly forty years after the war, some forty per cent of the Polish treasures officially 'safeguarded' by Germany remain missing and unaccounted for. All, or most, almost certainly still exist, in hiding somewhere, privately or in the vaults of museums. And that figure does not of course include the many things that were taken by individual looters, soldiers or scholars, or that caught the eye of the S.S. wives.

If Estreicher had doubted it before, Meeting 19 brought it home to him that the politics of occupied Germany were going to prevent the implementation of the new methods which he saw as necessary. So far, I have mentioned only three of these. In his American report of 1943 he had proposed a fourth:

> The occupation authorities of the United Nations should give to the liberated countries as securities or guarantees objects of art and culture from the German museums and libraries which would be returned to Germany after the Germans will have surrendered the looted treasures. *Only this straight way leads to assuring justice.* (Author's italics)

This was the most original of Estreicher's proposals in that it held out the idea of temporary reparation as a weapon of revindication. Here, unequivocally expressed, is the idea of holding Germany to ransom by retaining German art works as hostages, or, as Estreicher put it, 'securities or guarantees', for the return of looted Polish works. '*Only this straight way*' led to the simple justice that he sought, not the crooked path along which the Allies were dragging their feet. In fact, 'the occupation authorities of the United Nations' were to agree to no such scheme, but unlike Estreicher's other proposals this was one that did not require the active co-operation of the Allies: it required only 'objects of art and culture from the German museums and libraries'.

By the time of Meeting 19, Poland had discovered the Grüssau manuscripts in the eastern area of Germany that she had annexed as her Recovered Territories. If only in outline the magnificence and importance of the manuscripts were known. It was also known to Karol Estreicher, the champion of the 'straight way' to Polish revindication, and the manuscripts must have been very much on his mind during the meeting, as a hidden source of future bargaining strength. In the minutes, he makes an oblique reference to them. Referring to a complication of his revindication work in Germany – 'that in some causes the identification marks of German museums had been substituted for Polish ones' – he added that 'already, however, several small cases containing looted objects had been found in Silesia'.

But, by then, Estreicher knew very well that several hundred cases branded with the letters P.S.B. had been found in a certain Silesian monastery, and that, while there might be some looted Polish objects among them, the vast majority had never belonged to Poland. Here was an unexpected windfall which might make possible the pursuit of his 'straight way'. From the reference to 'several small cases' in Meeting 19, with its convenient rider implying that the P.S.B. stamp might hide Polish property, we can date the beginnings of the state secret. From this point, Poland committed herself to the secret implementation of a policy that had not been agreed under international law.

Estreicher knew about the Grüssau manuscripts from the man who had been his chief source of cultural intelligence during the war. He had known him before it and had met him again on his homecoming visit to Poland that summer, and now felt able to divulge his identity. 'In the past,' he told the delegates, his information 'had been based on reports submitted mainly by Mr. Lorenz, Director of the National Museum of Warsaw, who was a member of the Polish Underground'.

At eighty-two years of age, Stanisław Lorenz is still, in 1981, Director of the National Museum. Like Estreicher, he is an art historian, but his powers are both wider and deeper than that description might suggest. He is a senior member of the Polish Academy of Sciences, and of other official bodies. He is a long-standing member of the Communist Party, and has strong connections in the Soviet Union, which has bestowed on him its highest honours. For five years, between 1965 and 1969, he was a member of the Sejm, the Polish Parliament.

Most Poles know him as the man who restored the thirteenth century Royal Castle in Warsaw, after its razing by the Germans, and understandably regard him as something of a hero for that reason. The heroism of the restoration was in direct proportion to the work of destruction, and that was scientific and thorough. In occupied Warsaw, Lorenz experienced at first hand the horrors that Estreicher was documenting at long distance in London:

> At any cost we wanted to rescue the most beautiful Castle ceiling of the Old Audience Hall, representing 'The Apotheosis of Art and Science', painted by Marcello Bacciarelli . . .

When, unofficially, a few days later, I managed to get into the Castle, I could ascertain that the beams of the Old Audience Hall had been removed and carried away: the ceiling existed no more, and I could not even find in the rubble covering the floor the smallest crumb of the painting; the falling ceiling had reduced everything to powder.

He had also to deal directly with those 'academic gangsters' denounced by Estreicher, notably Professor Dagobert Frey: 'I can still see Professor Frey, whom I had known well before the war, admiring the beauty of a neo-classic fireplace in the King's bedroom – and giving in my presence the order to tear it away from the wall . . .'

The ransacking ended in December 1944, when the ancient Castle was systematically blown up. Against this background, it is miraculous that the massive silhouette of the Castle, or 'its plastic reminder . . . a true copy of it', as Lorenz says, stands out today in the old quarter of Warsaw.

The credit for this achievement is the best-known fact about Professor Lorenz. A lesser-known fact is that he found the Grüssau manuscripts.

CHAPTER FIFTEEN

The Convoy

Dieter Henrich, later in his career, moved from Berlin to take up a professorship at the University of Heidelberg, within easy striking distance of the new Grüssau monastery at Bad Wimpfen. From this favourable vantage point, he became the first searcher really to gather and to weigh the evidence of the monks.

The role played by the monks was vital, as we have seen. Without them, news of the convoy would have spread neither to the West nor probably within the eastern bloc to East Germany. Over the years, that one piece of information – the convoy – kept hopes alive.

But the role of the monks was as problematic as much else in the story. It was nine years after the war before the three monks who had witnessed the convoy joined the others in West Germany, and during those years the three were in a sense hostages in the East; Father Lutterotti died soon afterwards, and from the early 1960s the monks found themselves under a certain political restraint, asked as loyal West German citizens not to upset the delicate balance of Polish-West German relations.

The monks had also to be aware of their status as members of the Benedictine Order, and of the problems faced by Polish Benedictines in their relations with Poland's Communist Government. Those relations were not good. Statements by German Benedictines which could be construed as blackening the reputation of the Communists could bring reprisals down on the Polish Benedictines.

This further complicated the Bad Wimpfen community's already complicated relationship to the information at its disposal. Concern for the Polish Benedictines was surely the unspoken factor uppermost in the mind of Father Michalski when he wrote his first, not at all welcoming, letter to me. 'As a

Benedictine monk,' he said, 'I will not be involved in political affairs.'

The story of the Benedictine Rescue, of which, in one version or another, Father Michalski seems to have heard, was an additional complication. For example: Carleton Smith speaks of having investigated 'a monastery a few miles up the river from Kraków'. This was the Benedictine monastery of Tyniec, on the Vistula, re-established in the 1930s after having fallen into ruin in the late eighteenth century. It was also investigated by Peter Whitehead as a possibility, but the idea was firmly scotched by Father Michalski: 'Your suggestion that the crates might be at Tyniec is groundless. We have been in touch, and they would have said.' Father Michalski had other 'trustworthy' sources in Poland, probably in the Church, whose identities he wished to protect.

So the monks of Bad Wimpfen were not as free as they might have appeared. Conscience and a sense of responsibility prompted them to interest themselves in the problem, and to press for a solution; commonsense, diplomacy, a sense of decorum, and the conviction, where responsibility was concerned, that people took precedence over paper – all these told them to leave the problem be.

Throughout, the monks were careful to stress that the convoy could have been either Polish or Russian. We have already quoted Father Michalski in 1977: 'It cannot precisely be said whether it was Poland or Russia that took the treasure.' But from Dieter Henrich's researches we can be sure that the convoy was made up of Poles, and of no one else, and that Father Michalski knew this perfectly well. That in turn must lead us to suspect that the Father was consciously clouding the issue.

Dieter Henrich evidently succeeded to some extent in winning the confidence of the monks. But, when he came to approach them, only one of the three witnesses still lived – the Austrian-born Brother Günther Veith (Father Lutterotti having died in 1955 and Brother Florian Windisch in 1960). He was able to talk to Brother Veith, however, and to glean from the other monks their recollections of conversations with Lutterotti and Windisch. And, most importantly, Father Michalski dictated to him some letters from the Bad Wimpfen archive. They were by a monk who has not so far appeared in the story – Father Alexander Schlachta, who was the administrator of Grüssau during the war and, as such, responsible with Father Lutterotti for the upkeep of the buildings. He wrote the letters in July 1968, and February 1971, to Ruth Hörber, the Mozart-loving nurse mentioned earlier. By the time Dieter Henrich came to Bad Wimpfen, Father Schlachta had died, as had the former Abbot, Albert Schmitt, who had helped Carleton Smith.

Now, Father Schlachta was of course among the monks expelled in May 1946 – *before* the convoy. But there had been developments during that time regarding the manuscripts, as his letters make clear. He recorded that 'several Polish commissions' had visited the monastery, and that 'the affable Polish gentlemen showed great interest in the depot of crates'. He added that the Poles expressly asked the monks not to tell the Russians of the depot's existence. (The Russians were still strongly concentrated in the area.)

Father Schlachta, Brother Veith, and reports originating from the two dead witnesses all confirmed that the convoy did not come before the time of the expulsion. Reports of the witnesses indicated that Germans still living in the village of Grüssau had been requisitioned to help with the loading. This narrowed the date of the convoy down to a period of some three and a half months, from the expulsion to the end of August 1946, when the last Germans left Grüssau. (This is backed up by Father Lutterotti's diaries.)

This may seem an unduly long time – more than a year after the war's end – to leave the crates where they were. But we shall see that the timing of the convoy fits well into the pattern of other work that was being carried out in Lower Silesia at the time, and, as Dieter Henrich remarks, the monastery 'provided especially favourable conditions for protecting the treasures from the vagaries of war and plunder'. The monks were there to watch over them, as they had done for several years, and 'it was far too obvious', says Henrich, 'that this had to be some state property of significance'. Accordingly, when the monastery and parish churches were searched by the Polish militia in the first post-war months (on the last occasion, in September 1945), 'they left the great depot in the lofts untouched'. The manuscripts, in effect, had already gone into the limbo they were to occupy for the next thirty years and more.

The convoy came to make the limbo complete. According to Henrich, reports originating from the two dead witnesses, and one from Brother Veith in November 1976, 'unanimously confirm that it was Poles who took away the crates'. A detachment of the Polish army arrived in lorries, and the loading began. Later, Brother Windisch told the other monks that, as the crates were brought down from the lofts, the leaders of the convoy had some broken open, to see what was inside, then nailed them down again for the journey.

It must have been a fairly large convoy, to carry away not only the 505 crates from Berlin, but something like the same number from Breslau as well. One imagines that it did not set off all at once, but lorry by lorry, as each was loaded, or in groups of lorries.

Two roads led away from Grüssau, one almost due north, one almost due east. When Abbot Schmitt told Carleton Smith that the crates had been 'taken east', he would not necessarily have been thinking of the amorphous political entity which 'the East' later came to mean, so much as of the old map of Central Europe, in which Lower Silesia was part of the German Reich and 'the east' lay across the old Polish border. He would have had in mind the geographical direction of the convoy quite as much as its political origin.

*

Dieter Henrich's researches in Bad Wimpfen gave substance at last to the thitherto hazy idea of the convoy, and provided sound evidence – long overdue – that it had been Polish. But this still depended on the word of the monks, almost thirty years after the events to which they were testifying, and most of that testimony at second hand. To provide convincing proof, he needed to find evidence from inside Poland herself, corresponding to that which the monks had given him. I have already outlined the political difficulties inherent in any approach to the Poles, but there were other complications belonging purely to the realm of detection. To put it in a nutshell, only East Germany really knew *what* had been lost, only the monks in West Germany knew *how* it had been lost, and only Poland knew *why* it had been taken and where it all was. The problem was to combine all three areas of exclusive knowledge into a coherent whole. Henrich having tackled the first two, he then approached the third, and set himself the task of going through

135

the looking-glass, as it were, to see the story from the Polish point of view. To do that, he needed first to find evidence from Polish sources, a daunting prospect, but one in which, astonishingly, he succeeded.

His source was an obscure Polish document called 'The Paulinum Museum-Depot and the Revindication of Art Treasures in Lower Silesia'. It was published as a report in the 1948 Proceedings of the Polish Society for Art and Art History. Its author was Witold Kieszkowski, an art historian whom the Polish Encyclopaedia gives as having been active in the repatriation of Polish art after the war. He died in 1950.

It is a long and detailed report which gives the context in which the Grüssau manuscripts were found, and, more than that, actually mentions their discovery. For reasons which I shall explain, I believe that this mention was inadvertent, and that Kieszkowski himself had no idea of the significance of the find.

The Poles were interested in three broad categories of art works in Lower Silesia just after the war. The one that most concerns us, because it is the category to which the manuscripts belonged, is the one that concerned Kieszkowski least, simply because it was the smallest, and possibly, where he was concerned, non-existent. This category was of art works evacuated eastwards to Silesia from the western parts of Germany. Kieszkowski's reference to it is ambiguous, but of its insignificance he leaves us in no doubt:

> Only Silesian museum objects – both public and private – were found in Silesia, plus a large proportion of the things looted from Poland. Objects evacuated from the West, with the exception of a very few, were nowhere to be found . . .

We can gather how tiny was this category from the two examples which Kieszkowski gives. Both were culled from files kept by the German Keeper of Monuments for the area, Günther Grundmann, and which were found in Breslau by the Poles: a crate of paintings from a museum in Dessau, and silverware and paintings from a castle near Darmstadt owned by the Prince of Hesse. But by the end of the war, and the arrival of the Poles in the region, both groups of objects had already been returned West, the latter group taken by Grundmann himself. The Poles knew this. It was all on record in the Breslau files, as Kieszkowski was very well aware. This gives his two examples an academic rather than practical interest. Clearly the manuscripts from Berlin belonged in this category of 'objects from the west', and as clearly Kieszkowski knew that 'German' collections had been found in the monastery of Grüssau (or Krzeszów, to give its Polish name). But he did not list the collections under this category.

The mention of Grüssau, taking into account the years of Polish secrecy that were to come, is in itself astonishing enough. Could we have here a case of the left hand not knowing what the right was doing? One explanation that fits the facts is that although Kieszkowski knew about the collections at Grüssau, as he evidently did, he did not know their origin. If he had known it, he would either have listed the collections under the above category, or, much more likely, not mentioned them at all. No other explanation, indeed, seems adequate.

In describing the collections as 'German', I believe, Kieszkowski meant to imply 'German-Silesian'. He regarded them, in other words, as belonging to the second, non-secret category of objects, previously located in museums, galleries, and libraries in German-owned Silesia, and evacuated for their safety during the war from towns and cities into the Silesian countryside. The Poles were interested in collecting these safely and returning them to their proper homes in places they regarded as now Polish, the 'Recovered Territories' of the ancient Polish homeland.

The discovery of Grundmann's files greatly aided the work of revindication within Silesia. 'It meant,' said Kieszkowski, 'that part of it at least could be carried out in an organised manner, without having to rely on imprecise verbal reports or on intuition;' and we may note in passing that the files, in recording the destination of the Breslau library holdings, would have directed the Poles to Grüssau. It is even possible that the crates from Breslau at first created genuine confusion, but highly unlikely, I think. We may remember that, when Grundmann visited St. Joseph's Church in November 1944, he was able to notice *at once* that it housed crates from the Berlin library. This would have been equally evident to the Poles who came later.

Kieszkowski calls it 'staggering' that Grundmann's files gave no help at all when it came to the third, most important category of art works in Lower Silesia: those which had been 'safeguarded' by the Germans in Poland and moved west. We have already noted that Estreicher regarded Silesia as the likely destination of many of these looted works, and that Professor Lorenz was Estreicher's chief informant. Kieszkowski gives more details of the intelligence network on which Estreicher in London relied. 'Its headquarters,' he comments, "was the National Museum in Warsaw:'

> The work was carried out under Director Lorenz, and everyone took part – porters, workmen, drivers, anyone with information on where the treasures were taken. In this way, from all these scraps of information, a picture was built up of the movements of the treasures, both internally and abroad.

Again and again, Silesia figured in the reports. As a result, as soon as the war was over, it was given top priority by the Ministry of Art and Culture, and became the area where the work of cultural revindication was first carried out.

Throughout, transport was a great problem. Kieszkowski stresses this repeatedly, describing the loan of twenty-four lorries for a few days in the autumn as 'success beyond compare'. In mid-May 1945, Lorenz managed to borrow a single lorry that had been placed at the disposal of the Ministry of Culture.

In this lorry, Lorenz and five other revindication workers set off for Silesia, passing through Katowice and crossing the old border area into Upper Silesia. Then the expedition struck south towards the Tatra Mountains, and made its way west along them, stopping on the way at towns and sites that had figured in the wartime arts intelligence reports, and at others that occurred to them. 'The results of the trip,' comments Kieszkowski, 'surpassed all expectations. It emerged that a considerable number of works of art taken by the Germans from Warsaw after the uprising, a large number of collections from Katowice whose fate had been unknown, as well as collections evacuated at the eleventh hour from Kraków, had remained in Silesia.'

On the way to Jelenia Góra[1], which seems to have been the

---

[1] Hirschberg. I have left the Polish place names – which apply today – as Kieszkowski wrote them.

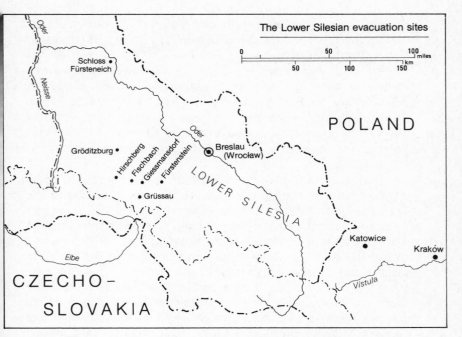

The Lower Silesian evacuation sites

0   50   100 miles
    50   100   150 km

POLAND

Schloss Fürsteneich

Gröditzburg

Hirschberg
Fischbach
Giessmansdorf
Fürstenstein

Breslau (Wrocław)

LOWER SILESIA

Grüssau

Katowice

Kraków

CZECHO-SLOVAKIA

Elbe

Vistula

Neisse

Oder

Oder

westernmost point of the journey, Lorenz and his team passed through the area in which the six Lower Silesian sites of the Prussian State Library were clustered. So the first commission of 'affable Polish gentlemen', Lorenz at its head, came to visit Grüssau: 'German collections were found near Kłodzko, in Kamieńcu and Henrykowie, and considerable collections of books (among them one in Krzeszów), and so on.' Kieszkowski mentions Grüssau a second time: 'Large deposits of books and archives were found in Karpniki, near Jelenia Góra, and in Jelenia Góra itself, in the monastery of Krzeszów, and in the castle of Pieleszkowicach.' Under the names of Fischbach, Hirschberg, Grüssau, and Gröditzburg Castle, these were all places to which collections of the Berlin Library had been sent.

These and other finds were made before Kieszkowski's arrival in Silesia, while Lorenz was still in direct charge of the revindication work there. But, at the end of July, Lorenz returned to Warsaw, just in time to meet Estreicher, who returned to Poland that month. He told Estreicher of his trip which had 'surpassed all expectations', and of the hundreds of cases bearing German identification marks. On the Vaucher

139

Commission in London two months later, Estreicher played down the Lower Silesian discoveries with his mention of 'several small cases'.

At the recommendation of Lorenz, the revindication work in Silesia was taken over by Kieszkowski and the Keeper of Monuments for the Kraków area, Józef Dutkiewicz. While Dutkiewicz supervised the transport of safeguarded treasures from their temporary storage points to Kraków, Kieszkowski worked on the spot in Silesia, gathering clues and getting to know the region.

Broadly speaking, the looted Polish treasures tended to be concentrated in the border areas to the west and east of the Prussian State Library's sites, while objects of Silesian origin were found to the east of them, in and around an inlet into the Tatra Mountains. Most of Kieszkowski's work was carried out in the south-western border area around Jelenia Góra. 'A great many crates of things from the National Museum were found in this area,' he writes, but he speculated also that the Germans may have been intending to move looted Polish objects across the border into Czechoslovakia, and from there to Bavaria, Estreicher's area. He heard stories of a train, loaded with looted Polish art, that had headed south towards Czechoslovakia, but had stopped in Cieplice before it could complete the journey. One night in Cieplice, finding a crate in the entrance to the library, he lit a match and saw on its lid the word 'WARSCHAU'. There turned out to be nineteen crates, filled with some of the finest of all the loot, old coins, paintings, silver, sculptures, church ornaments, and manuscripts.

Kieszkowski had nothing to do with the manuscripts at Grüssau. They were found shortly before he started work, and moved shortly after he left Silesia – on April 12, 1946. To this accident of timing, which enabled him to know about the manuscripts without knowing their exact identity, we owe his mention of them.

If the revindication work after Kieszkowski followed the same pattern, we can deduce that from Grüssau the manuscripts were taken eastwards to an intermediary depot. The Berlin Library holdings stored in the other Lower Silesian sites would have gone the same way.

At a secondary depot, the Grüssau crates which were

branded P.S.B. would have been separated from the crates of Breslau holdings and combined and piled together with the P.S.B. crates from other sites. The Breslau crates would then have been returned to the city the Poles called Wrocław: they presented no problem.

It is not hard to imagine the next step. The remaining crates would have been prised open with crowbars, and their contents examined. The carbon copies of the evacuation slips, the first things visible, proclaimed the P.S.B. to stand for 'Preussische Staatsbibliothek', but this the Poles already knew from the convoy, when some cases were broken open, and almost certainly from before that. Also, they must have had at least some idea of what they contained. At a secondary depot, however, the Poles could have begun to acquaint themselves with them at their leisure. How many crates did they have to prise open before they realised what an astonishing windfall they had? How many before they reached the music? Soon they would have realized that some of the finest cultural riches of Germany had fallen into their hands.

Whether the decision to appropriate the manuscripts had already been taken, or whether it was taken at this stage, we have no way of knowing. What is certain is that the Poles *must* have known their origin, and have had a good idea of their identity and importance, and that, whether or not they were taken first to an intermediary depot, they were certainly moved further east, behind the old Polish-German border, and hidden there.

But where? Kieszkowski's report again gave strong indications. It mentioned only three Polish cities behind the old border: Warsaw, the capital, Kraków, the former capital, and the Silesian industrial and coal-mining city of Katowice. Of these, only the first two are given as destinations of the Lower Silesian revindication transports, although we can surely assume that the rediscovered collections of Katowice were returned there.

Warsaw had been virtually flattened by the war, and had also been the Polish city that had lost most. It barely had room and facilities enough for its own returned collections. Kraków, by contrast, had survived the war virtually unscathed. It had both the space to store extra collections, and the facilities to handle them. The finding of suitable personnel must have been a problem, but that applied to all Polish cultural centres just after the war, and less to Kraków than to most.

And Kieszkowski's report made it clear, as Henrich put it, that 'from the beginning the Polish government had chosen Kraków as the place from which the work of revindication in Silesia could be most easily directed and supplied'. As early as February 1945, the Polish government in Lublin convened a commission in Kraków which was to have followed in the wake of the army to secure cultural goods. That plan fell through, but, as we have seen, a pipeline was later established through which cultural goods found in Silesia made their way to Kraków. In the early summer of 1945, special transport facilities for revindication work were set up there. The Grüssau convoy could have come from there, although it was more probably drawn from Polish military resources on the spot.

Most importantly, Kraków had the ideal place to store large quantities of cultural goods. The German occupation had used it for precisely that purpose, and Kieszkowski mentions it three times in his report, as somewhere which had 'large rooms well suited to the temporary storage of collections'. This was the complex of buildings on Wawel Hill, overlooking Kraków and the Vistula.

On the Wawel stood the city's Gothic Cathedral, the Renaissance Royal Palace, and other buildings including some nineteenth-century barracks. From Kieszkowski, we know that it was used as a store in the months before the Grüssau convoy, and from other sources that it was still being used as such in 1947 – for the trainload of Polish treasures which Karol Estreicher brought back from Bavaria. It seems reasonable to assume that it was used in the interim to store the very special Grüssau collection, which had no natural Polish home. But, according to a Polish art expert, 'the Wawel would not have been competent to deal with books or manuscripts. There was space there, but to my mind they would not have stayed for any length of time'.

CHAPTER SIXTEEN

The State Secret

The manuscripts were appropriated by the Polish government with its full knowledge and active participation. Dieter Henrich considered, but rejected, the other possibilities, firstly that the appropriation might have been the work of 'junior functionaries, perhaps acting on their own initiative'. Against this possibility he set the evidence of the monks that the monastery had been visited by a number of Polish commissions, the first of which, as was clear from Kieszkowski, had been led by the man officially empowered to carry out revindication work in Lower Silesia. But Kieszkowski provided other intriguing evidence that a particular Polish government agency was involved in the appropriation. Immediately after mentioning Grüssau, his report continued:

> . . . Contact was made with delegates of the Ministry of Education, representing library and archival interests, to whom, without delay, all details relating to library and archival collections were relayed.

The Grüssau manuscripts, of course, fell into that category, and Henrich remarks that 'one certainly has to assume that the Ministry of Education knew what the contents of the crates were before they took them away'. There Henrich assumes that the convoy was directly organised by the Ministry of Education, while I believe it possible that it was arranged on its behalf by the much better organised and better staffed Ministry of Culture. But the essential conclusion remains the same:

> The person who in 1946 was made reponsible for the Grüssau treasure had also the duty of looking after it and letting others know what had happened to it . . . But we have to conclude that this duty lay with the Government of the People's Republic of Poland. Its Ministry of Culture found

the Grüssau treasure and drew it to the attention of the then Ministry of Education. There are no grounds for assuming that the treasure could have been commandeered by some other office at so relatively late a time when the monastery had already been visited by several commissions on government duty.

Dieter Henrich also discounted the possibility of an administrative oversight. Since the war there have been a series of shake-ups and shifts in the responsibilities of various Polish ministries handling various aspects of culture, education, and research. In 1951, most significantly, responsibility for libraries moved from the Ministry of Education to the Ministry of Culture. Could responsibility for the Grüssau manuscripts, and even the knowledge of their existence in Poland, have slipped out of sight, as it were, in the gaps between these administrative change-overs? Henrich dismissed the hypothesis on the grounds that, 'in view of the size and significance of the treasure, and considering the mass of inquiries that have been initiated over the years, it would presume a total administrative chaos in whose existence we have not the least reason to believe'.

There remained only one reasonable conclusion:

> that Poland's government and some of its agencies denied the existence of the treasure under its control though knowing that this was not the case; or, which essentially comes to the same thing, feigned ignorance despite knowing the truth, evaded questions, or simply refused to answer them . . . the Grüssau treasure fell into the hands of the People's Republic of Poland and there is the greatest likelihood that it is still in those hands. All requests for information have met with either evasive or negative replies. Thirty years after the war it still refuses to say what the truth is.

Henrich wrote that in 1977, when the situation was still very unclear, but much clearer than when he began searching in 1960, and on the point of becoming clearer still. For, in the interim, there had been a vital turning-point in the search. From 1965, which I believe to be the crucial year, we can date the dénouement of the mystery. There is an essential difference between the search before and the search after that period. For before the mid-1960s the secrecy had been absolute; then there was a leak. Before, the history of the search is essentially the history of frustration set out in the first part of this book: then it began to produce results, small and confused at first, but enough eventually to break down the rigid Polish government position, ironically just as the findings of Henrich's marvellous piece of scholarly detective work were going to press.

So, for some twelve of the seventeen years of his search, Henrich was working under conditions that were in fact comparatively favourable. There is no reason why he should have known this, and no indication that he did, though oddly enough the article that he wrote does contain a piece of 'private information' which hints at the turning point: 'In Gröditzburg and Fishbach considerable parts of the Prussian State Library's newspaper section were stored. I would not like to say whether these also included items returned by the Poles in 1965 to the Unter den Linden State Library.'

After the turning-point searchers could at least feel confident that the treasures had survived:

> Since 1960 I have used every opportunity to ask library experts about the Grüssau treasure. Behind cupped hands, or in all openness – depending on the place where the question was asked – the name 'Kraków' was mentioned. This agrees with the information of others who came to ask about the Grüssau treasure in the course of their work. They are rumours, certainly, but they are founded on a considerable body of data, to wit, the existence of a microfilm of letters by Heinrich Heine in the Varnhagen Collection, which were made after the war and which were learned about in London. These came from Kraków.'

I do not know, but would be willing to wager, that the microfilm and the rumours of Kraków both post-date the mid-sixties.

We shall come to the dénouement in the next chapter. For the present let us consider some of the factors that led the Poles to pursue a policy of rigid secrecy, and make some guesses at the conditions under which the Polish state kept its secret so well, and for so long. For obvious reasons it is necessary to guess, but it is also possible, I think, for the guesses to be fairly well-informed. Particularly important is the watershed of the mid-sixties. If the conditions of the search can be seen to have altered after that time, then what, we may ask ourselves, was the situation that prevailed before?

Firstly, I am convinced, as others are, that the whereabouts of the manuscripts were a well-kept secret *within Poland herself*. I find it inconceivable, if this was not so, that it could have been kept so long, and that it was so is borne out both by the events of the mid-sixties and subsequent developments both inside Poland and in the search internationally. Before the trade secrecy could begin to develop properly outside Poland, the state secrecy had to be broken inside.

Dieter Henrich speculated that 'it is certainly not unrealistic to assume that after it was analysed the very politically sensitive contents of the treasure resulted in its being handed over to a special authority under direct Party control. The Ministry of Education would naturally have had to be aware of this.' That is possible, but I think it more likely that knowledge of the treasure was confined to an even smaller group, consisting of those, like Lorenz and Estreicher, who knew about it already, others perhaps who were trusted with the task of checking it periodically, particular government ministers, and the head of state himself. Certainly the state secret was known to Edward Gierek, First Secretary of the Polish Communist Party from 1970, and almost certainly to his predecessor, Władysław Gomułka, First Secretary from 1956.

It is likely that Gomułka, who at the time of the convoy was the minister responsible for the Recovered Territories, was one of those who knew the secret at a very early stage. The discovery of the manuscripts was made in the Recovered Territories, and if Gomułka learned the secret soon afterwards he could have taken it with him and continued to condone it right to the top of the Polish political hierarchy. This would have been far from inconsistent with his known views. Gomułka was militantly anti-German. In his biography[1], Nicholas Bethell remarks:

> . . . The new frontier, he said, was correct not only because it strengthened Poland, but also because it weakened Germany. 'The weakness of Germany,' he said, 'will be a condition of peace in Europe and the whole world for many decades yet.'

[1] *Gomułka, His Poland and His Communism*, Longmans 1969, Pelican 1972.

This view, fair enough perhaps in the Poland of 1945, was to persist. A quarter of a century later it was still the basis of Gomułka's foreign policy, almost his obsession. He was to propound anti-Germanism as a constructive idea, a contribution to the good of the world. Peace in Europe was only three months old, but already Gomułka was taking the lead in the anti-German (not anti-Nazi but anti-German) crusade. Several times he reminded Polish audiences how the Nazis were supported by 'almost the entire German people'. However much he might deny it, he was to become the spokesman for a national prejudice. Gomułka's anti-Germanism was originally as justified as any such feeling possibly can be, but it was later to become a negative ideal, a barrier in the way of a rapprochement, and as such probably detrimental in the long term to Polish interest.

It would be wrong to apply this too literally, but we may note that this prejudice of Gomułka's provided fertile ground for the state secret and its retention; also that, like the policy decision which dictated the appropriation of the manuscripts, it was an idée fixe, of uncommon constancy and strength, dating from the war: an evergreen grudge, Beethoven and Mozart posthumously held prisoner for the insufficiently punished crimes of their countrymen. Whatever the subtle, rational reasons for the secrecy, it would be wrong to overlook the element of revenge. Retention of the manuscripts certainly did nothing to strengthen Germany.

Another passage in Bethell's biography, concerning Gomułka's work as Minister for the Recovered Territories, gives rise to a further train of thought:

He had to administer 'state property', which meant almost everything there since everything German was automatically nationalised. Much of the movable wealth was being packed up by the Russians and exported east, and there are stories that this was the first bone of contention between Gomułka and the Soviet Union. He resisted the Russian depredations, regarded by them as legitimate war reparations, and ten years later was to denounce them openly.

The manuscripts were 'state property' which would have fallen within Gomułka's purlieu; the Poles may have begun by hiding them from the Russians and ended by hiding them from everybody. Gomułka was, understandably, protective towards assets that he regarded as Polish, not Russian, reparations, and touchy regarding the shaky Polish sovereignty – which it was his task to consolidate – over the Recovered Territories. The 'movable wealth' of the manuscripts could have been regarded as tied up with the legitimacy of Polish claims to the area.

I do not believe, however, that Poland started with the intention of incorporating the Grüssau manuscripts. Taken together, they do not fit the definitions, given in the revindication pamphlets, of treasures that could organically be grafted on to the body of the Polish cultural heritage. They were alien. The Poles did not wish to part with them, however, but to keep them as 'securities or guarantees', objects of future barter. At the same time (and here we have the essence of the secrecy), they could not admit to having them, because in this they were in defiance of international law.

The legal framework is complex and conflicting, and that is the essence of what needs to be known about it. Not only Polish law is involved, but the Allied laws dissolving the Prussian state (previous owners of the manuscripts), the laws of the Federal and Democratic German republics, and international law. The last, however, is quite specific. Article 56 of the Hague Convention of 1907[1] states:

> The property of municipalities, that of institutions dedicated to religion, charity and education, the arts and sciences, even when state property, shall be treated as private property . . .
> All seizures or destruction of, or wilful damage to, institutions of this character, historic monuments, works of art or science, is forbidden, and should be made the subject of legal proceedings.

The principles laid down in 1907 came, over the years, to be expanded into a widely accepted body of law ruling cultural objects to be *hors de combat*, and forbidding seizure of them as war booty – even when they have been evacuated away from their usual homes.

The quoting of Article 56 demands a few reflections. Firstly, whatever the Polish laws regarding the nationalisation of the Recovered Territories together with their fixtures and fittings

[1]'Respecting the Laws and Customs of War on Land.'

– including, for example, the monastery of Grüssau itself – in the matter of the Grüssau manuscripts the Hague Convention overrules them. They were not fixtures and fittings, but came to be situated east of the Oder-Neisse line only as a direct consequence of the war.

Secondly, there is the somewhat cynical reflection, which the Poles responsible for appropriating the manuscripts doubtless repeated to themselves, that possession is nine points of the law. If Article 56 of the Hague Convention were applied retrospectively, some of the world's best-known museums would stand to lose some of their finest pieces.

Against this must be set the fact that in recent years there have been moves towards the retrospective application of the ethics of ownership, and the preaching has to some extent been put into practice. There have been examples of the return to their countries of origin of objects unethically, but not necessarily illegally, taken from them, often during periods of colonial rule when the countries in question were too weak fully to look after their own interests.

These returns have been few, however, and have been carried out, not across the board, but fitfully by particular countries, notably the United States. Poland, which has been under colonial rule for much of her history, is still able to look eastwards and see in Russia objects taken during one or other of the three Polish Partitions. One example comes to mind: a bust of Voltaire by the seventeenth-century French sculptor Houdon, which stood once in the Royal Castle in Warsaw but is today in Russia.

More recent history provided stronger grounds for cynicism. Most importantly, after the war the Polish treasures evacuated to Canada through France and Rumania failed to return. The bulk of them, it turned out, had been appropriated by the government of Quebec. In 1949 Professor Lorenz wrote a pamphlet on the subject, 'Canada Refuses to Return Polish Cultural Treasures'. With it was an appeal signed by all the Polish cultural and intellectual bodies. It included two references to international law which might equally well have applied to Poland and the Grüssau manuscripts: 'The Polish Government wants to recall that the duty of a State to ensure on its territory the protection of the rights of other States is a principle which has long been recognised by international law.'

And secondly: 'It is a universally recognised principle in international law that a State may not plead the shortcomings of its internal legislation . . . as an obstacle to the claims of another State . . .' Poland had a legitimate grudge, but it was fourteen years after the war – 1959 – before the treasures returned from Canada. All that time their retention was yet another argument for Poland's own retention of the manuscripts. In the same vein, it was the late seventies before the Carter administration returned the Hungarian Crown of St. Stephen, which the United States had taken at the end of the war.

The main source of cynicism – the failure of revindication and reparations – has already been mentioned. Here we might note that the legal and ethical considerations were joined by political ones, and they like the rest tended to support the position that Poland in fact adopted: to sit tight on the manuscripts, but sit tight secretly. It was out of the question for Poland openly to use them to pick a quarrel with East Germany. That would not only have been an unsuitable way for one Warsaw Pact country to behave towards another, but, by questioning the adequacy of reparations, would have drawn the Soviet Union into the quarrel as well, since Polish reparations were supposed to have been settled out of the Soviet share. Secrecy had the advantage that it implicitly, but tacitly, criticised the Soviet Union by drawing suspicion on to her. This must have been a dangerous game, however. If the East Germans received assurances from the Russians that they did not have the manuscripts, and then approached the Poles with those assurances, Poland was in effect calling the Soviet Union a liar by denying that she had them either.

The ramifications are endless, but one last point must be made. When we try to apply the ethics of ownership to the Grüssau manuscripts it is by no means easy to come up with a simple answer. For if, by taking them, the Poles infringed Article 56 of the Hague Convention, how often during the war had the Germans infringed the same article of law? Of course, Poland received as compensation the eastern territory of Germany, but that was not the 'analogous' compensation for which the Poles were looking. The law, we may reflect, is not necessarily the same as 'simple justice': it can sometimes be a bitter pill, and this was one which the Poles stubbornly refused to swallow. Already during the war Estreicher was contemplating the futility of international law in defending the Polish cultural heritage, and the need for revising it if that heritage was to be reclaimed: 'International law, the Hague Convention, and other international agreements distinctly oppose the looting and destruction of art and culture . . . The Germans introduced a new law . . . We must think about new methods . . .' It is a short step from there, through disillusionment, to taking the law into one's own hands.

I am not saying that the decision to take the manuscripts and to sit tight on them was made by Karol Estreicher, although, like Professor Lorenz, he may well have been consulted: the two were, after all, Poland's chief experts on cultural revindication. What I *am* saying is that the policy behind the decision was formed on the basis of the conclusions which Estreicher reached during the war: that the only straight way to simple justice lay in new methods, one of which was the temporary take-over of German cultural property as 'securities or guarantees'.

This was illegal, but was it strictly speaking wrong? Two wrongs may not make a right, but, against the background of how many wrongs, does one in return come to seem, if not right, at least reasonable? As Dieter Henrich puts it: 'It is understandable that Poland should have felt herself justified in taking over cultural goods which had only been stored in the east and in carrying them off to the heart of the Polish homelands.'

I do not suppose it would be possible to find a single Pole, of whatever political persuasion, who would regard this as 'wrong'; and knowing the background one is inclined to agree.

In one very important respect, however, it *was* wrong. The whereabouts of the Grüssau manuscripts may have been no more spurious than those of other displaced treasures, including the Polish treasures in Canada between 1945 and 1959. But at least their whereabouts were *known*. Those of the manuscripts were not. Nor was it known whether they had survived. Nor were scholars and others able to see and to study them. This was undoubtedly wrong, scandalously so.

We return to the peculiar status of manuscripts, the music manuscripts in particular, part *objets d'art*, part priceless paper heirlooms, part invaluable *documents*, to which people

151

needed access for practical reasons, as they did not need access to things which were arguably of greater direct beauty.

This raises a paradox of the secrecy. It was necessary to continue Poland's retention of the manuscripts – a retention that the vast majority of Poles, had they known about it, would have regarded as right. But while it was being continued the status of the manuscripts as objects was being stressed at the expense of their status as documents and indispensable materials of research. The necessary secrecy was thus a necessary evil as well, as the Poles who kept the secret were probably aware. Whoever they were, they must have felt that the whereabouts of the manuscripts was the overriding consideration, and that the question of their accessibility came a long way second. The politics of revindication dictated this.

Scholarly ethics, however, dictate an opposite set of priorities. Accessibility of research material is all-important, its whereabouts a secondary matter. As one scholar-searcher put it: 'I am in no way concerned with who owns the stuff or whether it is kept in Warsaw or Berlin or Timbuctoo for that matter providing we can see it and work with it. It belongs to research and should be nothing to do with politics.'

One needs, perhaps, to be a scholar to appreciate that point of view, but by the same token no scholar would be *unable* to appreciate it, and in that I include Polish scholars. I do not believe that practising Polish scholars able to grasp the value of the manuscripts, and certainly no music scholars, were party to the secret. If Polish scholars were involved in the retention, they were those – like Estreicher and Lorenz – whose prime concern was revindication. There was no conflict in their position, or at least the conflict was small and easily borne. When the time arrived, after all, the manuscripts could always be conveniently 'discovered'.

The paradox – that the retention of the manuscripts was right, but that the inaccessibility necessary for this was wrong – surfaced only when practising Polish scholars came to learn of the secret. This I am convinced they did as a result of the mid-Sixties leak mentioned earlier. The known facts tally with this explanation.

With the leakage within Poland of the Polish state secret, the conflict, always latent, at last came to the fore. The scholars found themselves in an impossible position, bound as patriotic

Poles to condone the retention, bound by the ethics of scholarship to condemn the secrecy. They would not have regarded the inaccessibility of the manuscripts as a necessary, but as an unacceptable, evil.

The last phase of the Grüssau story is the resolution of that conflict.

CHAPTER SEVENTEEN

The Professor's Story

It was the late 1960s before the American pianist Malcolm Frager first heard about the Grüssau manuscripts. He was in Utrecht at the time, touring, and a Dutch fellow musician and friend, knowing Frager's interest in original sources, told him about these that had been missing since the war. Frager was astonished, and made a mental note to pursue the matter the next time he was in Poland or the Soviet Union.

Malcolm Frager is a very good pianist, as anyone who has heard him can testify. I heard him once, over the radio, playing Beethoven's First Piano Concerto, a fine performance which the announcer prefaced with a short introduction. Malcolm Frager, he told the listeners, was the winner in 1960 of the Queen Elisabeth of the Belgians Competition. He was then twenty-five. He had a strong interest in original manuscript research, and a strong belief in its importance. He spoke several languages, including Russian.

The announcer did not go on to add that Frager has visited Poland many times, nor that when in Poland he uses his Russian to make himself understood. Nor were we told that on one of those Polish visits, in February 1970, Malcolm Frager had had a most extraordinary experience, among the most extraordinary of his life. Earlier on the day of that radio concert, I had spoken to him about it, and as I sat listening to the Beethoven it continued to preoccupy me.

1970 was one of the years when he played in Katowice. While he was there, remembering the conversation in Utrecht, he asked a Polish musician friend about the manuscripts. The friend had never heard of them, but his interest was drawn as Frager's had been, and he wanted to satisfy it. He went into the next room and made a telephone call to Warsaw, returning a few minutes later, Frager remembers him, 'white-faced'. 'This

154

is a big political secret,' he said, 'and I don't know any more than that. There is only one person who may be able to help you, and that is Professor Lissa.'

Frager had not then heard of Professor Zofia Lissa, who at sixty-one years of age retired that year as head of the Polish Institute of Musicology. That position was as high as one could attain as a music scholar in Poland, and Professor Lissa had a string of publications behind her, many on the relationship between music and society, to back up the impression that she was not only the most powerful, but the best.

She was also a long-standing member of the Communist Party. As a Jew, she had managed to survive several years of the German occupation before fleeing to Moscow. From 1945 to 1947 she had served as cultural attachée at the Polish embassy in Moscow, before returning, 'a fervent Stalinist', according to some reports, to found together with two other scholars the Polish Institute of Musicology. From 1947 to 1949 she was vice-director of the Music Department at the Ministry of Art and Culture in Warsaw.

The Institute of Musicology was part of Warsaw University, and was located with the University's Music Division on the eighth floor of the Palace of Culture and Science, a Stalinist skyscraper which the Soviet Union built in Warsaw in the fifties, as a gift to Poland. 'The new institute benefited from its location in the seat of government', commented an American scholar in 1961, in an account which went on to outline the institute's work:

> . . . The development of a centre of documentation on Polish music at the National Library is progressing in close co-operation with the Musicological Institute at the University. Teams of advanced students are sent out to the provinces . . . to investigate and search after unknown musical sources. Whenever something of interest is found, it is then taken to the National Library for microfilming and then returned to the place where it was found. It goes without saying that the different musical collections are gradually being microfilmed also. In this way a general microfilm archive and card catalogue of Polish musical sources is being built up, which will gradually include the entire material of importance on Polish territory.

155

The institute was the centre of a web of search and research covering the whole of Poland. Little, one imagines, escaped its notice: that was part of its function.

In Warsaw on the same Polish tour, Malcolm Frager got in touch with Professor Lissa, and asked if he could come to see her. She agreed, and one evening he turned up at the house which she shared with another elderly lady on Miaczynska Street in Warsaw.

People who have met Professor Lissa at international conferences and the like describe her as 'short, dumpy, and formidable'. That was Frager's impression too, but in addition she seemed to him to be nervous, and even 'very scared'. They sat down in a room in which there was little other than a large desk and the many books lining the walls. There, after a while, she began to relax a little. 'I feel you have a face I can trust,' she told him. Frager took this as meaning their mutual Jewishness. (Jews in Poland had special reason for fellow feeling at that time, a wave of government-inspired anti-Semitism having swept the country in 1968 in the wake of the Arab-Israeli war.)

Professor Lissa produced a list of the missing music manuscripts of Grüssau which had been sent to her by Dr. Karl-Heinz Köhler of the East Berlin library. It was the first list of them that Frager had seen, and he was as bowled over by it as others had been, and would be. He asked if he might copy it, and the Professor gave her permission.

The list was identical in every particular to that which Carleton Smith had published in the *Book Collector*, except for one score, Bach's Cantata No. 111, which was on Smith's list but is not on Frager's copy. For a time I thought this significant; but it was an omission, either from Köhler's original, or the copy of it. One interesting feature of the new list, however, was the date on which Köhler had sent it from Berlin: October 12, 1966, after my 'turning-point' year of 1965, and roughly contemporaneous both with the East German Party-to-Party request concerning the manuscripts and with the period at which, according to Professor Lissa, they were found in Poland. Even more interesting was the explanation which she gave of their discovery.

Professor Lissa said that her Institute of Musicology and Polish music scholars in general had been actively searching for the missing music ever since the war, without success. Grüssau itself had been visited, but the scores were not there. So the situation had remained static for year after year, the Polish scholars aridly searching, just as their western colleagues had been, scouring their own country but failing to find anything.

Then, about 1966, something quite remarkable happened. A West German count contacted the Polish Institute of Musicology and told it the story which Professor Lissa then told Malcolm Frager: the story of the Benedictine Rescue. After hiding the manuscripts away in the church near Waldenburg, the monks had taken a vow of silence. In due course the term of the vow expired, and one of the monks, an aged man near death, possibly even on his death bed, decided to transmit the story to the count. He in turn told the Institute of Musicology, which in turn told the Ministry of Culture. A team was despatched to the parish church near Waldenburg, and the crates of music discovered behind the altar. They were taken over by the Ministry, in effect by the Polish Government. This all happened in the mid-sixties.

Professor Lissa had asked for, but been refused, permission to see the music. She had protested that she must be allowed to check the manuscripts' condition, and although she was again refused, one of her assistants was eventually allowed to do so.

And there, for four or five years, the matter had rested, bringing Professor Lissa near to despair. 'The manuscripts will never become accessible again,' she told Frager. 'It isn't possible that they will.' Frager reassured her: 'You mustn't believe that,' he said. 'You mustn't lose hope.'

*

To say that Malcolm Frager was a suitably receptive audience is not to say that he was gullible, but that he was in no position to analyse Professor Lissa's story. That, I am sure, is why it was told to him, in the hope that he would tell it uncritically to others.

It breaks down into two stories, that of the Rescue itself and that of its delayed-action dénouement, twenty years later. The first, I believe, is entirely and demonstrably untrue. That effectively disproves the second, the business of the aged monk, the German count, etcetera.

At the same time, I do not think that the latter was entirely false, but a *metaphorical* version of the truth, plausibly tailored

157

and laundered to exonerate the interests for which Professor Lissa was acting.

It is not hard to surmise what those interests were. Two attributes of the story as a whole are noticeable at once. The first is that it completely clears Polish scholars from any blame for the manuscripts' disappearance and their inaccessibility over the years; the second, that it absolves the Polish State from blame over the twenty years between the disappearance of the manuscripts and their dramatic 'rediscovery' in Poland. It does this at the cost of admitting that the State had kept the manuscripts inaccessible over the five years or so that had elapsed between the discovery and 1970; but in this, as Malcolm Frager had no way of realising, Professor Lissa was admitting no more than was already known.

Here we come to one of the key dates in the entire Grüssau story. Dr. Wolfgang Rehm of the "Neue Mozart Ausgabe', says that the N.M.A. learned *in the early part of 1967* that the manuscripts were in Poland. Dr. Rehm does not want to go into 'the long and complicated story' which resulted in 'the semi-official revelation' of that year. But the year itself is important. It is the earliest when we can be sure that foreign scholars knew for a certainty the whereabouts of the manuscripts. In talking to Malcolm Frager, three years later, Professor Lissa was giving away nothing that was not known abroad already. In other words, the poker-faced state secrecy was a thing of the past: that is one reason why the Professor was talking to Frager at all.

I do not mean to imply that Professor Lissa was one of those who had kept the manuscripts inaccessible. On the contrary, I believe she wanted them made available for study once more: as a serious music scholar she could hardly have wanted anything else. But that was not all she wanted, which is where her position becomes more complex, so impossibly complex that the truth no longer suited her purpose: it was necessary to invent. Professor Lissa had at heart the interests not only of Polish scholarship, but of the Polish State as well. As director of the Polish Institute of Musicology she had two masters, scholarship and government, and had to do her best by both of them.

This tied her in the kind of knot that tightens the more one struggles against it. For, if the Polish State had taken the manuscripts, Polish scholarship was in an impossibly embarrassing position. Either the scholars had not been told, in which case they should have been, or they had been told, in which case they should have told their foreign colleagues. The truth apart, what were other people to think? Polish scholars could emerge with their reputation intact only by blaming the Polish State, and blackening *its* reputation. The State could only emerge looking perfidious, the scholars looking foolish.

Therefore, the truth would not do. A substitute had to be found, a scapegoat. But who? The manuscripts could have been taken only by Poles, Russians, or the monks themselves. But the Russian option would not do. Its ideological impossibility needs no labouring, and anyway the manuscripts were known to be in Poland, which ruled out the Russians on practical grounds as well. That left only the monks. The monks would do very nicely indeed.

The possibility that the monks might have taken independent action had been explored before Professor Lissa, by Carleton Smith in 1950, and would be explored after her, by Peter Whitehead. For a searcher, the possibility was one of several to be investigated. And, even though that lead of Smith's had yielded nothing, it still made a suggestive backdrop to Professor Lissa's story twenty years later.

Another advantage of the Benedictine Rescue was the potent hold it exerted on the imagination. One *wanted* to believe it. Not only was it tailor-made for the sensation-seeking western press, and the thriller-reading western public, it even had its precedents in history. One, concerning the plunder of the Polish Royal Treasury in the eighteenth-century, had been recorded by none other than Karol Estreicher, and it bore astonishing parallels to the tangle of truth and rumour that grew up around Grüssau:

> ... Immediately after the plunder, in 1794, the Prussians proclaimed that they had found nothing in the Treasury; and as far as I know, the rumour that the Regalia had been saved was not heard till 1829. The Parisian newspaper *Constitutionnel*, on the occasion of the Coronation of Nicholas I, printed an article about the Polish Insignia. This reported the alleged rescue of the Insignia by two monks, who, in the company of six locksmiths, broke into the Treasury and safely hid the rescued Crown in some monastery in Lithuania.

159

This legend developed in the XIX century; though, as is the way with legends, the *dramatis personae* were often different. One version declared the rescuer to be the Father Guardian of the Capuchins, Father Tadeusz; another was for Father Sierakowski and the painter Stachowicz. The person who most of all contributed to the growth of these rumours was Father Wacław Nowakowski, who, owing to his erroneous interpretation of the Capuchin Chronicle, guessed that the Capuchin monastery in Vłodimierz in East Poland was the place where the Insignia were kept. The belief that the Regalia were hidden somewhere awaiting the true successor to the Polish throne was widely held among the Polish people until quite recent years. It even took hold of the Polish Government, who in 1920 ordered special enquiries and research to be made in Vłodimierz. What is more — even after the official Government announcement on the unsuccessful result of the search —certain scholars continued to believe that the Insignia were still hidden in some secret recess awaiting better times.[1]

I quote at some length not only to show the parallels, but to illustrate the potency and durability of this 'Capuchin Rescue' story, and its ultimate insubstantiality. Professor Lissa was planting a similar story in the hope that it would similarly take root and flourish as a rumour.

The beauty of it was that it recognised that the state secrecy had been broken; provided a rationale whereby there had never been any state secrecy; made it possible for Polish scholars guardedly to express their position and so preserve their credibility; and made it clear that the Polish State had a grievance and intended to hang on to the manuscripts until it was satisfied. It was not a question of the Polish State's having kept so important a musical secret from Polish music scholars, which indicated both culpability on Poland's part and an embarrassing mistrust of the scholars by government authorities; it was a question of scholarship and State learning simultaneously where the manuscripts were, and *then* disagreeing. It suggested a dialogue between Polish State and Polish scholarship which had never taken place.

The story required an admission that the Polish State had

[1]*The Mystery of the Polish Crown Jewels* (pamphlet), Karol Estreicher, Alliance Press Ltd., London, 1945, p.11.

been responsible for some years for keeping the manuscripts inaccessible, but what were those years compared to the total? And, for the total, the Polish State could not be held responsible. Another beauty of the story was that *no one* emerged from it blameworthy, not even the Benedictines. The action had not been taken by the Benedictine Order as such, but in chaotic and desperate times, many years before, by a bunch of well-meaning but misguided monks who were not even Polish, but German Benedictines. No one had acted maliciously, no one was really guilty, no one could really take offence.

All of this shows, I hope, both the convenience of the Benedictine Rescue story from the Polish point of view, and its plausibility as bait. Where the story starts to fall down, however, is when one starts to see it against its wartime background: the evacuation.

A major drawback of the story was that it concerned only the music, shelving the question of the other manuscripts. The Benedictines had not rescued those, but if they had taken only the music, where were the rest of the crates supposed to have gone? Professor Lissa made no mention of them, possibly because she was concerned only with exonerating her own branch of Polish scholarship, possibly because she knew nothing about them. But neither, of course, did Malcolm Frager.

The sheer size of the depot at Grüssau tends to rule out the idea of an independent action, and this is almost as true of the music alone as it is of all 505 crates. At no point did Professor Lissa tell Malcolm Frager that the Rescue had involved only *some* of the music. In fact, the success of the story hinges on all of it having been removed, since any remainder would have been found at Grüssau and would have become a Polish responsibility.

We are asked to believe, then, that the monks singled out the music. This was a total of some fifty crates, less than a tenth of the entire depot but having a combined volume of about three hundred cubic feet. Can we seriously believe that the monks moved that number of crates with the minimal transport at their disposal? Or that the space behind the Waldenburg church altar was large enough to take them all? Finally, Professor Lissa specified only four to six crates, enough to hold perhaps forty manuscripts, but no more. The music total –

excluding the old printed scores – was more than two hundred separate items.

So we come to the second stage of the double-barrelled Benedictine Rescue story: the revelation of it in the mid-sixties. At first glance, its most convincing feature is that 'German count' who set the dénouement in motion by getting in touch with the Polish Institute of Musicology.

A German count has already made an appearance.[1] The International Mozart Foundation in Salzburg, you may recall, learned of the convoy from one of its members, Count Johannes von Moy. He in turn had heard about it from a step-cousin, whose castle in south-western Germany was near the new Bad Wimpfen home of Grüssau monastery, and who had been in contact with the monks. The step-cousin's name was Count Hubert von Waldburg Wolffegg, and his castle, Schloss Assumstadt. He was the author of two books on the Hohenstaufen Dynasty, and he died in 1976, at the age of seventy.

I first heard about him in 1980, when he was four years past questioning. But, unless we suppose that the Grüssau monks had dealings, in the sensitive matter of the manuscripts, with two or more German counts, and that different counts, on different occasions, acted as Grüssau go-betweens, this was the man whom Professor Lissa had in mind.

We are required to believe, therefore, that Count Hubert *twice* acted as go-between for the monks, on occasions more than ten years apart and carrying contradictory information each time. The first time, he tells his step-cousin, Count von Moy, that the music manuscripts have disappeared in a convoy. On the second occasion, he tells the Polish Institute of Musicology, but not his step-cousin, that the music was hidden by the monks themselves.

Yet Count von Moy remembers Count Hubert as 'a perfectly honest, very nice man, very open, and with no reason to hide anything. He had no contacts in Poland, and if he had heard anything new about the manuscripts he would certainly have told me. The story is quite impossible'.

At the same time, Professor Lissa specifically made mention of a German count. How could she have come up with that impressive detail? One explanation immediately suggests itself.

[1] See Chapter Eleven.

Representatives of the Austrian search – the government, the N.M.A., possibly both – were in touch with Professor Lissa; this we know to have been so. The Professor could easily have heard about the German count through those Austrian channels. One can even imagine the conversation, the Austrian representative enquiring after the manuscripts, Professor Lissa, perhaps, having no idea where they were. 'We have heard, Professor, that the Polish army removed these manuscripts in a convoy.' 'Oh? and where did you hear that?' 'From the monks, Professor. One of them spoke to a *Graf*, who lived nearby. He told his step-cousin, who happens to work for the *Stiftung Mozarteum* in Salzburg. Until then, we hadn't even dared hope that the manuscripts might have survived.' And so on . . .

As the circumstantial detail is stripped away from the second part of the Professor's story it gradually reveals itself as a metaphor, built around a framework of truth. Yes, a German count *had* contacted an official music organisation – not the Polish Institute of Musicology, however, but the International Mozart Foundation; the music had become inaccessible as a result of the war, and remained so; Polish scholars genuinely *had* been in the dark, just as the Professor said, and just as their western colleagues had been; and, yes, they *had* been enlightened as the result of a dramatic revelation in the mid-sixties – not that of the Benedictine Rescue, however.

Malcolm Frager had no means of appreciating the analogies, and no means of testing the truth of Professor Lissa's story. The general impression was that at some personal risk she was unburdening herself of the truth. At the same time, however, it was clear to him that there was certain information which she was not prepared to divulge: the name of the parish church near Waldenburg; the place to which the music was moved after its recovery from the church (Frager assumed this was Warsaw); and the identity of the assistant who had been allowed to see the manuscripts.

There was one piece of information, however, which Frager also did not have, but which in addition he had no way of knowing that the Professor was withholding from him. It too had its metaphorical place in the story she had told. The revelation of the manuscripts *had* involved a death, not that of an aged German monk, but of a monkish, late middle-aged

Pole. A sort of vow of silence had been broken, but not by a Benedictine.

If Professor Lissa really was unburdening herself, and telling the truth, why did she not tell Malcolm Frager about the suicide? And, if the story of the suicide was true, which it was, how could that of the Benedictine Rescue be true as well?

CHAPTER EIGHTEEN

An Unexpected Death

There may even have been two suicides, but there was certainly one. It is the solid core of the Grüssau story.

The suicide was crucial in breaking the deadlock surrounding the manuscripts, and also in shaping the later stages of the trade secrecy, when knowledge that the manuscripts were in Poland began to be an open secret among scholars.

Whatever reasons they had for keeping silent before, this obscure death at last gave scholars one that was undeniably sound. If people could die because of paper, then silence was better than the risk of a repetition. The prime consideration became the dangers and difficulties faced by Polish scholars on the spot, for one effect of the suicide was to confirm once and for all that the manuscripts were in Poland, a Polish scholar having died because of them. One has more respect for the trade secrecy after the suicide.

It also alters our perception of the role played by the trade secrecy in the story as a whole. For the first time, the suicide put the scholars in possession of a real secret of their own, which they alone had the power to divulge. This both tightened the secrecy and placed it under greater pressure.

By its authority and finality, the suicide decisively broke the state secret within Poland. It then became in the interests of the State to hush it up as quickly and as securely as possible, to paint over the wide crack which it opened. In this aim it would have succeeded, except that a side effect of the death was to spread the poison of the state secret – like an infection of knowledge which could not be shaken off – within the bloodstream of Polish scholarship.

Thence, through the freemasonry of scholars, it spread more widely – but still only to a comparative few. Looked at in this light, the trade secrecy after the suicide was not another wrapping around the state secret, but the means by which, imperfectly but irreversibly, the state secret was eventually destroyed.

Slowly, in broken fragments, the story reached me, first as a dark hint dropped by Carleton Smith in the early summer of 1977. 'The people who are looking after these manuscripts," he told me, 'are in danger of their lives.' The statement was suitably chilling. What could it mean? I asked Carleton Smith, but he wouldn't say. I decided he was probably being theatrical, and was certainly being vague, and left it at that. Note that he made no mention of a suicide.

I was reminded of his curious remark, however, by a 'titbit' in a letter from New York later that year: 'While the manuscript issue was under discussion, two archivists committed suicide over the matter . . . vague about further details, but perhaps you could dig further.' I was intrigued, but finally unimpressed. It was, after all, just a 'titbit', and had all the hollow ring of rumour about it. I did not dig further. Then, in October 1978, more than a year after Carleton Smith's aside, I heard something else which convinced me that there must be some substance to the suicide rumour.

What decided me was the observation that the rumour came in unprompted fragments, from different sources. This time it was someone in London, who told me about a Polish librarian who had 'cut his throat' because of the manuscripts. Now, I did want to dig, but unfortunately my London informant could not for the life of him remember where he had picked up the rumour. So I wrote again to my source in New York. Where had she heard the story? Because of external problems, her reply would take a further sixteen months to arrive.

Meanwhile, in November 1979, I visited Berlin, where I was to meet Dr. Wolfgang Rehm of the N.M.A. Almost his first words to me revived, but this time confirmed, that disbelieving chill I had first felt in the summer of 1977: 'You do realise, don't you, that at least one person has died because of these manuscripts?'

Dr. Rehm spoke of 'the suicide in the late sixties of a man who was looking after the music'. This for the first time put an approximate date to the death, and for the first time specifically gave the music manuscripts as the background to it. Like the letter from New York, it raised the possibility that there may have been more than one suicide, but, unlike all the earlier clues, it confirmed that there had been 'at least one'. For the

166

first time, also, it was suggested that the suicide had been male. This was important: a great many librarians are women.

Dr. Rehm could also confirm that the suicide had been committed as a result of pressures directly related to the manuscripts. This was definitely so[1], but as to the precise nature of those pressures he had no idea. Before the motive could be examined, however, it was necessary to establish the identity of the person who had killed himself. There again Dr. Rehm could be of no help: he did not know the man's name.

Four months after that Berlin meeting, my New York informant at last replied, passing me on to the source from whom she had heard the story. This was a music scholar who at the time was in Israel. I wrote, and a month later received my reply:

> I remember that I heard what at the time was 'just a rumour' during a meeting of some Mozart scholars in Salzburg, in connection with the hidden Mozart autographs. As an 'outsider' in this particular affair I did not go into it further, even though somebody else – I do not quite remember who – told the story of the suicide(s) some time later as a certainty. So there must be something to it . . . At the time, the people who knew more also hinted that they would not check further for fear that this would complicate East-West scholarly relations to an extent that would make further exchange of information impossible.

Like Dr. Rehm, this source did not know the identity of the suicide. A further clue, however, came in a letter from Rehm which arrived soon afterwards. It referred to 'the supposed suicide of a librarian of the Jagiellonian . . . I have *never* learned who this librarian was'.

Now, at our meeting in Berlin Dr. Rehm had not said that the librarian had been an employee of the Jagiellonian, and at that stage it was by no means certain that the Jagiellonian Library in Kraków had been the home of the manuscripts since the war. One reason why it would be helpful to establish the identity of the suicide was that his place of work, and therefore

[1] This was confirmed to Dr. Rehm by two separate sources, both of whom were in a position to know, but neither of whom can be named. I myself do not know their names, only the relation in which one of them stood to the man who died. I am satisfied as to the authenticity of this source.

the location of the manuscripts at the time of his death, would be established as well. For a while, I confess, I thought that Dr. Rehm might be misleading me.

That he was not was confirmed by a German librarian whom I asked about the suicide in the summer of 1980. He too had heard the rumour, and though he did not know the suicide's identity, as far as he *did* know he had been a male employee of the Jagiellonian.

I assembled the scraps of evidence and reviewed them. I could, I decided, work on the assumption that the suicide had been a man employed in the Music Department of the Jagiellonian Library. Those were conditions which the candidate had to meet. In addition, I could guess that he had died probably by cutting his throat.

It remained to narrow down the date of death. Dr. Rehm had said 'the late Sixties' – a span of five years. Had I any clues that could help to pinpoint it more accurately?

In Berlin, Dr. Rehm told me that, in 1967, the year of the N.M.A.'s 'semi-official revelation', he had himself visited Kraków, and disingenuously, but unsuccessfully, asked after the manuscripts there. At a later meeting with him, after specifying that the N.M.A.'s breakthrough had been 'in the early part' of 1967, he said he could be sure that he had learned of the suicide after that time.

If one could assume that the suicide followed the semi-official revelation, that narrowed the time-span by half – from mid-1967 to the end of 1969. It was possible, of course, that events had occurred in an order different from that in which they had come to the notice of Dr. Rehm. But it was interesting, and possibly significant, that he dated his learning of the suicide by his memory of the semi-official revelation and his visit to Kraków the same year. Was there, possibly, a connection?

Whatever the background to Dr. Rehm's dating, it seemed reasonable to push the possible time span forward from 1965, and halve it. Could it be pulled back from 1969? There was one possible way. Both my main sources for the suicide story were music scholars, and both had worked on Mozart, Rehm as a member of the N.M.A. and the other as a delegate to that 'meeting of some Mozart scholars at Salzburg'. Judging from the Israeli letter, the story of the suicide seems to have been fairly hot news at the time of the meeting – 'a macabre curiosity', my source called it. Was that possibly because the suicide occurred not long before it, to join the body of the trade secret during the off-duty conversations at that meeting, to be heard there by Dr. Rehm and my other source *at much the same time*? The idea seemed worth trying, so I wrote to Israel again. My source replied:

> . . . I am in Salzburg at least once a year and thus it is very difficult to remember the occasion when the matter was talked about. I can only say definitely that I had no discussion of it with Dr. Rehm. Yes, I do remember that two suicides were spoken of – but again, this was so much 'in passing' that I would not swear on it . . . And most certainly I remember that an actual place was not mentioned.

Now, while one may visit Salzburg every year for the purposes of research, and while the city eats, sleeps, and breathes Mozart, it certainly does not play host every year to meetings – presumably international – of Mozart scholars. Was there a meeting 'in the late sixties' which fitted the bill? There was, and there appeared indeed to be no other that did. It had the very long-winded title of *Colloquium des Zentralinstitutes für Mozartforschung über Probleme der Instrumentalen Aufführungspraxis Mozarts'*, and it was held in the summer of 1968.

If my reasoning thus far was on course, I had narrowed down the possible time-span of the suicide from five years to one, the summer of 1967 to the summer of 1968. That was a considerable improvement, but there was another highly intriguing fragment which held out the possibility that the span could be narrowed yet again, by as much as three-quarters to a period of three months or less. This was a small news item reported by the Polish news agency P.A.P., picked up by Associated Press, and printed in Britain in the *Sunday Telegraph* for January 21, 1968: 'A previously unknown symphony by Haydn has been found in Polish archives, the official Polish news agency reported in Warsaw yesterday. The symphony is in F Major . . .' No manuscript of a Haydn symphony in F Major, and obviously no unknown ones by him, were known to have been evacuated to Grüssau. But still the news – to anyone acquainted with the Grüssau story – might have suggested some dramatic development in it. The suspicion would have been heightened by an even shorter story in the *Daily*

Telegraph three days later: "The reported discovery of an unknown Haydn symphony is a hoax, Warsaw University has announced . . .'

What was one to make of that? It is rarely enough that a researcher stumbles upon a manuscript which he believes to be an unknown work by a major composer, and when he does, and his belief is announced as fact, it is usually found that he has made a genuine mistake. This, however, was a hoax, and music scholars – by one of whom, presumably, and certainly if P.A.P. was doing its job properly, the Haydn symphony had been 'discovered' – are not renowned as puckish hoaxers when it comes to their work. Such a hoax, apart from its irresponsibility towards serious scholarship as a whole, would have been quite enough to ruin the reputation of the scholar perpetrating it.

Was it possible that the 'hoax' was an attempt to attract attention to developments in the Grüssau story, a cry for help in effect? Certainly, whether connected with Grüssau or not, it seemed to indicate a crisis of some kind, and falling as it did within the time-span of the suicide I felt justified in speculating that the hoax and the death were in some way connected. The hoax, an apparent act of professional suicide, might have been a sort of suicide note. Accordingly, in the corner of the index card recording the story, I wrote 'The suicide?' For the guess to stand a chance of being right, the hoax and the death would have to have occurred reasonably close to each other.

It remained, finally, to establish the identity of the suicide and the date of his death. Obviously there was no point in writing to Poland. I had to rely on the chance that the death had been recorded somewhere. But where? The only possibility seemed to be a house journal, and I discovered that the Jagiellonian had one – the *Jagiellonian Library Bulletin*, published twice yearly since 1957 and including in each issue a chronicle of the library life. To my relief, I then discovered that the Polish Library in London had copies of the *Bulletin* covering the relevant period. Before studying them, and going on the assumption that music librarians at the Jagiellonian do not die like flies, I decided that if I could find a suitable death within the right period that would be my man.

There was such a death, meeting all the conditions I had set myself, falling exactly midway between Dr. Rehm's 'after the

170

early part of 1967' and the Mozart conference in Salzburg the following year, and very close to the hoax, not shortly after, but shortly before it. That meant that it could not have been a 'suicide note', but falling as close as it did to the suicide, as well as being one of the clues that led me to it, in a sense the most exact of all, I did not dismiss it from the reckoning. I shall return to the hoax.

The *Jagiellonian Library Bulletin* in 1969 recorded the death, on January 4, 1968, of Władysław Hordyński, who had worked in the Music Department of the Jagiellonian since before the war, and directed the department from 1958. Hordyński's death at the age of fifty-nine was described as having occurred 'unexpectedly'. The Polish word, *niespodzie-wanie*, is quite precise and quite distinct from 'suddenly', for example. So disease wasn't the cause, and at fifty-nine neither was old age.

The evidence surely allows us to conclude that the man who was driven to kill himself by pressures arising from the matchless music of Grüssau was Władysław Hordyński, keeper of music at the Jagiellonian Library in Kraków.

*

Whether or not the manuscripts spent time in a depot on Wawel Hill, therefore, their eventual destination must have been the Jagiellonian. The move, I believe but cannot prove, was made shortly after the Berlin Library holdings in the crates marked P.S.B., including those of Grüssau, were brought together and sorted – in the middle to late 1940s.

Dieter Henrich had considered the possibility that the Jagiellonian, having the right facilities and more controlled atmospheric conditions than the Wawel, might have been the storage place. But he had rejected the idea: '. . . the venerable Jagiellonian Library would have been suitable as the administrator of valuable autographs, although there is good reason to believe that it was never brought into contact with the most important items in the treasure.' We shall look at that doubt of Henrich's. What matters for the moment is that the Jagiellonian *was* the post-war storage place of by far the most important of the Berlin Library holdings evacuated eastward, the Grüssau manuscripts, and certainly also of the vast majority of the holdings recovered from all the eastern evacuation sites.

171

Compared to the riches of Grüssau, most of the latter were dross – vast mounds of old German newspapers and printed German books, with a relatively small admixture of manuscripts. Whether all the contents of all the sites were stored together in one place at the Jagiellonian or indiscriminately in several places, we can be certain that at some stage the greater riches were carefully sorted from the lesser. It may be that the Grüssau treasure was put at the outset into a separate category of value, and stored separately.

Completed in 1939, just before the outbreak of war, the new library of the Jagiellonian University was considered the most advanced building of its kind in Europe, as well as one of the most stylish. It is built in an inverted 'T', the much larger front section looking out over Mickiewicz Street, the wing, containing the main reading room, extending into the library gardens. The section that concerns us is the front one housing the eight floors of stock rooms, with special yellow windows to protect their contents from sunlight. In these rooms the Berlin library holdings and the Grüssau manuscripts would have been stored. According to a 1963 guide book to the Jagiellonian Library: 'Special collections, especially valuable ones, like manuscripts . . . have their own stock rooms, safeguarded and protected by installations for the preservation of these irreplaceable materials.'

If special collections have special facilities, can we assume that the facilities for extra-special ones are extra-special? Certainly one cannot imagine that library staff were allowed to come and go as they pleased in those stock rooms that contained the German collections. They must therefore have been out of bounds, to most and possibly all the staff, a closed-off area, directly controlled by the state, within the Jagiellonian Library.

Dieter Henrich was inclined to rule out the Jagiellonian on information he received from a leading scholar, an expert on the Renaissance, who was told by the director of the library that the manuscripts were not under his roof. The conclusion to be drawn, when it was found that they were, was that the director had been lying.

That is possible, but there is a chance also that the director was telling the truth *as he knew it*. The directorship of the Jagiellonian is not a permanent post, but changes every few years, and it could be that the director himself was among those who were left in the dark about the presence and/or the nature of the German collections. It all depends on the date of his talk with the Renaissance scholar, for we shall see that after the mid-sixties that particular dark began to dissipate. Until then, in the store rooms of the Jagiellonian, known only to a tiny few in Poland, 'protected by installations' perhaps from the staff of the library itself, the books and manuscripts stayed. Still in their crates or stacked on shelves, they formed a huge but hidden paper monument to the war, gathering dust.

It is as though they were intended to be outside time: an illusion if so, for with every passing year time was building up pressures on them, and beginning to knock on the locked doors that hid them. The dormant German collections were most of them of small or no value to the state as reparations 'guarantees' and of no value to Poland as library holdings, and they took up a lot of valuable space. Every day brought new accessions to be processed, catalogued, and stored, books from Poland, the Soviet Union, the United States, and all over the world. Gradually, a critical point was reached, at which the administrators of the Jagiellonian found themselves unable to imagine where the new accessions could be kept.

There was another factor which, if the anonymous administrators of the German collections were aware of it, may have shaped the decision that was eventually taken. Among the German books there were many of Polish provenance, looted under the occupation and taken to Germany, stamped with German library marks and added to German collections, then evacuated east together with the rest. While the genuinely German holdings remained dormant, so did those of Polish extraction.

The most pressing consideration, however, would have been the need to accommodate the Jagiellonian's new holdings, which came in daily. The peaceful exterior of the building, the unruffled movements of the library staff, gave no hint of this pressure: no more does the deceptively quiet surface of Hordyński's life betray any sign of the pressures by which he was beset.

*

Władysław Hordyński was born in 1908 and educated first in Lwów, then in Kraków, where he would spend most of the rest of his life. His 'unexpected' death abruptly ended a life and career in which the unexpected can have played little part.

After a course in philology at the Jagiellonian University, he studied music and the piano at Kraków Conservatoire before specialising as a librarian. He started work at the Jagiellonian Library in 1930, and in 1936 took a degree in librarianship.

During the war, like the Polish Royal Treasury and Karol Estreicher, he went to Rumania; unlike them he stayed there for the duration. He worked on the music collection of the Rumanian Academy, and at the Institute for Byzantine Studies in Bucharest, and brought out a bibliography of musical Polonica in Rumania, of the fifteenth to eighteenth centuries.

In 1945 he returned to Poland, to resume work at once at the Jagiellonian Library. One of his first tasks was to sort out the inheritance left by Paderewski on his death in 1941. In 1949 he was very active in organising the exhibition commemorating the centenary of Chopin's death. His post-war publications were mostly on Chopin, or of works by Chopin, including facsimiles of those scores which were handed over by the East Berlin Library to mark the tenth anniversary of the outbreak of war.

In 1948 he became director of the special commission on musicology of the Academy of Sciences: this must have put him in regular working touch with Professor Lissa. In 1951 he organised the music section of an exhibition on the Renaissance at the National Museum in Warsaw. In 1954 he was decorated for his services. Four years later he became director of the Jagiellonian Library's Music Department.

Hordyński evidently behaved himself, and kept in good odour with those in charge of Polish culure and its administration. The picture so far is of a tried and trusted scholarly civil servant, and a studious and blameless life. Yet, somewhere in its background at some point, intolerable professional pressures started to build.

At what point? The answer is crucial, but, before coming to it, let us consider the likely nature of those 'pressures'. We know that they arose from the Grüssau music manuscripts, and it is hard to see how they can have been unconnected with their inaccessibility and the secrecy with which they were surrounded. Since Hordyński must have known about the manuscripts, he was evidently party to the secrecy, though that does not necessarily mean the manuscripts were accessible to him.

It is also hard to see how the pressures on Hordyński could have been sufficient to bring about his death unless his relationship to the manuscript was in some way *exclusive*. Whether or not he was solely *responsible* for the care of the manuscripts– which outshone anything in his own collection, but which were inaccessible – he must surely have been solely *accountable* for the spread of information about them.

I am suggesting that the pressures on him arose first from the daily deception of having to conceal the greatest hoard of missing music the world has known, then from the consequences of his refusal any longer to live with the deception. For a musician, and serious music librarian, who was also a state employee, one can hardly imagine a more damaging or conflict-laden predicament.

It had at first to be unique to Hordyński among Polish music scholars. For if the secret of the manuscripts had become known to other scholars before him, as is implied in Professor Lissa's version of events, or had become known to a number of scholars at the same time, the secrecy would already have been dissipated and he would have been under no greater pressure than anyone else. It would have been incidental that the music was being kept hidden in 'his' library.

But that, surely, is far from incidental. Is it not rather our factual starting point? For if the music was all along hidden in the Jagiellonian, and if its existence and whereabouts at some point then became known to Polish music scholars, would we not expect the Jagiellonian's Keeper of Music to be the first to find out? If he had then been free to tell others, there would have been no secret, no sole accountability, no pressures, and ultimately no suicide.

At some point, therefore, Hordyński had to become party to the state secrecy. He had either to see into the secret stock rooms of the Jagiellonian, or to discover what they contained. He had at some point to *know*, and at that point the pressure on him began. If Hordyński was not party to the secret from the start, there had to be a point at which he could have become party to it by accident, or at which it was considered necessary to make him party to it. How else could he have seen into the depths of those rooms in which, since the war, the manuscripts must have been stored?

In the history of the Jagiellonian Library from the end of the war to Hordyński's death in 1968, there is only one suitable point. Falling at just the period to which Professor Lissa attributed the revelation of the Benedictine Rescue – the mid-sixties – it also shortly predates the earliest moment at which we can be sure that Polish scholars knew about the music, and allows just under three years for Hordyński's predicament to intensify to the point it eventually reached.

*

The psychological pressures on Hordyński had their origins in pressures on the storage space of the library for which he had worked nearly all his life. The revelation, when it came, can have been no less dramatic than that outlined by Professor Lissa, but its root causes were rather more mundane than the dying monk and German count of whom she spoke.

In 1960, the Jagiellonian Library made space for itself by removing part of its secret German holdings westward to Łódz. This was a vast quantity of material, all fairly low-grade as far as Poland's needs were concerned. The bound volumes of German newspapers alone weighed twenty-four tons. In Łódz began the work of sorting out what belonged to whom. When it ended, a total of some five tons was found rightfully to belong to the Warsaw University Library, and another nineteen-teen thousand volumes to libraries elsewhere in Poland. The majority, however, were genuinely German.

This gave the Jagiellonian some *lebensraum*, but still not enough. The library had been built originally to hold one and a half million volumes, but, as the 1963 guidebook notes, one of its original architectural features had been that 'the principle of "organic extension" of the building was taken into consideration from the beginning of the planning'.

To this in-built 'organic extensibility' I believe we owe the discovery by Hordyński of the secret music collection within 'his' library. The extension work, we can judge from the 1963 guidebook, began the year after the transfer to Łódz:

> In 1961 began the first stage of the planned library extension. The new section (about 10,500 cubic metres) will consider-ably increase the number of readers' seats, special collections

rooms, and library workrooms. Construction work will be completed in 1963. The extension of stock rooms will be the next stage of library expansion.

The schedule reasonably allows us to place the extension of the stock rooms as having occurred around 1964-65, which means that it ties in with two other developments over the same period. The first was the involvement, soon afterwards and for the first time, of Polish scholars in the Grüssau mystery; the second was the operation called, by the few Germans who knew of it, 'Rü-Be-Pol', which took place in 1965. The extension work was evidently related to 'Rü-Be-Pol', and was possibly its starting point; and both form the background to the entry of Polish scholars into the mystery.

'Rü-Be-Pol' stood for 'Rückführung der Bestände von Polen', or 'Return of the Holdings from Poland'. It was an extraordinary operation, and a powerful clue to Grüssau, which makes it extraordinary that nothing was published about it in the west at the time, and nothing later, only that scrap of private information about newspapers returned from Poland which Dieter Henrich picked up. In East Germany the story was published only in two highly specialised library magazines, and nowhere else, as far as I know.

In 'Rü-Be-Pol', Poland sorted the chaff from the golden grains of wheat, and blew it back whence it had come. Over three months in the summer of 1965 eleven train wagonloads of German books, catalogues, and newspapers were returned to Berlin. They totalled 127,000 volumes, and came in seven wagons from Lódz and four from Kraków. Two smaller consignments followed later from Wrocław, perhaps inspiring Carleton Smith's Wrocław theory of that year.

All these had hailed from the Berlin University and City Libraries, the Berlin museums, and the High School for Music – which shows how many institutions had found wartime evacuation sites in territory beyond the Oder and Neisse rivers. The great majority, however, were from the former Prussian State Library. It could have been that the holdings were returned unconditionally, simply to relieve the pressure on Polish libraries arising from the retention of dormant German material. Or perhaps a deal was struck. According to one of the East German sources, the sorting at Lódz ended in the autumn of 1965, to be followed by a delay as talks between the Polish and East German Ministries of Education drew to a close. At these, the finishing touches could have been put to some reparations deal.

This, however, is incidental to the main point, which is that the extension work and 'Rü-Be-Pol' provided ideal conditions for the uncovering of the Jagiellonian's hidden music. The doubling of the library's capacity to three million volumes, and all the sorting and moving needed for 'Rü-Be-Pol', must have caused a massive disturbance – the biggest in the Jagiellonian's post-war history. In it, the Grüssau manuscripts could have come to light and to the attention of Hordyński by accident, much as a glacier, moving down its mountain, will sometimes give up the body of a climber twenty years dead. Or the music's hidden presence could have been disclosed to Hordyński on purpose, because he was required to help in the sorting work for 'Rü-Be-Pol', making him party to the state secret on the strict understanding that he was thereafter expected to keep it.

It matters little how Hordyński came by his knowledge. Whether the Polish authorities were caught out or whether they miscalculated can have made no difference to his response; to his responses rather, for he surely went through several. His first must have been the amazement of an innocent in a robber's cave. So much magnificent music! Perhaps he even saw some of it – *The Magic Flute*, *The Marriage of Figaro*, some of Beethoven's late quartets or his symphonies. Then, very soon afterwards, the deeper implications would have begun to crowd in upon him. Almost certainly he had heard about the missing music. To think that, since soon after the war, since his late thirties, he had been sharing the same building with these treasures! Day after working day, as he was dealing with the public, with problems of research, all the time they had been hidden there, a secret hoard which in its majesty and importance outshone all the music – even his beloved Chopin! – for which he was responsible. Not five floors, not twenty doors from his own.

It was marvellous! It was scandalous! What a mixture of elation, anger, and despair, and what a fool he must have felt, Hordyński, the lifelong musician and diligent music librarian! How long before the turmoil began to subside, and he could bring a clear head to bear on the issue?

For there was an issue. The concealment of the music broke all of the rules by which he had lived; it could not be allowed to continue. For the first time since they had been taken hostage, the manuscripts had come to the notice of someone capable of seeing them, not just as objects of great financial value, German cultural property which was useful as a 'security' or 'guarantee', but as part of the sublime inheritance of civilised man as a whole, and as unique material invaluable for research. Hordyński's training, a lifetime of experience, told him this was so.

For the first time, in Hordyński, there was someone in whom the paradox could take root – that a morally defensible position, Poland's retention of the manuscripts, had been sustained under morally indefensible conditions, the long inaccessibility of those manuscripts. The dilemma, one could say, had been lying dormant, waiting for someone to come along who was capable of grasping both of its horns, someone like Hordyński. As a Pole with experience of the war, he would easily have been able to understand why the manuscripts were in the Jagiellonian, and as a patriot he probably thought that the Jagiellonian was where they should stay. But as a musician he could not accept the inaccessibility which was a consequence of the secrecy. Perhaps he tried to argue his position, but if so to no avail: the old policy was to be continued.

It must have been at this stage that Hordyński began to slide towards despair. Not only had the manuscripts been inaccessible since the war, which was terrible enough, they were to remain so indefinitely, and that, as Professor Lissa implied to Malcolm Frager, hardly bore thinking about. Having looked under the bushel, and seen the light, Hordyński was expected to help, or at least co-operate by his silence, in replacing the bushel. To say that this put him in an invidious position is to understate the issue: he was forced to choose, in effect, between betraying the policy which representatives of the Polish State considered to be in Poland's best interests, and betraying himself – all he had lived for and all in which he had believed. On a more everyday level, he was expected to turn up for work at the Jagiellonian as usual and to keep to himself the knowledge that much of the greatest music ever written was being secretly hidden by Poland, by the Jagiellonian Library, and by himself.

For, although Poland returned a very great deal of German material in 1965, she returned no treasures of the first importance, that is to say none of the music and none of the holdings from Grüssau. It was in 1965 or 1966, during or after 'Rü-Be-Pol', that the East German Communist party formally asked its Polish counterpart whether the manuscripts were in Poland. The reply that they were 'not on Polish soil' makes it clear that the Poles were planting the idea that the manuscripts, wherever they were or whatever had happened to them, had had *a separate history* from the rest of the material evacuated eastwards: the idea that the Russians must have taken them, or the monks, or that they had been destroyed, perhaps in a fire at the monastery.

In 'Rü-Be-Pol', Poland had apparently played her whole hand, but only after palming the court cards and the aces. The astonishing and risky deception shows just how important the manuscripts were regarded as being, and the Polish determination, despite the shake-up of 'Rü-Be-Pol', to maintain the old, war-vintage policy of which the manuscripts were the cornerstone.

In this, Poland over-reached herself. Less than two years after East Germany's Party-to-Party request, and Poland's denial, the N.M.A. in Austria learned for a fact not only that the music was in Poland, but that it was in the Jagiellonian Library. In the mid-sixties, after 'Rü-Be-Pol' but before Hordyński's suicide, the Polish State lost control of its secret, and the suicide lends weight to the explanation that it did so as a result of an indiscretion, or indiscretions, calculated or not, by Hordyński.

He need not have spoken directly to foreign scholars about the manuscripts. It would have been enough to break the Polish state secret to Polish scholars. An obvious first choice would have been Professor Lissa, Poland's most powerful musicologist, who was trusted by the government and known to Hordyński since 1948 at least. He may have been her 'German count'. Through Polish scholars, the secret could have begun to spread abroad, to Austria, and possibly to East Germany. There are signs of East German activity over the same period, not only the Party-to-Party request, but enquiries in Poland by Karl-Heinz Köhler, and Köhler's letter and list of the missing music which he sent to Professor Lissa. The significance of these developments must remain murky, but if

180

East Germany had come to learn the truth soon after Poland's denial that the manuscripts were on Polish soil – worse, if it had known the truth *before* – the Polish government would not have been pleased.

How the secret travelled we cannot know[1], only that it did travel, to reach the N.M.A. in Austria by the early part of 1967. That was embarrassment enough. It required only one searcher who knew the truth, and could prove it. And the next development of which we have certain knowledge is the death of Hordyński, six months after the N.M.A.'s 'semi-official revelation'.

The breaking, then the dissemination, of the state secret created the need for a new policy, more subtle than the old sphinxlike stance of sitting tight and saying nothing. This must have become clear before Hordyński's death, but it is after it that we first see the new policy in operation – one part of it being Professor Lissa's conversation with Malcolm Frager, early in 1970. It is almost as though there had to be a death, if the secret were to die, as though the old policy needed a sacrificial victim before it could become the new.

---

[1] But it can be said that the first stage of the secret's journey outside Poland was at the 1966 meeting of the International Association of Music Librarians, which, by coincidence, was held that summer in Warsaw. It was at that meeting that Dr. Köhler made his enquiries. Soon afterwards he sent Professor Lissa the list of missing music. It can safely be assumed that Hordyński was also present at the meeting.

CHAPTER NINETEEN

The One That Got Away

The theory has it that, as the secret began to spread inside Poland, after 1965, Polish scholars were united in one respect and divided in another. The agreement was on Poland's right to have taken the manuscripts in the first place, and, if she so decided, her right to keep them in perpetuity. The division was over the conditions under which the right had been exercised, and would be exercised in future.

Here we have to draw a distinction between the inaccessibility of the manuscripts and the secrecy with which they had been surrounded, because at that stage the distinction was a fact. Previously, the inaccessibility had been inseparable from the secrecy. Now, the secret of the manuscripts was no longer watertight, while their inaccessibility still was.

The first group, the hawks, argued that what mattered above all was that the manuscripts should stay in Poland, inaccessible if need be. Their inaccessibility was even desirable. It was part and parcel of the punishment, which was necessary to the policy under which they had been appropriated. By keeping them inaccessible, Poland was squeezing the maximum advantage from her possession of them, thereby increasing pressure on the Germans to fulfil their long-overdue obligations in the cultural revindication and reparations field. As for the secrecy, the hawks argued that, as long as their opponents, the doves, kept their mouths shut, it was not beyond repair.

Gently, the doves replied that the hawks were being unrealistic, adding hastily that they were every bit as patriotic and as mindful of Poland's best interests as the hawks were. But the hawks failed to realise that Poland, by keeping the manuscripts inaccessible, had punished and was continuing to punish, not only Germany and German scholars, but scholars all over the world, including Poland. It was unrealistic of the hawks to expect Polish scholars, just because they were Polish, not to respond as scholars as well. As Poles, they approved of the retention of the manuscripts; as scholars, they were appalled by their inaccessibility. A way would have to be found to break the deadlock, for as long as it continued they would be divided against themselves. It was unrealistic to expect someone to *unknow* something, simply because he was never supposed to have known it, and even more unrealistic to expect him then to keep it to himself, if by doing so he was helping to prolong a situation which was intolerable to him. It was unrealistic, therefore, to expect the secret to be contained, and unrealistic to expect that Poland, the secret blown, could continue to keep the manuscripts inaccessible. A new policy was needed, incorporating the aims of the old, but subtler, more imaginative, acceptable to Polish scholars as well as to the Polish State.

There are certain expensive hydraulic systems that have to be overhauled if so much as a drop of water enters them. For twenty years the secret had been hermetically sealed, the manuscripts out of sight and out of most minds behind locked doors and yellow window-panes. Then the disturbance at the Jagiellonian broke the seal, and as soon as Hordyński *knew* what was in those closed-off stock rooms, whether or not he saw for himself, the drop of water entered. Then the resultant rust of knowledge had begun to spread to other scholars. Those were the doves.

Gently they let it be known that their knowledge of the situation must thenceforth be considered an inalienable part of the situation. They had always had a right to know, and now that they did know they did not approve. The hawks listened and disagreed, but could hardly blame the doves for knowing. How they felt about the person who had been responsible for the first leak with which corrosion of the secret had begun was another matter.

They would not have felt any more charitable towards Hordyński after the early part of 1967. Let us assume that the first hawk-dove dialogue took place before the leak reached the N.M.A. in Austria, to be resumed after it in the knowledge that it had occurred. Setting aside the question of how the secret reached the N.M.A., the very fact that it was now known abroad meant that the situation could never be the same again. The game-plan had altered. There you are, the doves would have been able to say, we told you the secret couldn't be contained for long. Now the old policy *has* to be overhauled. The N.M.A. knows today; tomorrow or the day after everyone will know. How will the Polish State be able to continue with its denials then, without looking both perfidious and foolish? How will we, the Polish scholars, be able to face our foreign colleagues?

How did the hawks reply? By accusing the doves of acting as foreign agents? By threatening to withdraw their travel visas? Perhaps. But perhaps, also, some of them gave a guarded welcome to the 'new game-plan'. Good, they might have said, that turns the screw a little tighter. Poland has nothing to be ashamed of! The leak might even serve as a discreet advertisement for Poland's legitimate grievance. But there matters must remain. The affair was in the hands of the State, and the scholars must cease their 'semi-official' meddling. We do not know how the N.M.A. achieved its break-through, but we do know that nothing was changed. The hawks again prevailed.

The next development, in January 1968, was Hordyński's suicide. The act, with its implicit assertion that the rights of scholars to the manuscripts as music must take precedence over the State's right to keep them hidden as objects, thrust the moral and ethical issues to the fore of the discussion. The doves were able to adduce the death as a demonstration that their arguments were correct, and as the tragic but inevitable consequence of the stubbornness of the hawks. They could point to it as evidence that the problem had no easy answer, as the doves had recognised all along, as Hordyński had recognised at the cost of his life, and as it was now time for the hawks to recognise. The doves doubtless recited all their earlier arguments with new vigour, and some of the hawks were perhaps impressed into taking them more seriously.

At any rate, it is only after Hordyński's suicide that we have the first evidence of Polish scholarship beginning to communicate with the west about the secret; and I believe that the Haydn symphony hoax, only sixteen days after the death, may have been a first confused attempt at that communication. I simply do not believe that a music scholar would have perpetrated so apparently pointless a hoax for its own sake. A fortnight after Hordyński's suicide, however, it makes sense. Horrified and angered by the death, and themselves frightened, a dove or group of doves could have perpetrated it, in order to draw attention to a real and much bigger hoax, the one into which Hordyński had been forced but which ultimately, and honourably, he refused.

As people will dream the acts they dare not commit, so they will sometimes state, obliquely in a metaphor, the truth they dare not speak. Like the Benedictine Rescue, the hoax has metaphorical parallels with the cover-up of the manuscripts. It is not the truth, but a veiled clue to the truth, which by forcing the State into a denial that a German music manuscript was in Poland forced it to sound the echo of earlier denials. By this reading, it was a frantic signal, a kind of poem which stated crookedly the truth that could not be stated straight. People in the west knew the background to the story. Had they, the Polish scholars, not been hearing it for years? But westerners were ignorant of its most recent development inside Poland. The outside world had half the telegram; the hoax was the torn-off other half.

The parallels, this time, do not implicitly exonerate, but implicitly accuse. Literally, the story of the Haydn symphony was a falsehood, its retraction the truth. Seen metaphorically against the background of the Grüssau story, it was the other way around: the Haydn symphony *was* in Poland, and the Polish government, not Polish scholarship, was the hoaxer. At the same time the hoax was a sort of posthumous suicide note sent as a marker to the predicament that had killed Hordyński, and which, despite his death, was to continue.

The retraction came from Warsaw University, by which we can surely understand its Music Department and Institute of Musicology, presided over by Professor Lissa, 'in the seat of government' high on the eighth floor of the Palace of Culture and Science. Again I stress that I do not believe she wanted to conceal the manuscripts; but I do believe that she was in the business of papering over the embarrassment of their revelation, and of defusing the explosive element which the suicide had introduced. She was the scholar delegated to double as diplomat in the delicate surgery needed to heal the breach between Polish scholarship and the Polish State. Her job was to represent the hawks to the doves, and the doves to the hawks, to achieve a compromise position, and then if necessary to represent that compromise to foreign scholars. She had to be dove and hawk in one. She may even have been the

185

architect of the new policy, but she was certainly its chief exponent. Where foreign searchers were concerned, she was not to speak unless spoken to, and then to break things gently, with the gentleness of a dove . . .

The new policy was built not only around the principle that foreign scholars had a right to know what had happened to the manuscripts, but around pragmatic acceptance of the fact that some knew already, and more would know in time. In pursuing it, Poland took the initiative, and in a sense enlisted both the complicity of foreign scholars in the deadlock surrounding the manuscripts, and their sympathetic understanding of the causes of the deadlock. So, gradually, the closed state secret was turned into the open trade secret.

Information was passed on in scraps, on the understanding that it was privileged. Foreigners were given to understand that their intervention was unnecessary – since Polish scholars were well aware of the problem and doing their responsible best to solve it. Foreign intervention would also be potentially embarrassing and even dangerous, in that it might prejudice not only the positions of the Polish scholars personally but also the hoped-for successful outcome of their efforts. Yes, there were political difficulties – were there not always, with governments? – but it was confidently expected that there would one day be a satisfactory conclusion, even if hopes did sometimes flag.

So the problem came in a way to be institutionalised. The problem now was not one of detection, as it had been back in the fifties and sixties, but of diplomacy – not finding out where the manuscripts were, but getting Poland to admit that she had them, without loss of face, then getting her to make them once more accessible. Great delicacy was required, the foreigners were told. One wrong move could spoil everything, and put the clock back twenty years.

Honesty is sometimes the best policy, and this policy certainly had the advantage that there was a great deal of truth in it. But it was also very skilful. By accepting the inevitable, and then controlling its development, Poland bought time for herself – time in which it slowly came to be accepted that the manuscripts were in Poland. In this way, the central aim of the old policy was imperceptibly furthered as well.

The secret was no longer contained and under Polish state

control, but, by the simple expedient of making Professor Lissa solely responsible, the spread of it was. Polish scholars were required to refer their foreign colleagues to her, and so the possibility of another Hordyński incident was minimised.

So it was that, when Malcolm Frager asked his colleague in Katowice about the manuscripts, he returned from his telephone call saying that 'only Professor Lissa can help you'. Frager had no way of knowing that – by then, two years after Hordyński's death – some at least of the music was in Katowice itself.

*

Professor Lissa's conversation with Malcolm Frager, and her face-saving story of the Benedictine Rescue, is the first solid example we have of her involvement in the Grüssau story, in February 1970. Towards the very end of the same year she was to crop up again, and, at exactly the same time, so was Carleton Smith, after several years' absence from the story. Katowice was then to be openly mentioned.

The first hint of it as a storage place for the missing manuscripts, however, dates from soon after Hordyński's death, and this time the evidence stands up as sound, not another will o'the wisp.

In 1976, a retired music librarian of the Library of Congress in Washington, William Lichtenwanger, read an article which Peter Whitehead had written about his search for the American music magazine, *Notes*. Remembering an encounter from years before, he wrote to Whitehead:

> What I remembered when I saw your article in *Notes* was that in, I think, the late sixties I showed a Polish woman librarian around the Music Division at the Library of Congress. We were in our vault looking at some of our autograph manuscripts and I made (not entirely by accident) a casual reference to the former Berlin autographs that were reported to have gone east and never come back. She, with what I took to be a certain amount of embarrassment, said in effect: 'Some of those manuscripts are stored in my library.' I said 'Do you mean they've been added to your collections?' She said, in effect, 'No, they are merely stored there until we get further orders.' I have no recollection of her name, and not much of the date, but I do remember that 'her' library was in Katowice– which I see by the map looks to be some 40 miles

WNW of Kraków . . . Over the years I have thought of this incident and recounted it to perhaps eight or ten people.

Lichtenwanger seemed to remember that the Katowice library 'was connected with a conservatory or some kind of music institution'. More digging around in Lichtenwanger's memory, and more digging around by him in his files, established that it was the library of the State Higher School for Music in Katowice. As for the year of the lady librarian's visit to Washington, Lichtenwanger said that his 'best guess' was 1968, the year that had begun with Hordyński's death. The implication, surely, is that the music was moved as an immediate response to Hordyński's death, perhaps to distract attention from it by distracting attention from the Jagiellonian Library.

The second Katowice lead came less than two years later, at a time, and against an immediate background, that were especially propitious for new revelations about the Grüssau secret. That is not hindsight: a seasoned searcher after the manuscripts – such as Carleton Smith – would have been able at the time to look around him and realise that conditions had never before been so favourable, and were unlikely to be as good again. Smith had hoped for great things from the 'mood of reconciliation' following the Geneva Summit of 1957, thirteen years before. But that had been nothing compared to the mood of 1970.

It was as though a fisherman who had spent his life trying to catch a particularly exotic and cunning species of rare fish, and expert in its habits and habitat, were to wake up one morning, look at the weather, gaze out over the sea, and just *know* that the day had arrived. All the signs were there, all the omens were right; all the factors were present that could possibly encourage the strange mixture of musical and political priorities which the Grüssau secret had become, to emerge from under its rock and swallow the hook that could haul it into the open.

The year 1970 not only possessed a high significance to the music world and to music-lovers generally, marking as it did the two hundredth anniversary of Beethoven's birth; it was also a year which saw dramatic developments in West Germany's relations with Poland and the eastern bloc as a whole, and political ferment within Poland itself. In a space of a fortnight at the end of the year all three would come to a head almost simultaneously.

In the autumn of the previous year, Willy Brandt's Social Democratic Party had swept to power on Brandt's reconciliatory *Ostpolitik* and *Deutschlandpolitik* ticket. In just over a year, Brandt as Chancellor then succeeded in completely transforming the post-war political map of Europe, incidentally helping to prepare the ground for the politics of détente. The events were profound and manifold, and overtook one another with almost bewildering speed. They began before 1969 was out, with the drafting by East and West Germany of a treaty on the establishment of equal relations. In the summer of 1970 West Germany signed a treaty with the Soviet Union, incorporating West German acknowledgment[1] of the Oder-Neisse Line between Germany and Poland.

The big diplomatic prize of the *Ostpolitik* – because of the territorial question and the war background – was Poland. In October 1970, West Germany signed with Poland a five-year trade agreement granting the most beneficial terms yet extended to a Communist country: Poland was accorded most-favoured-nation status. 'We hope,' said a German representative, 'this treaty will be a sort of inspiration.'

Just over a month later, representatives of the Federal German Republic and the People's Republic of Poland drafted a treaty providing for the 'Normalization of Mutual Relations' between their two countries. Its most important clause was that the Oder-Neisse Line 'shall constitute the western State frontier of the People's Republic of Poland'. On December 7, the German-Polish treaty, one of the most significant historical documents since the Second World War, was signed in Warsaw.

It was the year that Willy Brandt knelt down at Auschwitz, a heady year, politically the equivalent of being swept off one's feet. The importance of the *Ostpolitik*, Brandt had said, was that through it Germans could come to an acceptance of German history in its entirety. In its wake, Gomułka's *Westpolitik*, the anti-Germanism which he had preached for fourteen years as the cornerstone of his foreign policy, looked

[1] According to the 'Zgorzelec formula', stopping just short of full recognition under international law, worked out at the Zgorzelec, or Görlitz, treaty signed by Poland and East Germany in 1950.

pitifully inadequate. It is almost as though the Polish people, after the tension that had surrounded the status of Poland's western border since the war, collapsed in relief, and as they did so their confidence in Gomułka collapsed as well.

The disillusionment had begun back in 1968, with the anti-Zionist-*cum*-anti-Semitic campaign of that year[1], the repression of student demonstrations, and Poland's participation in the invasion of Czechoslovakia. It had been a year of moral disgrace, hysteria, and cultural stagnation. The Communist Party, jittery and brashly lacking in confidence, had 'papered' Polish universities with its own often unsuitable and under-qualified appointees; there had been a clamp-down on the degree of free expression to which Poland had become accustomed, and individual writers – seen by Gomułka as threats – had been criticised by name.

At the same time, Poland's rulers were having to contend with the country's economic stagnation, which was keeping basic foodstuffs and other necessities from the shops and putting queues on the streets, and in 1968 Gomułka launched plans for a national economic break-through. The plans were subsequently revised, and re-launched, again and again, but the break-through failed to materialise.

In his foreign policy, however, Gomułka was having more success. On the evening of December 7, 1970, after the signing of the historic treaty with West Germany, he went on television to announce the triumph to the Polish people. He should have left it at that, and retired in a blaze of glory. But Gomułka saw the treaty as the political sugar coating around the bitter economic pill which he believed it necessary for Poland to swallow. And on December 12, just five days after the signing, the Polish Council of Ministers announced, with no softening-up preamble whatsoever, swingeing price increases on a wide range of products: of just under twenty per cent on flour and meat, and almost a hundred per cent on coffee.

Professor Lissa was not then in Warsaw, but in West Berlin. All over the German-speaking world – in Bonn, Beethoven's birthplace, and in Vienna, where he lived and died – the bicentennial celebrations were proceeding apace, building up to the

---

[1] A campaign tolerated, and to some extent restrained, rather than supported, by Gomułka, whose wife was Jewish.

climax on December 16, two hundred years to the day after the birth. The Professor was in West Berlin to make her own contribution to the festivities, a talk on Beethoven's arrangement of Polish folk-songs which she was to deliver before a meeting of music scholars.

The atmosphere so near to Christmas must have been festive, against the background of the reconciliation with West Germany only a few days before, the Beethoven celebrations, and the fuss that was being made of her, the distinguished foreign visitor. The temptation must have been strong, suddenly to break off her talk and galvanise the gathering of Beethoven scholars with the best Christmas present she could possibly give them; to announce: 'I am happy to be able to say that the Ninth Symphony is safe, as are the Seventh and the third movement of the Eighth, the Piano Concerto No. 3, the late quartets Op. 127 and 130, 131 and 133. Not to mention a number of other items. You have probably been wondering what has happened to them.'

But Professor Lissa did not believe in Christmas and, if the temptation was there, she resisted it. She did not remain silent, however, but discreetly took some scholars aside and told them about the manuscripts. They were in Poland, she said, but alas inaccessible. There were political problems. It was necessary to have patience. Did she repeat the story of the Benedictine Rescue?

A week at most after this very private meeting, Carleton Smith reappeared on the Grüssau trail. This time, he had received a cable from 'a very reliable man working in Poland' – a Polish professor from Breslau 'who is paid for his research work into the whereabouts of the manuscripts by the National Arts Foundation'. I do not believe in the existence of this 'reliable man'. I think that 'he' was Professor Lissa, and that Smith was being confusing on purpose in order to protect his source. The coincidence of the cable from Breslau with Beethoven's birthday, and with the private meeting which we know Professor Lissa to have had in West Berlin, is too much to accept. She, I think, was the 'Professor from Breslau'. It is interesting to note that Smith chose the exact day of Beethoven's two hundredth anniversary to make his new information public.

The information was that the manuscripts were in 'the

191

libraries of Katowice', and Smith, who was in London at the time, told a journalist of the *Daily Telegraph* that he and his aides were 'flying out there on Saturday'. The journalist began his report on an optimistic note, with Smith expressing the cautious hope that the search for the Beethoven manuscripts, worth a million pounds or more on the open market, 'may end soon'.

This, I am convinced, struck exactly the right note, for if Smith had been in touch with Professor Lissa he had made the most important break-through in his long search. The end was tantalisingly near, a 'plane flight to Poland away. But the note of healthy scepticism with which the report ended was also exactly right: 'The fact is that although Dr. Carleton Smith and his colleagues are confident that their search may end soon, they will not know until their visit to Katowice this weekend.'

The weekend was too late. In Poland, after the announcement of the violent price rises, protest demonstrations broke out across the country, to be as violently put down. The protest was concentrated in the northern ports and shipbuilding cities, where, ten years later, the Solidarity free trade union movement would originate. In one of those towns, Gdynia, on the morning of December 17 – the morning after Beethoven's birthday, as the news of Smith's Katowice break-through was published – the Polish militia fired on a peaceful group of shipyard workers. Several dozen are believed to have died in one of the most horrifying incidents of a week of violence which saw several hundred deaths (forty-five is the official Polish figure).

Three days later, on December 20, Gomułka was removed from power. His replacement as First Secretary was a former coalminer from Katowice, the liberal Edward Gierek, whose first act was to revoke the punitive price rises. The workers returned to work. The Polish crisis subsided. The Russians did not invade.

But neither did Carleton Smith come to the end of his search. He was extremely unlucky. He had, at last, been on to something, but as the last moment forces outside his control snatched it from him. It was as though the ideal conditions for hooking the secret had involved the gathering storm, but not the storm itself. At just the wrong moment it broke, and his elusive prey took fright.

The immediate turbulence died down, but conditions in its wake were still too uncertain for Smith's delicate mission. Poland had a new leader. It was necessary, again, to be patient, to wait and see which way the wind was going to blow. Smith would have to wait almost another four years. Whether or not he made his 'plane-flight to Poland that weekend, he had missed the real connection. The Katowice break-through, at least in the short term, proved fruitless.

Only in the spring of 1974 would Smith make the vital flight, his final foray on to the Grüssau trail which he had begun to follow a quarter of a century before. To his own satisfaction, if not to everyone else's, he would accomplish his mission, and return with the most dramatic news of the Grüssau manuscripts to emerge since their disappearance.

CHAPTER TWENTY

The Copernicus Connection

Carleton Smith claimed to have seen the lost music. The story appeared in the *New York Times* of Thursday, April 11, 1974. It was really two stories in one. The base of the whole was that Smith – 'the chairman of the National Arts Foundation based at Vaduz, Liechtenstein' – had been taken by three Poles 'to view the manuscripts "in a safe, well protected, locked-up room" in the vicinity of Kraków'. There 'they opened one crate and let him see one act of Mozart's *Figaro* and a Beethoven quartet'.

We can build a little on this base, but not much. In conversation[1], Smith has told me that he saw into four or five crates, which had been opened for him before he arrived. 'I took out enough material from each box to make sure that what I wanted was there. I saw manuscripts of Mozart and Beethoven: two acts of *Cosi Fan Tutte*[2]; two acts of *Figaro*; *Titus* also; the Piano Concerto No. 3; and a good many of the printed collection. I did not see *The Magic Flute*.' In an article in the *Smithsonian Magazine*, in December 1975, Smith wrote: 'The contents of two cases were shown to me. Holding these old manuscripts in my hands again after 40 years was like meeting one's first love after four decades, only the manuscripts have not aged. They have been carefully cared for and are in good condition.'

Let us call this the first story. The second goes as follows. The find, Smith said, 'was seen as a sensitive political issue because Polish officials have so far denied any knowledge of the existence of the art treasures', and he therefore 'declined to give their exact whereabouts or name the persons in whose custody they are'. He said that 'the persons involved feared

---

[1] On October 28, 1978.
[2] Only the first act of *Cosi* was at Grüssau.

imprisonment for disclosing to him the existence of the treasure. They told him that they needed "political authority" from the Warsaw government before making any public statement'.

Few people except journalists, and often not even they, bother to scrutinise newspaper stories in much detail. But the source of this story was a former journalist, publicist, and 'image builder'; it was told to and written up by a journalist, and printed rather than spiked by an editor. If we analyse its construction as a newspaper story we come up with some illuminating insights.

The most noticeable aspect of the story as a whole is that nowhere does the *New York Times* give it its imprimatur as being the truth. It is all, as it were, in quotation-marks, attributed to Smith. Therefore the *New York Times* did not *necessarily* believe it. The reason for that is not hard to see: at no point does Smith come up with any positive proof that what he is saying is true. The story is presented therefore on a 'take it or leave it' basis.

Why then did the *New York Times* see fit to print it? That, too, is easily explained. Although the story is of the kind that British newsmen label 'iffy', American newsmen label 'a flyer', and the man-in-the-street calls 'fishy', it is, for all that, what newsmen everywhere call 'good copy'. Before analysing the story more closely in the light of that idea of 'good copy', let us retrace the process by which it came to be printed.

Ellen Lentz has been Berlin correspondent of the *New York Times* since 1960, and remembers first meeting Carleton Smith in the sixties, when he was passing through Berlin. In March 1974, she paid a visit to New York, and met him again at the paper's offices. In the first week of April, he turned up again in Berlin, en route for Poland, and told her that on his return he might have a story for her.

Soon afterwards he was back in Berlin, with news of the manuscripts. According to the story as it appeared in the *New York Times*, 'he went to East Berlin after his discovery to encourage East German officials to ask Poland for a return of the treasure.' In East Berlin, he visited the British embassy just down the Unter den Linden from the library. There he spoke to K. H. M. Duke of the embassy, who in February 1975 wrote to Peter Whitehead:

. . . Curiously enough I had a visitor . . . last year – who may be able to help. He is an American named Carleton Smith . . . He had just returned from Poland and was greatly excited because he had located a number of important musical manuscripts.

He was interested in getting advice on press correspondents in West Berlin to whom he might explain his discoveries . . .

P.S. I would be most interested to hear if you discover anything further, as an old friend of mine is interested in the Humboldt Nachlass[1] which formed part of the same batch.

Smith's story did subsequently appear in West German newspapers, but it was published first in the *New York Times*. It appeared as told to Ellen Lentz, and Smith did not confide to her the name of the place where the manuscripts were, nor the names of the people who had shown them to him – but he did vouchsafe one significant piece of information. The manuscripts, he told her, were in the keeping of a 'religious order'. 'The characters,' Ellen Lentz told me[2], 'these monks, took him into the building and showed him the depot.' This information was not for publication, because it would have helped the Warsaw government to identify the guilty parties who had acted without its authority.

We have already taken a good hard look – as Ellen Lentz had not – at the story of the Benedictine Rescue, and at Smith's brush with it way back in 1950. Here we have him mentioning monks again twenty-four years later, just after a visit to Poland, and four years after Professor Lissa spoke to Malcolm Frager. Five years later still, in early 1979, Smith would tell me that Peter Wackernagel's reference to the help he received from 'the gentlemen of the Catholic Church' was 'a crucial phrase'.

We may observe that Smith's version of the involvement of monks in the story, as privately told by him to Ellen Lentz, differs markedly from Professor Lissa's, as told to Malcolm Frager. By 1974, according to Professor Lissa's account, the manuscripts were under the direct 'political authority' of Warsaw, and had been since the mid-sixties. While disagreeing

[1] i.e. bequest.
[2] On October 16, 1978.

with the Professor that monks played the major role in the story that she ascribed to them, we may certainly agree with this part of her account.

So, in telling Ellen Lentz that monks were involved, Carleton Smith was being intentionally misleading. If he saw the music manuscripts, he saw them at the Jagiellonian Library in Kraków, or in one of those 'libraries of Katowice' which he had mentioned four years before; probably the latter, if we are to believe his reference to the location as 'in the vicinity of Kraków'. We have other independent confirmation of this from a letter which a Polish music scholar sent to an Oxford don in the summer of 1972. The manuscripts, he wrote, were in Kraków, then he added the qualification that, if they were not in Kraków itself, they were in the area: more evidence that the music was moved after Hordyński's suicide. The same letter went on to say that the fate of the manuscripts would be decided *unilaterally*, and that the matter was being considered at a very high level. This confirms that they were, in 1972, directly under Warsaw's political authority.

Was the mention of monks, then, a smokescreen laid down by Smith to protect those who had risked their necks to help him? Surely not, because if Smith had been concerned with protecting his helpers *he would not have told the story to a newspaper*. In the *New York Times* it was freely available to all and sundry, including the Warsaw government from whose vengeance Smith was so anxious to protect people that he would name no names. But if the manuscripts were under Warsaw's political authority, as Smith implies, and as we know they were, then Warsaw knew where they were and the names of 'those persons in whose custody they are'. If the music was scattered in several places, Smith's reference to 'one act of *Figaro* and a Beethoven quartet' would have enabled Warsaw to pick the right one. If Smith's helpers *had* risked their necks, then Smith had said too much simply by saying that he had seen the manuscripts and – the very thing that his story emphasises that he did *not* do – had betrayed them.

If Smith was not betraying a confidence, he was lying, and if he was not lying, he was betraying. Smith's background gives us no grounds to think of him as a betrayer of confidences; on the contrary, there is plenty of evidence of him as the soul of discretion, well able to keep a secret. The last chapter provides an example: not only would Smith not name the 'Professor from Breslau', but there is reason to believe that he invented 'him' in order to protect Professor Lissa. If he suddenly decided to be indiscreet in 1974, we must face the question of why he did not go the whole hog and name names, instead of elaborately refusing to do so, as he has refused ever since.

Smith's career, on the other hand, does provide evidence of a less than literal respect for fact. There is the story of Smith in his nightcap, sleeping with Bach, or Smith in top hat, at Ambassador Dodd's credentials ceremony, both dating from before the Second World War; there is his claim that the National Arts Foundation, after the war, 'verified the existence' of 10,500 music manuscripts. To those, I suggest, we add his story of 1974 that the people who helped him to see the manuscripts 'feared imprisonment for disclosing to him the existence of the treasure' without the 'political authority' of Warsaw.

If Smith was not betraying confidences by telling the story to a newspaper, then he must have known, or at least must have *believed*, that when he was shown the manuscripts this was not *without* the authority of Warsaw, as he stresses in his story, but ultimately *with* such authority.

If he believed this, why did he not say so? Because he had already promised, before seeing the manuscripts, that a condition of his doing so was that the story would be unattributable – he would name no names. The obligation which Smith had to honour, and which explains the factual gaps in his story, was not to people acting in defiance of Warsaw's authority, but to Warsaw itself.

Now, another searcher, if he had seen the manuscripts in 1974, and verified their existence to himself, might have been satisfied with that. But Smith was not that kind of man. It was not enough for him to know, and to have been the first, he had to let the world know as well. If the Warsaw government allowed him to see the manuscripts on certain conditions, and if Smith abided by them, then he was not precluded from publishing the story in a newspaper. A man with Smith's 'noisy' record cannot have been expected to keep to himself the information that he had at last seen the manuscripts for which he had been searching since he was forty years old.

The trouble was that that was about all he *could* say, if he was to honour his obligation; and, if he was to say only that, and nothing else, he would be unlikely to get the story into print. He had experienced something marvellous, which was worth repeating as widely as possible, but if he was to repeat it he would in effect be acting as the channel for a controlled leak from Warsaw. Not only was he obliged to give no hint of that, any such hint would have been enough to scare off any self-respecting journalist or editor. Western newspapers do not like to act as publicity sheets, no questions asked, for eastern bloc governments.

With a little ingenuity, however, the problem could be solved. A compromise was needed. A little judicious bending of the strict journalistic truth, a little Communist knocking copy – slightly damaging to Warsaw, but without breaking any of the conditions – could provide a colourful and water-tight rationale for the factual gaps, neutralise any suggestion that he might be acting as Warsaw's errand boy, and achieve the overriding aim of telling the world the wonderful news: the music had survived, and was safe, he, Carleton Smith, had seen it with his own eyes and held it in his own hands.

In his hotel in Berlin, he picked up the telephone and dialled Ellen Lentz . . .

This may seem outrageous, but at least I have accepted the core of Smith's story as true: his claim that he actually saw the music. In 1974, there were those who did not believe even that. I am saying only that Smith told an untruth in order to get a truth into print. By the other interpretation, Smith's first story was untrue, as well as his second. By an apparent paradox, I am vindicating Carleton Smith, because I believe that the ingenuity of the second story was directly related to the truth-fulness of the first. Smith *was* telling the truth when he ended his search in 1974 with the same claim he had truthfully made when he started it: 'When I told Truman that I had had these manuscripts in my hands . . .'

The difference was that Truman had believed him. For what I am proposing was not, and is not, generally accepted among those who know the story of Smith's 1974 claim. Those who were steeped in the Grüssau story were inclined then to dismiss it as another antic. Some of the scepticism made its way into print. For example, the *Christian Science Monitor* of December 18, 1975:

Some musicologists believe the . . . missing manuscripts are somewhere in Poland, taken there clandestinely . . . Dr. Smith says he knows for a fact that (they are) in Poland; he says he has seen the manuscripts there and they are still in good shape, despite repeated denials by the Polish government of any knowledge of the manuscripts.
Other U.S. music historians are skeptical of Dr. Smith's statement . . .

Individual sceptics were mentioned by name in an article by Peter Whitehead for *Notes* in 1976:

. . . in February 1975, I was able to visit Berlin and to discuss with the Directors of the Music Departments in both East and West Berlin the question of the lost Grüssau manuscripts and in particular the alleged discovery made by Mr. Smith. Both Dr. Karl-Heinz Köhler and Dr. Rudolf Elvers expressed doubts about this 'find' . . .

This was understandable, given the questionable nature of the claim itself, and, according to the sceptics, the questionable quarter from which it came. But I believe that the scepticism – while stemming from a professed 'scientific' objectivity – was in fact grounded in an essential misunderstanding of Smith. Nothing in his background, and nothing in the background of his search, justifies the assumption that he concocted stories wholesale. The stories of bedtime with Bach, his presence at Ambassador Dodd's ceremony, or the National Arts Foundation's sterling services as a 'verifier', were not inventions so much as elaborations which took off from a platform of truth. In the sober Puritan weave of 'the truth, the whole truth, and nothing but the truth', one could say, he embroidered colourful, Catholic *variations* upon the truth.
As for his search, it is true that in 1950 and 1957 he jumped the gun, and announced, in 1950, that the music had been 'rediscovered', and in 1957 the return of the manuscripts to Berlin and their imminent return to the world of scholarship. But these announcements were faults, not of integrity, but of patience. Races have false starts, but searches have false finishes, and one can assume that Smith was in the search at least partly for his own glory. He wanted to be the first to find,

and that was one reason for the scepticism when, in 1974, he declared that he *was* first. It was all too neat, too predictable, and too insubstantial.

In 1950 and 1957 Smith had been like an athlete who believed himself to be running the mile when in fact he was running the marathon. Imagining that he was breasting the tape, he had announced the end of the race (the search); but in each case he had picked himself up and continued. After 1974 he stopped searching and consistently behaved as if, for him, the search was over. If he was not telling the truth, then he had dropped out of the race by the simple expedient of declaring himself the winner. But, if he did decide on that expedient, why did he wait twenty-five years to do so?

The sceptics have also to explain the gradual 'warmness' of Smith's search from his Wrocław theory of 1965, to his Katowice break-through of 1970 – a warmness which, we have seen, ties in very well with developments inside Poland. His claim of 1974 not only seems a natural development of his search, but, when we set it in the context of the previous two chapters, a logical development of the new Polish policy towards the manuscripts. Through Smith, scholars abroad were being reassured, indirectly, that the manuscripts had survived, in such a way that Warsaw could pull back if necessary. Warsaw was taking the temperature of the deep end into which it was preparing to dive. And what a wonderfully ambiguous ambassador it had in Smith! Viewed in this way, the questionable nature of Smith's claim to have seen the manuscripts was engineered by the conditions under which he was permitted to see them, and the scepticism with which his claim was received was *anticipated*. It was all part of the process of 'breaking things gently'; with the gentleness of a dove. Not even Smith need have been told in so many words what the position was. It could have been broken gently to him too, quietly intimated, that if he were to serve Warsaw's purposes in this affair he would be advancing the interests of the manuscripts at the same time: by lifting the veil a little on this occasion, he would hasten the day when the veil would be lifted completely. He must have believed that Warsaw was behind this 'semi-official revelation', and must have believed that it was right to pass it on obliquely, on Warsaw's conditions. For my part, I do not believe that he would have agreed to act as a broker on these terms unless – as he claimed – he was allowed to see the manuscripts for himself.

So in defending Smith against an outrageous accusation – that he was lying when he said that he had seen the long-lost music of Grüssau – I advance a slightly less outrageous proposition: that he was lying in his outline of the *basis* on which he saw the music. Like Professor Lissa's story, his was true, and was not true. Evidence to support a position of qualified scepticism can be found not only in the Polish new policy as implemented by Professor Lissa, but in the background to Smith's search between 1970 and 1974, developments which had their roots in the origin of the whole story – the war, and the period of Polish revindication just after it.

*

I first heard of Karol Estreicher in July 1977, from the then British ambassador to Poland, Norman Reddaway. I was at the British embassy in Warsaw.

'He's the man who brought back the Kraków altarpiece,' said Mr. Reddaway. 'You should look him up when you're in Kraków.' He took down a copy of *International Who's Who*, and his secretary made a photocopy of the entry on Estreicher.

Half an hour later, I was round the corner at the Polish government press bureau, Interpress. There I was told that arrangements had been made for me to go to Kraków, and that I had an appointment there with – to my astonishment – Karol Estreicher.

The following Monday I flew to Kraków, and turned up on the Tuesday at the Collegium Maius, the fifteenth-century university building which was the home of the Jagiellonian Library until World War II. It has since housed the University Museum and the Institute of Art History.

Professor Estreicher was expecting me in a medieval office up a short flight of stairs overlooking the central courtyard. I was met by a short, barrel-chested bearhug of a man, who did not conceal his annoyance that I was late. It quickly evaporated, however, as he smiled and we shook hands. His eyes were bright and shrewd. He was wearing a tweed jacket of some greyish mix, and he spoke the English he had learned in London during the war, with a thick accent. I apologised for my lack of Polish, and told him how beautiful I had found the Veit

202

Stoss altarpiece, which I had seen in Our Lady's Church earlier that day.

The rest of our conversation was mainly about the war, and very interesting it was; but none of it was as illuminating as something that occurred in a pause halfway through. He offered to show me some of the collections that were kept in the Collegium Maius, and we walked from the medieval office down narrow corridors to storerooms with bare wooden floors. In one he showed me a painting of Sir Thomas More; in another, a whole gallery of paintings that had been cut from their frames by the Germans. All had been lovingly repaired. The Poles are world-renowned as restorers, but for all their skill they had been unable to restore these to exactly their former state: the cuts of the knives and bayonets still showed under a thick scar-tissue of paint.

From there we moved down another corridor, and from behind me I heard Professor Estreicher call that I was going too fast, there was something he wanted to show me. I turned. He had stopped in front of an alcove, roped off from the corridor. Inside it, there was the gleam of brass and bronze. They were scientific instruments – astrolabes, globes, and a combined compass and sundial called a torquetum, which was used in astrology. Among them was an Arabian astrolabe dated 1054, a celestial globe dated 1480, one of the largest to survive from the Middle Ages, and the Gold Jagiellonian Globe of about 1510. This was an object of great historical interest – showing as it did the newly-discovered continent of America – and great beauty in its own right: inside the globe there was a clock mechanism which turned the world to indicate hours, days, months, and the position of the sun. It was considered the most valuable object in the Jagiellonian's collections, even if, after five hundred years, the globe turned in a day of twenty-six hours.

Professor Estreicher was saying all this, and I was listening, but my mind was on something else. I was thinking that the medieval university town of Kraków had been especially famous for the so-called 'Black Arts', and, related to them through astrology, the study of mathematics and astronomy. Dr. Faustus was reputed to have studied at the Jagiellonian University, and the discoverer of the great truth that the earth dances attendance on the sun, and not vice versa, was known to have studied there. Nicholas Copernicus, the father of modern astronomy, had been at the Jagiellonian from 1491 to 1495.

Most of the instruments before me in the alcove would have been in use when Copernicus was a student, for the demonstration of truths which he would later disprove. Copernicus himself would have handled those finely-tooled pieces of brass and bronze. Beside me, Professor Estreicher was saying that most of the instruments had belonged to Martin Bylica, a wealthy professor of the Jagiellonian, who later worked in Hungary. On his death, he willed his collection to the university, and on the day the instruments arrived the Rector cancelled all classes. That was in 1491, and Copernicus, then in his first year, was one of those who stood in awe before the instruments as they were unpacked.

This started me off on another train of thought. Back in December 1975, in his article in the *Smithsonian Magazine*, Carleton Smith had given an outline of the means by which he had eventually been able to see the lost music manuscripts. 'In the spring of 1974,' he had written, 'some Polish associates told me that if I went to Poland and remained there for several weeks, they would arrange for me to inspect the manuscripts – but only on the condition that I would not say where they were or who had shown them to me. After endless preliminaries and being passed from one intermediary to the next, I was taken to the place where the manuscripts are kept.'

This gave a more detailed – but still vague – account of the cloak-and-dagger 'second story'. It shows Smith having to undergo 'endless preliminaries', passed from one cautious intermediary to another along an obscure chain of command: a kind of initiation ceremony. By the end of it, Smith had been fully primed and his trustworthiness fully tested. At the same time, the 'chain of command' had been long enough for Smith to be able to reconstruct it only with difficulty, and only with difficulty decide on the status and allegiance of this or that intermediary. He was in a foreign country, among strangers.

Still, Smith could take confidence from his knowledge of the first link in the chain. That was the vital clue, and in December 1975 – the same month as his *Smithsonian Magazine* article, and the month I first met him – Smith had said something to me that seemed a possible pointer to that clue. Here it is, complete with pauses: 'I was told by some great friends . . . It came about through a visit to America of the . . . of Copernicus's memorabilia and things, and through the contacts we made then we finally were told that . . .' I interrupted to ask the date of the American visit, and Smith in his reply threw in the *reason* for the visit: 'Copernicus's anniversary was five years ago or four years ago . . . And we found friends and people whose confidence we got, and finally, on the condition . . .'

Standing in front of the alcove in the Collegium Maius in Kraków, I was thinking back to Smith's reference to 'Copernicus's anniversary', and to the American visit of 'Copernicus's memorabilia and things'. Weren't some of those 'memorabilia' staring me in the face?

The result was that, with new eyes, I stared into the face of Professor Estreicher. Back in the medieval office, I asked him – had he ever met Carleton Smith? He asked me to repeat the name; I did, and he shook his head. We went on talking about the war.

*

Copernicus was born in 1473 and died in 1543. His great work *De Revolutionibus Orbium Coelestium* was published in the same year. Neither date squared with the varied years Smith had given as the one in which he picked up the first 'link in the chain' – 1974, in his *Smithsonian Magazine* article, and 1970 or '71 in his interview with me. However, the year before Smith's secret meeting in Poland – 1973 – would have been the five hundredth anniversary of Copernicus's birth, worthy indeed of celebration.

Like the Beethoven celebrations of three years earlier, the Copernicus anniversary of 1973 saw a unique and benign convergence of the currents of politics and scholarship. It was celebrated all over the world, by many countries with special postage stamps; but nowhere more than in Poland, where he was born and educated, and the United States. The U.S. space programme was setting out, as Copernicus had done, to plumb the secrets of the heavens. Only four years before, Americans had landed on the moon; that very year, Skylab was orbiting the earth: the earth that Copernicus had 'moved'. As the old Polish adage has it: 'He stopped the sun, and moved the earth/The Polish people gave him birth.' The parallel was drawn by the Polish ambassador to the United States. 'Today, in the era of space flights,' he said, 'Copernicus stands before us in a new light of scientific fame.' In the American press coverage, Copernicus was referred to as 'The Father of Space Exploration.' In Warsaw, the Polish government proclaimed 1973 as 'Polish Science Year'; the Copernicus anniversary was its highlight. Hundreds of astronomers gathered in Torun, the birthplace of Copernicus, to compare theories on the study of the universe.

As well as a source of Polish pride, the anniversary was an opening for the celebration of the special relationship between Poland and the United States, with its huge Polish immigrant population. Détente was in good repair: only the year before, President Nixon had visited Poland, and the joint communiqué had included a reference to the Copernicus anniversary and the need for more scientific co-operation between Poland and the United States. American dollars poured into Poland to finance a new Copernicus Centre in Warsaw.

A wealthy Polish-American, Edward J. Piszek, chairman of Mrs. Paul's Frozen Foods, Inc., of Philadelphia, set up 'The Copernicus Society of America' to promote the anniversary. The society set out to make it an occasion that could be celebrated by scientist, scholar, and common man alike. It imported a shipload of books on Copernicus; backed a Copernicus film; promoted competitions in schools. Almost half a million 'Copernicus' lapel badges were also shipped in from Poland. One American columnist commented: 'Have a care with those Polish jokes, fellows. It's not every man who can boast that he put the sun in its place!'

The Copernicus Society was also involved in the two main scientific celebrations: an international symposium on 'The Nature of Scientific Discovery' in the last week of April, and a travelling exhibition of those same scientific instruments – globes, astrolabes, and torquetum – that I saw in the alcove in Kraków. It was their first ever showing outside Poland, and travelling with them were the maces of the Jagiellonian University, on which, in 1491, Copernicus had sworn allegiance.

The Smithsonian Institution in Washington, with the National Academy of Sciences, was joint organiser of the symposium. It was also the venue for the first American showing, in the second week of April, of the exhibition of scientific instruments. Carleton Smith is listed as a consultant to the

Secretary of the Smithsonian Institution, and it was in the *Smithsonian Magazine* that he chose to publish his skeleton account of the background to his secret meeting of 1974 – a background which he also dated to 1974.

It was there, in Washington, that Smith the veteran seeker met Estreicher the veteran hider. Their handshake was the first link in the chain along which Smith was to feel his way to the lost music. The noisy self-appointed ambassador who had been 'creating hell' about the manuscripts for twenty-four years met the man who, all these years and more, had been sitting on his knowledge of the 'several small cases' found in Silesia. The mystery that had hidden met the mystery that had sought. The champion of Poland's interests met the champion of music's. The two pasts, both rooted in the war – the past of concealment, and the past of search – intersected in the present: Washington, April 1973.

In his introduction to the book which he edited on the Washington symposium, the astronomer Owen Gingerich says of the 'special loan exhibition of rare scientific instruments from the Collegium Maius' that it was 'arranged through the co-operation of Professor Karol Estreicher'. But Estreicher also travelled with the instruments to the United States – almost exactly thirty years after his crucial wartime visit – and with them around the country.

By the middle of June they were in Milwaukee, which has one of the largest Polish communities in the United States. The *Milwaukee Journal* published a picture of Estreicher unpacking the exhibits, which were touring America 'in a special car provided by Edward Piszek'. Asked to describe the precautions that were being taken for their safety, Estreicher refused. 'A doctor does not tell you how he cures a patient,' he said. 'A museum director does not like to tell about precautions. I assure you everything that can be done is done. We travelled, and nothing happened. I touch wood.'

In October 1978 – almost three years after first telling me about the Copernicus anniversary – Carleton Smith filled in a little more of the background. He had evidently forgotten his reference of three years before. 'We got these people to the United States,' he said, 'on another mission, nothing to do with the manuscripts or with music, to do with the anniversary of a great Pole. *These people were sent to look after the exhibi-*

tions[1]. They are people of great responsibility in whom I had confidence – in whom the present Communist leaders have great confidence – whom I had befriended.'

Smith uses the plural form, but, if we look at the programme of the Copernicus anniversary in America, there was not only no other exhibition of Copernican 'memorabilia', there was no other which involved Poles visiting the United States: only the exhibition of instruments, which was in the sole charge of Professor Estreicher. And the Professor, we have already established, was one of the very first to know the secret of the manuscripts.

In February 1979, I suggested to Carleton Smith that his contact had been Karol Estreicher. 'Then print that,' he said, 'but loyalty makes it impossible for me to say either yes or no. I have promised,' he continued, 'that as long as I live I will not say where the manuscripts are and who showed them to me.'

When I mentioned Estreicher's connection with the Copernicus anniversary, Smith replied, very slowly, 'Then I did meet him.' I asked him where, and he said, 'Kraków.' I suggested Washington, and he said, 'Maybe. I don't know.'

Smith remembered meeting Estreicher, who had not remembered meeting Smith; yet Smith is nothing if not memorable. Two days later, I asked Smith how inflammatory the information was. 'Very, I should think,' was his reply.

A few days after that I received a letter from him. 'Now I think it only fair to tell you,' he wrote, 'that the "lead" you guessed . . . is not the correct one . . . I wish only that I were free to tell you all, but I am not.' There *were* occasions, it seemed, when he was prepared to say no.

The point need not be laboured. Carleton Smith's contact in America was Karol Estreicher, the old war horse and champion of 'the straight way' to Polish revindication. Since Hordyński's suicide, and the watershed of 1965-68 (when he had seen Smith's article in the *Book Collector*), the man whose ideas had shaped the old policy under which the Grüssau manuscripts were taken hostage had become a practitioner of the new policy. Since the replacement of the hawklike Gomułka by the dovelike Gierek, the doves had won, and the

[1]Author's italics.

208

hawks, reluctant realists, had been required to go along with them.

The olive branch looked out of place in a hooked beak, and Smith, while hardly daring to believe his luck, must also have wondered what was going on. As he passed from link to link of the chain which originated with Estreicher, however, he must have begun to understand. '*People of great responsibility*,' he told me, 'in whom I had confidence – *in whom the present Communist leaders have great confidence. . .*' Warsaw, for its own purposes, wanted to lift the veil a fraction; officialdom wanted to be semi-official, a government wanted to be quasi-governmental. Well, if he could achieve the mission on which he had first set out – 'to verify the existence of all the autograph manuscripts of the great German composers, from Bach to Brahms' – he would go along.

Because he believed this, he felt that it was safe to tell the story, embroidered a little in the telling. So, by a strange marriage, hide found common cause with seek, on strict conditions. If Estreicher the hider would show certain things, then Smith the seeker would hide certain things.

*

Other evidence shows that Carleton Smith was in possession of vital information about the lost music before he went to Poland and actually saw the manuscripts for himself. In the first week of March 1974 – more than a month before his Polish visit – the chief of the New York Public Library's Music Division took a telephone call and scribbled a note: 'Manuscripts in Poland from East Berlin, 90-80-100 items, Jan. or July 1976.' A few days later Thor Wood of the library wrote to Carleton Smith: 'Frank Campbell has told me of your tantalising idea of perhaps exhibiting the lost manuscripts from the Berlin library here in New York . . . Mr. Campbell and I are both intrigued and curious to know how this could possibly happen.' Smith did not satisfy their curiosity, but asked Wood to write to him at the Austrian embassy in London, where he was staying, with answers to two questions of his own: '(1) How many manuscripts could you display? (2) When in 1975 or 1976 would you have time in your schedule?'

The correspondence and telephone calls continued after Smith's trip to Poland to see the manuscripts, and then, Thor Wood remembers, about the middle of May there was a subtle changing of the subject. 'As nearly as I can understand it,' says Wood, 'he began talking about manuscripts in Poland and then unobtrusively switched to those which had been and are in East Berlin (in my notes on a conversation of May 13, 1974, I have references to the first two acts of *Figaro*, the St. Matthew Passion, Schubert's 'Heidenröslein', Beethoven conversation books).' The correspondence collapsed soon after that. The lost Grüssau music did not come to the United States, as Smith —perhaps over-confidently, perhaps with reason – had hoped; but original scores from the East Berlin library did cross the Atlantic for a while, in the American Bicentennial year of 1976. Smith had been hoping for a great coup, but had to rest content with a lesser one.

This exchange with the New York Public Library is important because it shows that Smith was firmly in possession of the essential information – that the manuscripts had survived, and were in Poland – before he had his secret preview 'in the vicinity of Kraków'. He was even thinking in terms of an American exhibition of up to a hundred of the manuscripts. He saw the enterprise, therefore, as one of some solidity, and continued so to think of it for about a month after visiting Poland. This clinches my argument. Smith may have been able to see the manuscripts in Poland in defiance of the 'political authority' of Warsaw, but how, without access to that authority, would he have been able to think in terms of staging an exhibition of them outside Poland, in the United States? This shows clearly enough the allegiance of Smith's contacts, who led him on, then put him off.

The importance of the Copernicus Connection is not so much the light it sheds on Carleton Smith. It is the insights it affords into the subtle diplomacy through which the Poles were seeking to resolve the dilemma of the manuscripts. That diplomacy was very skilful indeed, calculated to perfection. Every move seems brilliantly stage-managed – right down to the scepticism with which Smith's claim was received. The process lasted almost exactly a year – from Smith's meeting with Estreicher in Washington, to the moment in Berlin when he lifted his telephone to speak to Ellen Lentz. As in a dance, we can almost see the interests of the hider merging with those of the seeker – the gathered past moving towards its resolution in the present. It is as though the Polish State wanted to force its own hand of court cards and aces – the manuscripts it had palmed eight years before. There was one final stage in the process, before the Grüssau mystery could at last come out into the open.

CHAPTER TWENTY-ONE

Three Red Boxes

By the spring of 1974, Peter Whitehead had been searching for the lost picture of *Piquitinga* for three years, and was no nearer discovering whether the little Brazilian fish was a herring or an anchovy. All he had to show for his labours was a large file labelled 'Grüssau'. It bulged, its fatness a testament to his failure.

The next and final phase of the search returns to where we began – with a stubborn man trying to fit the right name to the right fish. Peter Whitehead was collaterally related to the late Basil Rathbone, the actor most famous for his film portrayals of Sherlock Holmes. But he was finding the going far from 'elementary', and beginning to feel more like Dr. Watson than the great detective. He had begun his search by writing to the Polish libraries – in Warsaw, Wrocław, and elsewhere, including the Jagiellonian in Kraków. Not one replied. In desperation he turned to a Polish zoologist he had met once at a conference: 'Please forgive me for troubling you, but you are the only person I know in Poland.' He asked her to explore the possiblity that the manuscripts had been secreted in a Silesian salt-mine.

It is interesting that each of the searches had something of the national character of the person pursuing it. Smith's was a flamboyant piece of showmanship; Henrich's was methodical and tightly argued; Whitehead's, by the same token, was extremely English. There was an element of haphazard eccentricity to it, not suprising given his background. Born in Kenya, he entered the world just fifteen minutes too late to inherit the family baronetcy (motto: 'By Virtue And By Industry'). It went instead to his first-born twin brother. When he was seven, his parents divorced, and he was sent to school in England. He attended a good English public school, and Cambridge. His young manhood was rebellious: he married an Irish revolutionary firebrand, several years older than himself. White-head's father threatened to cut him off from the family fortune. He went back to Kenya, where he first 'got into fish', or rather, oysters and crabs, floating about the mangrove swamps, like a true Victorian naturalist, with net and collecting jars. It was in the swamps, perhaps, that he picked up his habit of referring to cold, wet, scaly and crawly creatures almost affectionately as 'little fellows'.

Whitehead brought something of this adventurous eccentricity to his search, but also, like a good Englishman and cricketer, he remembered to 'keep his eye on the ball'. *Piquitinga* was the point of his search, and no amount of Beethoven and Mozart was going to let him forget it. 'I am looking only for the six *Libri Picturati*,' he told his Polish correspondent in 1972. As typically English was his disdain of the political background, or at least his attitude that, if the world was not one great big Parliamentary democracy, then it jolly well ought to be. 'Of course this affair is in part a *political* one,' he wrote to Poland, adding, 'I do not care about the political arguments.' In August 1972, he wrote to Hermann Knaus of the West Berlin library, 'Why are the manuscripts hidden? This does not help anyone – scholar or politician.'

With no idea that he was following in the footsteps of searchers before him, Whitehead explored the Russian option. Two letters which arrived to enrich his file in June 1972 both raised the possibility. First, Knaus wrote that just after the war the manuscripts 'fell into the hands of the occupation army, first Russian, then Polish'. Soon afterwards, a letter came from Poland 'I have little hope that you will be able to find, here among us in Poland, the books you are searching for . . . In my opinion it is more likely that they are in Russia.' His correspondent had by then exhausted the possibilities of the Silesian salt-mine idea. Whitehead replied: 'You are perhaps right. The manuscripts may be in Russia. If this is true, then they must be in Leningrad (all manuscripts pre-1800 are there; post-1800 in Moscow archives).'

His next step was to get in touch with Edgar Breitenbach, a former member of the wartime Monuments, Fine Arts, and Archives Division of the U.S. Army. 'It occurred to me,' he wrote, 'that you might happen to know if there were Russian opposite numbers to yourself who could be contacted, even at this late stage. Or else, what more can I do? There must be other avenues. I have taken steps to stir up the Polish librarians again, but what if this material went westwards? I *assume* that the lorries that collected it were Russian, but what if they were German?' Breitenbach replied early in 1973: 'I am afraid I can add nothing . . . The strange attitude of the Polish librarians seems to indicate that the books survived the war, and the Poles are unwilling to return them. Any official steps, such as diplomatic channels or trying to persuade the Russians to intervene on your behalf would, in my opinion, get you nowhere. Sometimes personal contacts are helpful . . . However, the matter may well be fraught with political pitfalls.'

There in outline is the progress he had made by April 1974. Small wonder that, on the evening of the 23rd, he was something less than his usual cheerful self. In the kitchen of their Berkshire home, Greta (his second wife) was doing the washing-up. The children were watching television. Whitehead was in his study, catching up on some clupeoid correspondence; the herring catch in Icelandic waters, a rare anchovy specimen sent from Vienna.

He went outside and rolled himself a cigarette. In the English garden, Central Europe seemed more than a world away, and his search for the manuscripts worse than hopeless. He felt alone and tired, and had a mind to abandon his *Piquitinga* problem there and then. Herring or anchovy – the world could get by.

He felt much as Carleton Smith must have felt in the mid-fifties – looking without knowing where to look, and seeing no end to his search. He would have felt better had he so much as heard of Carleton Smith, and known that he was not searching in a vacuum. If he could have set his personal quest in the context of the search as a whole since the war, he would perhaps have seen that by beginning it in 1971 he could not have begun at a better time. The position overall had never been more hopeful than at that moment when he felt most dispirited.

Really, his proper search was just about to begin, in as much time as it takes to finish a cigarette, stub it out, and walk back across one's lawn to the kitchen, early on a spring evening in Berkshire. In the kitchen, his wife was drying the last dish, and turning to him with a smile. 'The B.B.C.'s just broadcast something,' she said, 'about those blessed manuscripts of yours.'

One way to describe Whitehead's response is to say that, if he had worn a monocle, it would have fallen out. Watson-like, he uttered the one word 'No!' as his wife hurriedly explained that she had been listening to the radio, but with only half an ear, so she hadn't caught everything. But she had heard the name 'Grüssau', and the mention of manuscripts, musical ones, no mention of a fish. An American had found them.

Whitehead's house is in a quiet country village where at that time of day even a passing car is an event, but the noisy Dr. Carleton Smith had managed to reach that far, and break the silence. So Grüssau was not so remote, in time and space, and he was not alone after all. It was the most encouraging news he had heard since his letters to East and West Berlin three years before. It put new heart and hope into his search.

Now, far from abandoning the *Piquitinga* trail, he began to pursue it with new vigour. From now on, his correspondence would snowball. His first letter was to Smith, sent in the hope that they could pool their information and merge their searches, but Smith, to his surrprise, turned out to be as reticent as any Polish librarian. He managed to get him on the telephone, but all he would tell Whitehead was that he was 'grateful, perhaps more than you can realise, for your letter'. Correction: he *was* alone. The end of Smith's search was not his. He would have to pursue the trail to his own version of its end.

After the Russian option, it was the Benedictine Rescue. He passed on the news of Smith's secret preview to his Polish correspondent, and she replied: 'The Berlin manuscripts can only have been hidden in a Benedictine *convent*. Father Lutterotti was in charge of archives and left after the war taking with him cases of the most valuable documents, which, one isn't sure.' She gave the monastery of Tyniec as one of the places between which the remainder had been shared, and Whitehead, seeing Tyniec to be 'in the vicinity of Kraków', guessed that it might have been the scene of Smith's preview. The Polish letter appears genuinely to confuse the monastery's own archive with the Berlin manuscripts, but from then on the confusion became Whitehead's as well. He passed on to Hermann Knaus the news that Father Lutterotti 'took with him some boxes of the most valuable manuscripts', then enquired at Tyniec, to no result. As we have seen, Father Michalski later disabused him of the idea that Tyniec might be the place.

More difficult to weigh up was a bad-tempered reply which he received from the Manuscript Department of the Jagiellonian Library. Jan Pirożyński deplored Whitehead's 'poor Polish' and, in what seemed a wilful misunderstanding, took his enquiry about the original *Libri Picturati* to be instead about the printed *A Natural History of Brazil*; yes, he said, the Jagiellonian had it.

By then – the summer of 1974 – the burden of knowledge that Hordyński had to carry was being borne by a number of Polish scholars, including Pirożyński, and one way out of the embarrassment was to refer, like Pirożyński, to the catalogues. In the same month, the Polish National Library in Warsaw told Whitehead: 'None of the manuscripts mentioned in your letter . . . is listed in Polish catalogues.' The East Berlin Library was meanwhile keeping up its side of the masquerade. The Keeper of Manuscripts, Hans-Erich Teitge, wrote to Whitehead about this time: 'I do not know where Carleton Smith got his information. It is not known to us, and we have assumed that the material evacuated to Grüssau was lost during the war.' It was the old pretence that had served for thirty years, but which was now beginning to wear thin – as thin as the patience of the Polish scholars.

Pirożyński's, for example, had worn thinner still by the end of 1975, when Whitehead wrote to the Jagiellonian on behalf of the ally he had enlisted in his search. This was a German-born conductor and scholar, Hans-Hubert Schönzeler, a specialist on Bruckner. In 1972, Schönzeler had heard from two confidential sources that there existed sketches for the final (fourth) movement of Bruckner's Ninth Symphony. (Bruckner had been writing the Ninth, which is dedicated to God, right up to the day of his death in 1896.) One of Schönzeler's sources had seen some sketches in Berlin before the war, and had intended working on them – then he was called up, and the sketches were evacuated, he was sure, to Grüssau; the other knew of the sketches, and had heard, soon before Schönzeler spoke to him, that they might be in Poland. Whitehead wrote to Pirożyński: 'If you see some boxes in a storeroom tell me how Bruckner sketched the end of his 9th symphony!'

Pirożyński's reply was apoplectic: 'It is rather absolutely improbable for me, even being full of good intentions, to describe for you e.g. the finale of the IXth symphony by Bruckner . . .'

The Polish scholars were being ground between an upper millstone – the demands made on them by foreign scholars in persistent enquiries like Whitehead's – and a nether – the stubborn intransigence of their government. Over the year ending late in 1976 the tension was tuned to its highest pitch, as knowledge of the Polish whereabouts of the manuscripts spread further afield than ever, and as, at the same time, the Polish authorities screwed the lid down even tighter. Seeing that year in retrospect and in context, one realises that the breaking point was being reached.

Late in 1974, the West German Christian Democrat member of the Bundestag, Lorenz Niegel, tabled a written question. 'To what extent,' he wondered, 'has the Federal Republic co-financed the "Baroque" exhibition in Warsaw, although the Federal Republic is aware that after the war the People's Republic of Poland appropriated in Grüssau several crates of national cultural property belonging to the Berlin State Library, and has refused the return of these even to the German Democratic Republic?'

The question was indicative of a feeling that the Federal Republic was allowing itself to be crippled by war guilt, and in failing to be assertive enough was losing the political advantage to East Germany. Towards the very end of 1974, the President of the Bundestag, Anne-Marie Renger, visited Poland but failed to raise the question of the missing manuscripts. This came in for some criticism from the *Kölner Rundschau*, which, in an article headlined 'Poland Guards the Treasure of Grüssau', wondered whether the Federal Republic was not being too passive and circumspect; The G.D.R., it said, staked its claims loudly and clearly. The article all but urges that West Germany should actively try to do a deal with the Poles, who are assumed to be keeping the Grüssau treasure as a 'political trading object'[1].

The explicitness of this article – in the summer of 1975 – was matched by the open and confident reference by the music

[1] But, even at this late stage, the article does not discount the possibility that the convoy may have been Russian.

critic of the *New Yorker*, Andrew Porter, in an article that December, to the 'Polish hiding place' of the manuscripts. Like cobwebs, the brackets and question-mark were blown away from Landon's guess of twenty years before. Yet, only a month later, the Poles attempted to reinstate the brackets. In January 1976, after a long enquiry first set in motion by Peter Whitehead, the Ministry of Culture reported that it could find 'no trace' of the manuscripts in Poland.

The origins of the enquiry go back to November 1974, in London, where Whitehead met the Director of the Ministry of Culture's Foreign Department, Mme. Orchowska. Whitehead showed her the 1964 list of more than a hundred lost Mozart originals. Mme. Orchowska was surprised that such great treasures were missing, but thought it highly unlikely that they were in Poland. After the war, she said, all art-objects had been documented, 'down to the last picture in the last church'. She spoke of Whitehead's 'passionate search'.

Soon afterwards, Whitehead made contact with the British embassy in Warsaw. Through these channels the Ministry search – supervised by Mme. Orchowska herself – would come about, but the British ambassador's first thought was a different one. Inadvertently it went straight to the roots of the manuscripts' disappearance. 'I would propose,' he wrote, 'to consult with Professor Lorenz of the National Museum . . . a long standing and close friend of this Embassy.' Three months later an embassy official reported on his meeting with Lorenz. The man who had found the Grüssau manuscripts – a fact unknown both to Whitehead and the embassy – 'explained . . . that he is not a specialist in this field himself'. He suggested letters to the Jagiellonian and National Libraries, and to the National Archives, and did not discourage the idea of an approach to the Benedictine Order in Poland. Tyniec, he thought, was the Order's principal Polish monastery.

All these 'leads' drew blanks. The director of the Jagiellonian wrote that the manuscripts were not in his catalogues, but added, 'If the present position alters I will inform all interested in it.' The head of the Archives suggested it might be worth approaching someone among the generation of scholars who had been active in 1946 – the most prominent of whom, he might have added but did not, had been Lorenz and Estreicher. Whitehead commented: 'We might just as well have asked about pre-war railway timetables, instead of some of the most important musical documents in our European heritage.

The 'we' by then included Hans-Hubert Schönzeler, through whom Whitehead grew into an awareness of the importance of the music originals. His underlying goal remained fixed – to see the picture of *Piquitinga* – but it was easier to interest and impress people by citing the music. The strategy was like trying to catch a shark in order to net a particular pilot fish.

At the end of 1975, Schönzeler succeeded in enlisting the former organ scholar and British Prime Minister, Edward Heath. He got in touch with the then Foreign Secretary, James Callaghan, who early in 1976 passed on to Heath the result of the Polish Ministry of Culture's 'search':

> I am sorry to have to tell you that the Ministry's enquiries revealed no trace of them; and they have pointed out that the evidence that they are still in Poland was far from conclusive. Since, as you will appreciate, H.M.G. have no formal standing to pursue this matter further with the Polish authorities, I am afraid there is nothing more we can do officially.

Mme. Orchowska, it seemed, had written to the British embassy that 'there has never been any [such] collection in any of the Polish libraries'. She told the British Council representative in Warsaw that 'In the turmoil of the late forties, all kinds of hearsay had got about which could not be substantiated'. She knew of no evidence 'strong enough to prove that the manuscripts had been seen in Poland since shortly after the war'; if there were such evidence, she would be glad to hear of it.

When the British diplomat suggested that the manuscripts might be 'in the care of, or at any rate in a place known to the ecclesiastical authorities', Mme. Orchowska replied, very properly, that the Church administration was independent of the State's and that she could offer no suggestions as to how best to approach it.

The 'end of the official road' had been reached; the brief involvement of the British government – at the instigation and at the service of Peter Whitehead – had come to the same impasse as the other governmental searches. But Mr. Whitehead, the Foreign Secretary pointed out, was perfectly free to continue privately if he wanted to, 'as long as he doesn't start the Third World War!'

Whitehead's next step was to try to get the manuscript question on to the agenda of the 1976 U.N.E.S.C.O. conference in Nairobi. Yehudi Menuhin was enlisted, and made discreet representations at the organisation's Paris headquarters. The plan failed, for the same reason as all the official searches had failed – the official Polish admission was lacking, and the people with the unofficial proof could not or would not be cited. Professor Lissa, for example. In the summer of 1976, Whitehead heard about her and about the Benedictine Rescue, and wrote to her excitedly: 'Six boxes of manuscripts . . . wonderful news . . . Will you write what you know?' In July, the Professor replied: 'Unfortunately I am not entitled to supply you any information on the question. What you should do is approach the Ministry of Culture . . . I should like to ask you not to mention me in your negotiations with U.N.E.S.C.O.'

Less than six months after the unsuccessful outcome of the Ministry of Culture's search, therefore, another Pole with strong government connections was implicitly admitting *to the same person* – Peter Whitehead – that the manuscripts were in Poland, so making a nonsense of the Ministry's search. At the same time, strengthening the brew, the Professor specifically referred him to the Ministry of Culture. The gap between official governmental 'reality' and the unofficial truth had never been wider.

It widened still further in the autumn of 1976, when a visiting British musician was told by a Polish composer in Warsaw that the lost music was indeed in Poland. 'Let us leave it at that,' the composer said, adding somewhat mysteriously (to the musician), 'We have suffered enough at the hands of the Germans.' On the same visit, the musician was given to understand that the whole affair was in the charge of Professor Lissa, who had earlier told Whitehead that he should ask the Ministry of Culture, which earlier . . . etcetera.

This un-coordinated stumbling is too clumsy to be called a policy. Most striking is the categorical nature of the Ministry of Culture's denial. This must have been a conscious deception, whether or not Mme. Orchowska was party to it. At that stage it is inconceivable that the Ministry could not have known where the manuscripts were, which makes it all the more strange that it should choose, at that stage, so firmly to deny that they were in Poland. What we have here is another bout of secrecy officially imposed from above, of the kind that Carleton Smith had encountered in the fifties. In context, the Ministry's flat denial seems as old-fashioned as leeching seems to modern medicine: no cure at all.

The 'new policy' implemented about 1970 was itself getting fairly old by then. Professor Lissa, at this period, keeps a low profile. What has happened in the interim is that the old policy has been given a new lease of life; the doves and hawks have reached some sort of truce, and from 1974 to 1976 it is the turn of the hawks to dictate. If we look again at the *New York Times* report of Smith's secret preview, we find signs of an important shift. According to the report, Smith said: '. . . that the East Germans told him they were ready to draw up proposals to their counterparts in Poland suggesting that certain Polish cultural treasures now in German hands should be exchanged for the scores.' In other words, the purpose for which the manuscripts had originally been taken – as 'securities or guarantees' – was at last to be implemented. Despite international law and Warsaw Pact practice, the Poles and the East Germans were to negotiate over the treasures. This in itself amounted to an admission that there was justice in the Polish cause. It was a crucial development, to which, I believe, we owe the apparent 'freeze' of the new policy in these years of Whitehead's search. The dominant question was the outcome of the Polish-East German negotiations. Foreign searchers were an intrusive nuisance, to be sent packing even at the cost of Polish credibility.

The talks between Poland and East Germany were conducted in absolute secrecy. The most that can be said about them is that they concerned the future of the manuscripts in the light of Polish treasures in Germany, that they started in the late sixties to early seventies and were still in progress in 1978. It may be that the talks were/are the sort of dialogue between two countries that never reaches a firm conclusion.

In December 1975, Smith commented that 'the East German Minister of High Schools, who controls the present German State Library, has been shuttling back and forth to Poland. Negotiations are under way and one hopes, before too long,

221

the manuscripts will be returned to East Berlin . . . Nevertheless,' he added, 'competent Polish authorities still do not admit
their existence.' In the same month he told me: 'I think it's part
of the double talk that goes on at various levels in all dictator-
ships and Communist countries, and my own feeling is that
there will be an exchange made between East Germany and
Poland, and that these manuscripts will eventually be found
"officially" and returned . . . This will become a barter arrangement.' After seeing the manuscripts, he said, he went to see
Gierek, and 'he said they weren't there, he didn't know anything about them'. In the summer of 1977, in Poland, I was
told that the negotiations with East Germany were being conducted at the highest level up to Gierek and his East German
counterpart, Erich Honecker.

The Ministry of Culture's denial must be seen in the context
of these high-level, highly secret talks, at which, thirty years
after the war, battle had at last been joined with one Germany,
at least, if not Germany as a whole. The specific purpose for
which the Ministry's 'search' was mounted must also be borne
in mind. It came about directly at the behest of the British
diplomatic presence in Warsaw, and indirectly at Peter Whitehead's, and its phony outcome was perhaps intended specifically to throw Whitehead off the scent, in the hope that he
would lose hope, search elsewhere, or stop searching altogether.

If that was the hope, it was mistaken. Whitehead was less a
detective, proceeding by deductive method, than a doctor,
testing the body of European and Polish scholarship by touch,
trying to find a tender point. He noted, for example, the yelp of
pain arising from the contact with Pirożyński. At the same
time, he became a carrier of the disease he was diagnosing –
'the Grüssau bug', he called his own infection. After the 'official
road' turned out to be another cul-de-sac he continued with his
by then labyrinthine correspondence. As he gathered scraps of
information, so he spread them, by a kind of contagion, like
addresses in a chain letter. 'Each rumour,' he remarked, 'was
more promising than the last and there was an almost geometrical progression in the numbers of correspondents.'

There is neither the space to go into all his initiatives, nor the
need. Most were unproductive. Typical of one sort of response
was the enquiry of a Polish music scholar: 'What has zoology

to do with musicology?' Slowly, however, some sort of progress was made. Dieter Henrich heard of Whitehead in the summer of 1976, on a visit to the Berlin libraries, and wrote to him 'with regard to a problem we obviously have in common'. Henrich said that on a visit to Warsaw in 1975 he had 'tried to attract the attention of a few members of the Polish Academy. But I had the impression that there was hesitation that cannot be fully explained in terms of ignorance'. Another tender spot. Then in the autumn Henrich wrote: 'I am nearly in a postion to be able to prove that the Poles themselves have conceded that they found the Grüssau boxes.' Against the background of the situation inside Poland, Henrich's and Whitehead's searches were both converging on the same goal, from different directions. In October, Whitehead's Polish correspondent reported on a letter she had received from Professor Lorenz. 'I hope,' he had told her, 'that I shall soon be able to announce, both to you and to Mr. Whitehead, some positive news.'

Whitehead was very close. In context, that remark of Professor Lorenz assumes a greater importance than it seemed at the time to possess. Indeed, Whitehead was only fully struck by it *afterwards*. It appears to indicate a relaxation of the rigid official 'reality' of Poland's position at about this time – a side effect, perhaps, of the secret talks with East Germany, their breakdown, or their arrival at some sort of conclusion. Probably significant also was a slightly later development: a one-day meeting between Gierek and Honecker at the end of February, which stressed 'the importance of seeking out and returning cultural properties of both nations, as a factor in the constant strengthening of their friendly co-operation'. At this meeting, surely, the next stage of the Grüssau revelation was agreed.

After thirty years, the Grüssau secret was hanging by a rapidly fraying thread. The biggest barriers had fallen, with the death of Hordyński, the consternation of Polish music scholars, the noisy search and the secret preview of Carleton Smith, and the patient detective work of Dieter Henrich – then nearing its conclusion. The break-through was only the thickness of a single sheet of paper away – a letter yet to be sent by a person whose name was yet to be added to the 'almost geometrical progression' of Whitehead's snowballing correspondence.

The name was Professor Jan Białostocki, a Polish art historian and expert on the Renaissance in eastern Europe, who was
suggested to Whitehead by a colleague of his in West Germany.
In the first week of 1977, Whitehead wrote to him – a letter
that was by then routine. 'I understand that these manuscripts
still exist. The problem is to get official recognition of this fact.
Scholars do not care who *owns* these precious manuscripts:
the important thing is to make them *available*.' He enclosed a
copy of his 1976 article for *Notes*.

Among Białostocki's posts was that of Curator of Foreign
Paintings at the National Museum in Warsaw. In his office –
just a few doors down from that of the Museum's director,
Professor Lorenz – he opened Whitehead's letter. The reply
which he wrote suggested that he was not familiar with the
problem which Whitehead raised, but had come across similar
problems in his time. This one, however, struck him as 'very
tricky, if after so many attempts the missing manuscripts did
not appear':

> . . . I shall try to inquire about the musical and other manu-
> scripts, which are reported to have been deposited at the
> Krzeszów monastery, and as soon as I learn anything I shall
> let you know of the results of the inquiry. I presume however
> that there must be some special difficulty in this specific case
> if no earlier questioning brought any results.
> I can only promise to do my best to find out how things are.
> There never was any fire there. The monastery is very well
> preserved.

Whitehead marvelled at the understatement – 'some special
difficulty' indeed! – but so far the letter was just another sub-
heading in his bulky file.

In Warsaw, Białostocki contacted the President of the
Academy of Sciences, and then the head of the Academy's
Section One (covering Social Sciences, Philosophy, History,
Philology, Literature, Art, Economics, and Law). Exactly what
he was told, and more importantly exactly why he was told it,
we do not and cannot yet know. What matters are the unprece-
dented *conditions* on which he was told. Could it be that the
authorities decided that this was the way the story should
end – not with a German or devout Austrian in search of
Mozart, but with an Englishman in search of a fish? The result

was that last thickness of paper between the unofficial truth and the artificially imposed official 'reality' – paper on which was written a letter as matter-of-fact as its contents were sensational:

> Dear Mr. Whitehead,
>   I am very glad to be able to tell you that the problem of the lost manuscripts has been cleared up. I have been authorised to tell you that the manuscripts exist, are preserved in good shape, and an official communiqué will be issued soon to make it known.
>   I cannot tell as yet when the manuscripts will be returned, but as far as I can gather the whole affair should be brought to an end and the materials will be accessible.
>   I hope this will be satisfactory to you for this moment. As soon as I learn more details I will write to you again.
>   With best regards,
>   Sincerely yours.

Białostocki's letter arrived in the middle of March, and for a little while at least its contents were known only to Whitehead and other scholars inside the charmed circle of international scholarship. Whitehead's first step was to write back to Białostocki:

> . . . Are you responsible for this miracle? The discovery will be applauded by hundreds of musicologists, historians, art historians, biohistorians and others who believed that the material was destroyed in the war.
>   Obviously, I am impatient to learn how many of the manuscripts have been found. Can I hope to see one day the famous *Libri Picturati* volumes? Now what shall I do?

Next, he typed a circular and sent it to all those to whom he had written over the six years he had been searching. Typical responses were those of the West Berlin music librarian, Rudolf Elvers – 'The best news to me since the end of the war, 1945' – and the West German lady who had put Whitehead on to Białostocki – 'If only my husband had lived to see this!' Whitehead was elated, but still worried that the promised 'communiqué' might not materialise. To put the development on record, he contacted the press, with the result that in the first week of April the story was carried all over the world, from Australia and the Arabian Gulf States to the Argentine, and in the United States everywhere from Fort Worth in Texas to San Francisco.

The story was naturally good copy, as that of Smith's secret preview had been, with plenty of openings for puns on 'scales', Peter Whitebait or Whiting, and so on. There was a strong element of the absurd in it. 'In the meantime, why not name the fish Beethoven?' joked the *New Yorker*, and one German newspaper, in a baroque simile, compared the stave line to a net, and the musical notes to little fishes caught in it.

It is almost as though Whitehead were specially *chosen* to be the recipient of the news. Coming from him, it sounded more unreal than it might otherwise have done – almost light-hearted. At the same time, his story had more solidity than Smith's, backed up as it was by the 'authorised' letter from Poland. But what was the 'authorisation'? Did it extend, for example, to Whitehead's passing on the story to the press? Week followed week, and still the communiqué did not appear. Had Whitehead acted prematurely, and scared the secret back into its shell?

Now it was his turn to come in for criticism. In Berlin, Rudolf Elvers seemed to have cooled somewhat. 'The only solid information we have,' he remarked sceptically, 'is this letter . . . from which we don't know where the manuscripts are at present.' In Heidelberg, there was just time for Professor Henrich to add a postscript to his article before it went to press:

> Whitehead certainly did his middleman no service when he decided not to wait for the official announcement but gave in to the temptation to link his name in public with the credit for 'finding' the Berlin manuscripts. For it's still uncertain in what circumstances and under what conditions the Poles will reveal (them) or return them to the G.D.R. . . .

Henrich also pointed out that it was still unknown both what had been 'found' and what would be returned – just the manuscripts of Grüssau, or those of all the eastern sites. Ever since the Munich crisis, it seems, the world has mistrusted Englishmen who wave bits of paper that promise something –

peace in our time, or the rediscovery of lost German treasure.

The Grüssau story was living up to its tradition: never quite ending, but leading instead into a vanishing perspective of endings. Smith's secret preview, but no proof. Białostocki's letter, but still no communiqué. And, even when the communiqué was issued, if it was going to be, there was still the question both of the future whereabouts of the treasure and its accessibility to scholars.

In the event, the communiqué appeared, in the last week of April, as a tight-lipped little news story by the government agency, P.A.P. After referring to 'earlier reports that part of the precious collections of the ex-Prussian State Library . . . might have been found somewhere on the territory of Poland', the report continued: 'Systematic and scrupulous search has recently been rewarded with a successful result. The regained collections are now undergoing introductory research, examination, and sorting.'

The Grüssau manuscripts had been officially found, exactly as Carleton Smith prophesied they would be, after having been officially lost for the length of a short lifetime. It was just over thirty-five years since the scarred and war-wounded Dr. Poewe had evacuated them from Berlin; just over thirty since the mysterious convoy had come to Grüssau to collect them; and just over nine since the lonely death of Hordyński. On the Unter den Linden, the music librarian, Dr. Köhler, read the news and smiled to himself. In Berkshire, Peter Whitehead opened a bottle of his wife's home-made wine, and raised his glass in an ironic toast: 'To Grüssau! And to *Piquitinga*!'

*

One month after the official communiqué, at the end of May, Edward Gierek boarded an aeroplane at Warsaw, bound for East Berlin. He was going to ratify a new treaty between Poland and the G.D.R., 'of friendship, co-operation, and mutual assistance', and, befitting the occasion, he took a token of friendship with him. It was perhaps the most precious property that one head of state has ever handed over to another as a gesture. It travelled in three smart red boxes, like the dispatch cases that busy government ministers take home with them.

These too held documents, but not the usual array of statistics that civil servants compile for politicians to pore over.

They were nowhere near neat enough, although just as incomprehensible to many, and were not in themselves state documents at all, although they had been secretly pressed into service as such for many years. Since the war, they had been hostages; now they were about to become ambassadors, and, as ambassadors are, they had been carefully chosen for their posting. In one red box was Beethoven; Mozart and Bach filled the other two. In them were seven scores, a small selection of the Grüssau music representing all three of Germany's greatest composers and a good cross-section of their greatest and most popular works.

In the Beethoven box was the original orchestral score, minus the choral finale, of the Ninth Symphony, nestling together with the Third Piano Concerto. The Mozart box was the biggest, holding as it did the richest prize of all, the whole of *The Magic Flute*, the Mass in C-minor which Mozart had written to celebrate his own marriage, with a part for his wife-to-be Constanze, and the Jupiter Symphony. The smallest was the Bach: one of his most unusual manuscripts – the Concerto for Two Harpsichords with, thriftily, on the bottom three stave-lines of each page, a sonata, No. 3 in A-flat for Flute and Harpsichord.

The choice was clever. For among these scores were some that had, for thirty years, been the slowly burning touchpaper on Poland's musical time bomb: works like *The Magic Flute* and the Ninth Symphony, having the most intense significance nationally and the widest internationally. The ordinary German thought of them as most bound up with his own national soul and identity; the ordinary music-lover, anywhere in the world, as most synonymous with 'classical' music.

In choosing to surrender them, Poland was defusing and rendering harmless the bomb which had been ticking away all those years, and which had already blown up in a few faces. As Gierek's plane touched down at East Berlin's airport, these scores, at least, were only hours away from freedom: the moment when they would cease to be documents of state and could become once more the music that Beethoven, Mozart, and Bach had written.

But there were lies to be told, and smilingly accepted as true, there was cant to be spoken, trumpets to be blown and cymbals clashed, before the transition could be made complete. At

the signing ceremony, Gierek said that the originals had been
'found in the course of action taken to protect cultural goods
... and safeguarded from destruction', sounding an echo,
surely conscious, of the return of the Dresden paintings twenty-
two years before. There was talk from both sides of the scores
as a 'symbol of national friendship'; the speakers reiterated the
importance of finding displaced cultural property. Then everyone applauded, as one politician placed the three red boxes in
the hands of another.

'All Men Shall Be Brothers', blared a headline in the East
German *Neues Deutschland* – a reference to the Ode to Joy
which ends the Ninth. Below it, was an uncomfortable exercise
in rhetoric by the usually sober Dr. Köhler. 'No finer symbol of
friendship,' the article had us believe, 'could have come from
our Polish brethren than the original copy of . . . the immortal
Magic Flute, Mozart's great German opera.' It ended by extol-
ling 'the spirit of friendship between two socialist brother
countries which was displayed on the 28th May, 1977, and
which is so meaningfully exemplified by the humanitarian
message of Mozart's *Magic Flute* and Beethoven's Ninth
Symphony'.

It was a quieter Dr. Köhler whom I met in his office on the
Unter den Linden, a month later. 'Now for the great moment,'
he said, and went to his wall-safe. He took from it three red
boxes, and handed me two of them – the Beethoven and
Mozart. His hands were trembling, and so was his voice. I
though of a sentence from his newspaper article: 'The librarians
of the *Deutsche Staatsbibliothek* will watch over these valuable treasures like their own eyeballs . . .'

He led the way to a music room on an upper floor of the
library, and there we spread out the original scores on the lid of
a piano, as though for a sing-song. We actually did hum the
opening bars of the Jupiter together, from the open score
which Mozart himself had written, but never heard performed
in his life-time; then Köhler closed it again. It had been well
studied before the war, he said, and photographed; there was
nothing new to be learned from it.

Over the month since the friendship treaty, he had been
looking closely at *The Magic Flute*, and had confirmed from its
page-numbering that Mozart composed it in snatches as the
mood took him, then pieced the whole together. 'Look,' he

said, pointing to page after page, 'here, and here . . .' I thought
of the letter that Köhler's wartime predecessor, Georg Schünemann, had written in 1942, saying that *The Magic Flute* was
spending the war 'in a little South German corner', and could
not be consulted 'until after the war was over'.

How confident, even arrogant, Schünemann had been! My
thoughts turned to a nasty little episode I had come across in
my research. During the war, Schünemann – the expert on
Beethoven – visited France on a buying expedition for Hans
Frank, the 'Butcher of Poland'. Frank was interested in some
mementoes of Chopin, potential Polish trophies, that had
turned up in Lyons; Schünemann advised him on their quality,
and how best to get them for the lowest price. Yes, he too had
been an 'academic gangster', mixing scholarship with politics,
ideology, and preferment, muddling spirit and power. And
there before me was *The Magic Flute*, part of Poland's considered revenge for that corruption.

But this was not Schünemann, but Köhler, and he had
moved on to the Mass in C-minor. In its front was a piece of
paper, and on it, in ink almost as faded as Mozart's, the
signature S. T. M. Newman, Newcastle-upon-Tyne, and the
date, 1937. It was the last time the score had been studied
before its evacuation. When Köhler opened the Ninth Symphony, a similar piece of paper fluttered to the floor, a pre-war
moth disturbed in its sleep.

He picked it up – Eunice Crocker, Massachusetts, 1937 –
and replaced it in the score. That was one of the years when
Carleton Smith was in Berlin. I thought of him – a young man
whose mind was music – in the 'treasure house' of the Unter
den Linden, under the irritable vigilance of Schünemann, un-
consciously doing the groundwork for his long search. I turned
a page of the Ninth, and realised for myself what it had meant
to him, to have 'had these manuscripts in my hands.' I felt –
even though I was neither musician nor scholar of music – the
reverence that he must have experienced.

There was one piece of original research which I felt to be
within my scope. I wanted to see the date on the Third Piano
Concerto, first performed in 1803, and believed by some
scholars to have been composed then, but generally attributed
to 1800. Beethoven's slapdash way with the pen was the cause
of the problem, and this was one original that had not been

photographed before the war. Dr. Köhler produced a magnifying glass, and I peered at the date on the flyleaf. What was it? I thought 1803, but Köhler was the better judge, and I handed him the glass. 'Let me see,' he said, and peered in his turn.

I looked at him, and wondered how much of a prison his life would be without that intellectual eagerness he was showing. It was almost time for me to go – as he could not – back through the Berlin Wall over Checkpoint Charlie, just two blocks down the road. But I waited, treasuring this moment which had nothing directly to do with politics or post-war history, which had to do with a date, and yet was curiously timeless. I thought of Carleton Smith's strange remark: 'The people who are looking after these things are in danger of their lives.' A man had died to make this humble moment possible, and with it the search and the story ended: a man with a magnifying glass, a music room in East Berlin or anywhere in the world, the faded scribble of a genius.

CHAPTER TWENTY-TWO

Conclusion?

Four years later, in 1981, only those seven original scores are back in the place where they were collected. The rest of them, and all the Grüssau manuscripts, are still in Poland, and look like staying there, if not for good, then for a long time to come. There is no sign at all of their returning to the Unter den Linden, and yet the East Berlin librarians are quietly confident that they will return. Why, they will not say. They have, perhaps, powerful friends in Moscow on whose intervention they are counting; certainly it is hard to see what other grounds for confidence they could have, for if Poland has made one thing abundantly clear it is that she attaches enormous value to the manuscripts, and will not give them up without a fight.

In the meantime, however, the East Germans are far from satisfied, and are reliably rumoured to be less kindly disposed towards Poland and Polish scholarship than they have ever been. Relations are *sehr schlecht* – very bad indeed. For, just as certainly as the Poles will not surrender the manuscripts except on their own terms, so the East Germans will not be happy until they are back in Berlin.

Everyone else is happy enough because, for two of the last four years, the manuscripts have been accessible, and one after another scholars have gone to Poland to study them in the Jagiellonian Library. At last – from the Polish point of view – the back of the paradox has been broken. The manuscripts are both in Poland and available for study and – the demands of state and scholarship both satisfied – the grounds for internal Polish disagreement have evaporated.

This has required, and will continue to require, something of a balancing act. Having played one dangerous game, Poland is now deep in another. For the resolution of her own internal conflict, and satisfaction of the needs of foreign scholars, has been at the cost of alienating the East Berlin library, and thereby the East German state. It is worse, from East Germany's political point of view, that Poland is making the manuscripts accessible. Not only does it deprive East Berlin of the support of foreign scholars, who, as Peter Whitehead stressed in letter after letter, are concerned not at all with the whereabouts of the manuscripts; it also ominously suggests an arrangement that could become permanent. By satisfying the scholars, therefore, Poland can be interpreted as openly defying East Germany.

Yet Poland no more sees herself as 'owner' of the manuscripts than either Germany sees her as owning them. Back in 1977, Karl-Heinz Köhler criticised an East German newspaper's 'mistaken' description of the three red boxes as a 'gift'. Dr. Peter Wackernagel made the same criticism: 'We collected them, looked after them, took them to safety during the war. They are ours'.

One can give only that which it is in one's gift to give, and Dr. Köhler and Dr. Wackernagel – on either side of the Berlin Wall – agreed in withholding that right from Poland. But the trouble is that Wackernagel's 'ours' is out of date; he was thinking of a time, now receding into history, when the German people was one, in a united Germany.

Here, there is unexpected support for Poland's present position, its now open pursuit of the policy previously pursued in secret: the keeping of the manuscripts as 'guarantees'. For, on balance, West Germany is happier that the manuscripts remain accessible in Poland than that they return to East Berlin. Their return would give East Germany a propaganda coup, and strengthen her claim to be regarded as the true guardian of 'German humanistic culture'. Nations, like newspapers, most resent those 'scoops' that go to nations in the same competitive stable.

Or, even worse, to non-nations. In the summer of 1977, Lorenz Niegel returned to his attack of three years before and tabled two questions in the Bundestag in Bonn. In the first he asked: 'Has the Federal Republic made it clear that [it] is the legal successor to the German Reich and is therefore entitled to these German cultural possessions . . .?' In the second, after referring to 'the autograph scores illegally handed over to the S.E.D. regime', he asked: 'What steps has the Federal Government undertaken, or is it contemplating, in order to protect the interests of the Prussian Cultural Foundation?'

Niegel received a letter from a Minister of State at the West German Foreign Office, from which he learned that West Germany had already by then strongly affirmed her own interest in and right to the manuscripts. This was done in the few weeks of May, 1977, between the Polish official communiqué and Edward Gierek's visit to Berlin. What the letter did not state in so many words, though it refers to it in a veiled way, is that West Germany had gone much further than that. She had evolved and floated a plan to buy the manuscripts from Poland, for an enormous amount of badly needed foreign currency. How far the plan floated before it foundered, one cannot be sure, but the Minister of State's letter – with its reference to lack of 'feasibility' – suggest that the West German government went so far as to take soundings in Warsaw. If that was so, and it seems more than probable, then the Poles remained true to their original revindication policies of thirty years before: 'Having lost objects expressive of culture, we demand only analogous objects . . . it is beside the point to try to fix up the "market" value of the reparations due to us' . . . Here is part of the Foreign Office's letter:

> . . . our embassy in Warsaw made representations to the Polish government and unequivocally expressed the Federal Republic's interest in these German cultural works.
>
> Even though a return to the Prussian Cultural Foundation was not feasible, the Federal Republic made it clear that it did not accept that Poland and/or the G.D.R. were solely competent to decide the fate of the autograph scores, and that it will energetically oppose the legal implications of this action.

This has only one conceivable interpretation: West Germany, regarding herself as the long-term rightful owner of the treasure, prefers that, in the foreseeable short term, it remains in Poland. Its 'energetic opposition' could have no other effect. This provides Poland with a strong argument for her present position. So, by a kind of levitation, these opposing claims and rivalries keep the manuscripts suspended where they are, which is legally nowhere, in limbo.

But they are accessible. In July 1977, I was shown into a room at the Jagiellonian, and there on a coffee table was a pile of the Haydn scores: a brief foretaste of the wealth of treasures that the trained eyes of specialists would later see, and trained minds study. My special treat was a cover-up, so to speak, of the cover-up. I will not embarrass the person responsible by naming him; he was just another scholar caught in the political web, and it was not his fault that he felt he had to lie. *'We never tried to hide anything from the world,'* he said, adding that the manuscripts had been found in the Jagiellonian around 1974. Enquiries from foreign scholars prompted the library to accelerate its routine, non-stop work on the huge uncatalogued collections, a backlog of the war. In that backlog they were found. 'From their position on the shelves we judge them to have been here since the early fifties.' And where were they before? Here I had my own taste of the Benedictine Rescue. 'We think,' I was told, 'that they were stored in a monastery, not far from Kraków.' Which monastery? 'We are not sure which.' He laughed: 'Look, I was only ten years old at the time.'

In 1978, the American pianist Malcolm Frager was able to see some of the Mozart manuscripts at the Jagiellonian, and made an interesting discovery. The wartime evacuation list of the Grüssau music was not accurate, but heavily underestimated the true number of the originals. The reason for this, apparently, was that the wartime librarians, in their hurry, had often listed only the first work in a binding that contained two or more. So Frager was told by Karl-Heinz Köhler; but I am not convinced. From my conversations with Dr. Wackernagel, who actually worked on the evacuation, I have the impression that the packing and listing were very carefully done. And how is it that *neither* score on the important Bach manuscript returned to Berlin in 1977 is listed as having gone to Grüssau? This has yet to be properly explained: it may be, for example, that original manuscripts from another site were moved east of the Oder-Neisse line during the war. For the tidy-minded, there are still some aspects of the paperchase to be tidied up.

It was not long after this that the Poles and East Germans fell out and relations reached their present low point. In 1978, Dr. Köhler wrote that 'the commissions of the Polish and G.D.R. governments are at present in negotiation and we hope for a good result'. That hope must have snapped soon afterwards.

Early in 1979, Köhler left the Berlin library for Weimar, though he had told an American music scholar that if there were the slightest hope of the music returning he would stay in Berlin. And, not long after that, the Polish government began to make the manuscripts accessible to foreign scholars, indicating a decisive breakdown of the negotiations and marking a new phase in the strange history of the treasure.

Since then, scholar after scholar has taken the high road to Kraków, once the narrow, unmarked, and perilous Grüssau trail. The N.M.A. was sent microfilms of the missing Mozart originals; the Haydn and Bach were filmed and sent abroad. An American scholar, Deborah Hertz, went to study the Varn-hagen Collection. Hans-Hubert Schönzeler saw the Bruckner sketches: they turned out to be disappointing scraps. The first fruits of research began to be gathered, among them the dis-covery that the date that Köhler and I had puzzled over *was* 1803. Edward Heath, speaking in Brussels, remarked how a Mozart concerto among 'the Polish manuscripts' had turned out to be markedly different from the accepted performing version. And so on, and many yet to come: the small victories of light over darkness, of the magnifying glass over the yellow window-panes.

One of the victories deserves special mention. In September 1979, eight years after first stumbling upon the *Piquitinga* problem, Peter Whitehead stood waiting in the foyer of the Jagiellonian. He was met by a young man in his thirties, who introduced himself as Piotr Hordyński. He was the Jagiel-lonian's Keeper of Manuscripts, and must presumably have been related to Władysław, as he wrote the 1968 obituary of him. So a second generation of Polish scholars is learning to live – a little more comfortably – with the Grüssau manu-scripts.

He ushered Whitehead upstairs, and went to get the *Libri Picturati*, leaving Whitehead to wonder 'what I was really feeling. Would I weep? Would they be borne in on a huge red cushion, or on a golden handcart, or might they not just float in? In the event, a small trolley entered, pushed by a stout woman . . .'

The moment was finely stage-managed. Hordyński took one of the volumes and opened it at a place previously marked. 'There,' he said, '*there* is your *Piquitinga*.' Eight years of searching ended in an instant of recognition, recorded by Whitehead in his diary:

> . . . the problem was solved. For there before me was not an anchovy but a herring. The mouth, the upper jaw, the opercular series, even the scutes – all are superbly observed and drawn and proclaim 'Clupeid'. A herring-like fish is not easy to paint. The colours defeat the eye because they come and go as the eye moves. Yet, by spots or lines of white, the artist accurately caught the truth, more than three hundred years ago. The blood which has suffused a canal near the eye, the contusion near the pectoral base, the silver of the lateral stripe, the highlight at the tip of the maxilla, the dark of the small clupeid mouth, only just open. These are things you see in fresh material . . .

At the same time, Whitehead did some close observation of his own. 'I noticed a curious thing,' he wrote in his diary:

> . . . Hordyński treated these 350-year old volumes without any ceremony. He did not of course maltreat them, but he showed none of those reverential gestures with which a librarian handles his treasures. He even implied a kind of disdain for them. He admired the pictures and talks enthusiastically about the collection, but not with any proprietary pride.

The director of the Jagiellonian had earlier spoken to Whitehead about the grievous Polish war losses and their relevance to the manuscripts. 'Perhaps we will keep them,' he said. They have, so far, but to keep is not the same as to own. One does not strike up an emotional relationship with a hostage. It was just that 'proprietary pride' which Whitehad found lacking in Hordyński, which I had noticed in Köhler's handling of *The Magic Flute* and the other scores. There are things that *belong* in particular places, just as people belong.

There are things that belong in Poland – the Czartoryski Raphael, the vases of Gołuchow, all the thousands of stolen things hidden in secret places all over Germany, Europe, and by now the world. They were looted by "academic gangsters", who in their handling of Polish culture were conspicuously lacking in 'reverential gestures'. There are episodes in history that do not heal over – for many years, or ever – but scorch themselves into the national mind. This one scorched itself into Poland's.

I think of an old man in the icy November rain, standing shaven-headed under the Sun of Sachsenhausen; and his son in wartime London, working to salvage the past from the bloody present. I think of the deep scars around the paintings in Kraków, and the painting crushed into powder on the castle floor; of the castle itself, blown up, then blown up again; and sometimes of the scene which haunted Professor Lorenz, the man he had known before the war, standing to admire the fireplace of the king, then 'giving in my presence the order to tear it away from the wall'.

These images have nothing to do with music. Have they? Why then, when I listen to *The Magic Flute*, the Ninth Symphony, or to any of the Grüssau music, do they sometimes steal into my mind? They neither reduce nor enhance the beautiful sounds I hear, but flicker in the wings, as though angels could cast the shadows of devils, or as though, in paper of the purest white, the watermarks were images of war.

Index

Breslau (see also Wrocław), 6, 49–51, 136, 198, (*Wrocław*) 116, 191
Brezhnev, Leonid, 109
British Government, involvement in search, 202, 218–20, 222
British Museum (Natural History), 20
Browne, Patrick, 23
Bruckner, Anton, 216–17, 236
Bücher, Haus der, 91, 93
Budapest, 104
Bug, River, 62
Bylica, Martin, 204

Callaghan, James, 219–20
Campbell, Frank, 209
Canada, 6, 149–50, 151
Capuchin Rescue, 159–60
Cataloguing, 30–3, *letters* 91, 111
Catholic Church, 73, 79–80, 85, 88, 196–7, 219
Cherubini, Luigi, 37
Chopin, Frédéric, *evacuation of Chopiniana* 4–5, 61, 63, 149–50, *Preludes and Études, gift of G.D.R.* 84, 122, 174, *Memorabilia of in France* 230
Churchill, Winston, 61, 63, 93, 125
Cieplice, 140
Cistercian Order, 49
Clay, General Lucius, 78
Collegium Maius, 202–3, 207
Copernicus, Nicholas, 204–8
Crocker, Eunice, 230
Cuvier, Georges, 23
Cyrankiewicz, Jósef, 84
Czartoryski Collection (Kraków), 7, 237, *Museum at Gołuchow* 12
Czechoslovakia, 49, 55, 78, 123, 140, 190

Danilewicz, Maria, 12
Dehn, Siegfried Wilhelm, 106
Deutsche Staatsbibliothek, see: German State Library
Dillon, Douglas, 70
Dodd, William E., 67–8, 198, 200
Dodd Stern, Martha, 68

Dresden Museum, paintings of the, 40, 44, 56, 94, 98, 101, 109, 121, 122
Drobeck, Johann, 50–1
Duke, K. H. M., 195–6
Dutkiewicz, Jósef, 140

East Berlin Library, see: German State Library
East Germany, (G.D.R.), *relations with West Germany* 42, 233, *with Poland* 111, 146–7, 221–3, 227, 232, 235–6, *Party-to-Party request of mid-sixties* 108, 111, 156, 180–1, *search* 42–4, 111, 113
Eckhout, Albert, 25
Eisenhower, Dwight D., 98
Elbe, River, 53
Electoral Library, 13–14, 33
Elvers, Dr. Rudolf, 108, 200, 225, 226
Espagne, Franz, 60
Estreicher, Alojzy, 1–2, Dominik 1, Karol (elder) 1–2, 12, Professor Karol 3, 5–13, 117–21, 151–2, 159–60, 218, *visit to the U.S., 1943/44,* 119–20, 124, 129, *to the U.S., 1973,* 202–5, 207–8, 209, Stanisław, 2–3, 6–7
Evacuation, *of the Berlin Library* 15–17, 30–8, 53–4, 64, 161–2, *of Paris* 3, 15, *of Poland* 3–6
Evacuation sites, *German Ministry of Defence* 15, 53, *others* 16–17, 18 (*map*), 53–4, 83, 139 (*map: Lower Silesia*)

Facsimiles, 27–8, *European agreement on (1929)* 47
Fallersleben, Hoffman von, 34
Festschrift, see: German State Library
F.G.R., see: West Germany
Fichte, 35
Fischbach (Karpniki), 139 (*and map*)
Forrestal, James, 72
Forster, Dr. Karl, 79

240

Veith, Brother Günther, 81, 89, 133–5
Véscey, Jenö, 104
V.O.K.S., 99
Voltaire, 149

Wackernagel, Dr. Peter, 13 (*footnote*), 17, 36, 53–4, 59, 67, 77, 79–81, 88, 107, 233, 235
Wagner, Richard, 56, 58, 75, Siegfried 57, Wieland 58, 82, Winifred 56–8, 75
Waldburg Wolffegg, Count Hubert von, 162–3
Waldenburg, church near, 88, 157, 161, 163
Walker, Frank, 91
Warsaw University, 155, 185
Wawel Hill, (see also: Poland, Polish Royal Castle), 5, 142, 171
Wegener, Dr. Hans, 26
West Berlin Library, see: Prussian Cultural Heritage Foundation, State Library of the

West Germany, *relations with Poland*, 111–12, 132, 146–7, 188–9, 190, 217, *with East Germany* 42, 217, 233, *search for the lost music* 111–13, 234
Whitehead, Peter, 20–28, 133, 159, 200, 212–27, 233, 236–7
Wiesbaden, 92
Windisch, Brother Florian, 81, 89, 133, 135
Winters, Peter Jochen, 106 (*footnote*)
Wittelsbacher Ausgleichsfond, 58
Wolf, Hugo, 37, 91–2
Wood, Thor, 209
Woolley, Sir Leonard, 118
Wrocław (Breslau), 116, 177, 191, 212

Yalta Conference, 62

Zallinger-Thurn, Meinhard von, 100
Zhukov, Marshal, 77

246